W9-CAI-679

CONTENTS

INTRODUCTION & ACKNOWLEDGEMENTS

Regardless of the motivations leading to their creation, certain vehicles possess a combination of style, price, image and performance that destines them for automotive immortality. Among those emanating from America, few can equal the universal admiration, respect and recognition that the CJ Jeep commands.

Sixty years after the end of World War II, awareness of and admiration for the role that the CJ's military predecessors played in that conflict seems to increase with the passage of time. Whenever owners of military Jeeps display them at shows, they are invariably among the top attractions. In recent years, these Willys MB, Ford GPW and, upon occasion, Bantam BRC Jeeps have been joined by examples of the postwar civilian Jeep models, ranging from the CJ-2A, to its successors, the CJ-3A, CJ-3B, CJ-5, CJ-6, and CJ-7.

Owners of these Jeeps – along with Jeep enthusiasts and historians – are no less passionate and just as enthusiastic and knowledgeable about their Jeeps as their military Jeep counterparts. Many of these fine people generously gave of their time, experiences and knowledge to assist with this book.

Stirling Parkerson, who ranks as the dean of MA Jeep historians, was not only a valuable source of the history of the rare military Jeep, but did so in an engaging and humorous fashion. Joe Caprio, owner of a unique CJ-3A Jeep with less than 1800 miles on the clock, was equally generous with his time and knowledge of Jeep history.

My very good friend and mentor (in more ways than he realizes), Bruce Phillips, shared his experiences with a 1948 CJ-2A in the back country of the Adirondacks. His recollections of purchasing and owning a rare diesel-powered CJ-5 equipped with Warn overdrive, provided a first-hand account of operating a Jeep that, even as a new vehicle, was seldom seen on or off trail.

CJ-2A historian and chronicler, Harold West, was an ever patient, always helpful and invariably insightful source of information about the early CJ-2A Jeep. Similarly, Jeep collector and enthusiast, Todd Kerzig, was a cordial host and reliable source of various aspects of civilian Jeep history. Thanks and appreciation are extended to photographer Bob Christy for his photos of his Jeep and those of several other vintage models.

Details of the Ford Pygmy's design and the acquisition of a Ford GPW in 1943 by Fred Heine, who many believe was the first civilian to own a surplus Jeep, were provided by Randy Windrow of the Alabama Center for Military History. His assistant at the museum, Milt Aitken, was a faithful source and provider of photos and documentation of those two Jeeps that are today owned by the museum.

Photos of his 1958 CJ-3B, "Cherry Red," which were taken by his daughter, Carol Lynne, were supplied by Steve Perialas. Mr Perialas also shared his knowledge of and affection for civilian Jeeps in correspondence with the author over a period of several years.

Marshall Rimland, owner of the 284th CJ-2A to leave the Toledo, Ohio assembly line in 1945, not only arranged for his Jeep to be photographed for this book, but also provided the author with access to his extensive collection of Jeep memorabilia.

I also want to acknowledge the support of my good friend and MB Jeep owner, Bill Fredette, who listened when a good listener was necessary, and gave words of advice and encouragement when they were needed.

Robert C Ackerson
Brainards Forge, New York, USA

4

1 ORIGINS

Interpretations of events leading to the selection of Willys-Overland's design for what became one of the most famous vehicles of all time are often divisive, argumentative and controversial. Whether defending Willys-Overland, or maintaining that Bantam Motors or Ford was more deserving of this role in automotive history, partisans have for decades been stating their positions. This lack of unanimity is likely to continue even after the last shred of historical evidence is discovered and subjected to an objective analysis.

What is generally accepted is that a trail does exist leading to competition in 1940 between three contenders – Willys, Ford, and Bantam – for a government contract to produce a "¼-ton 4x4 truck."

In his 1981 book *The Jeep*, J-G Jeudy M Tararine refers to several military officers who regarded the Jeep as "a universal idea, which no one person invented, created or discovered ... an evolution and not an invention ... the fruit of specifications defined by the military over a long period. The idea of the Jeep originated with the infantry, which needed a low, very powerful vehicle with four-wheel drive."

Both military and civilian visionaries considered the use of motor vehicles before and during World War I to be a prelude to much wider and significant participation in any future conflict. In spite of numerous obstacles, such as limited budgets, the development of more refined, reliable and functional motor vehicles in the 1920s reinforced and refined this perception.

In mid-July, 1919, with new car prices falling and increasing automotive ownership stimulating demand for improved highways, a US Army convoy of sixty trucks, a dozen cars, and a number of motorcycles left Washington DC for San Francisco. This two month long journey demonstrated the shortcomings of the motorcycles, particularly for scouting purposes, as they had difficulty crossing streams, and were often left incapacitated in deep sand and mud. Years later, in 1943, Herbert R Rifkind, in his classic work *The Jeep – Its Development And Procurement Under The Quartermaster Corps, 1940-1943*, noted that "The motorcycle, even when equipped with a sidecar, was recognized as a notoriously poor performer in this regard, and dangerous to operate off the road except in the hands of a most expert rider."

The expedition's other vehicles didn't fare much better. When the convoy reached the west coast, about half of the trucks were no longer operable, validating the 1919 Quartermaster Corp's recommendation calling for the acquisition of a new type of vehicle for military operations. This should be of light weight and compact size, with a low silhouette and high ground clearance, and possess the ability to carry weapons and men over all sorts of rough terrain.

Pursuing these goals the Quartermaster Corps, in 1921, evaluated fifteen prototypes generically described as "farm tractor type" vehicles at the Aberdeen, Maryland Proving Ground. The results, as well as subsequent evaluations of modified medium duty trucks by the Ordnance Department, indicated that much smaller and lighter vehicles were needed for successful military operations over difficult terrain.

One participant in the Aberdeen tests, Colonel Carl C Terry, evaluated them in a 1944 paper *Test and Development of Light Cross-Country Vehicles at Aberdeen Proving Grounds, Maryland*. His oft quoted comment, that the military "learned mostly what not to do," underscored the need for fresh approaches to the challenge of building a modern "Cross-Country" military vehicle.

Financially restrained (in November 1932 the purchase of a $286.75 American Austin by the Fort Benning, Georgia, Infantry Board was only possible by using a special Quartermaster General's fund), for more than a decade the military tested inexpensive civilian cars converted into "Cross-Country" vehicles. These hybrids combined low cost, adequate ground clearance and a low silhouette.

One version, constructed in 1923 by Carl C Terry (then an Army Captain) and William F Beasley, head of the automotive engineering section of the US Army Ordnance Department's technical division, was a stripped down, 1100lb Model T Ford with cut down wheels and balloon-type aircraft tires. Years later, in his memoirs, Beasley asserted that this vehicle "contained within it the basic

The pilot model Bantam 4x4. After completion on September 21, 1940, it was road tested and, following some minor adjustments, driven to Camp Holabird two days later. It arrived 30 minutes ahead of the contract deadline and, prior to evaluation, its specification and construction were checked and recorded. Regardless of the wide variety of published opinions about this vehicle – ranging from criticism for a lack of power and the number of 'bugs' found in its construction – to praise for its overall performance, recognition by historians as 'Jeep #1' and 'Old Number One,' makes its significance in Jeep history obvious. (Author's collection)

concept of what was later to become the Jeep."

Beasley was not alone in staking a claim to Jeep parentage. In a letter published in the December 1943, issue of *Infantry Journal*, Colonel W B Wallace, Infantry (retired) wrote that "The true story of the development of the now famous Jeep should be told and full credit given to the Infantry School (tank section) before it was moved to [Fort] Benning."

Believing it inappropriate to give full attribution to a single person, since "so many different ones had a hand in it," Colonel Wallace detailed work led by the 1st Tank Regiment's commander at Fort George S Meade in the early 1920s. Utilizing a ¾-ton Ford truck chassis and motor taken from the Fort's salvage dump, the service company's maintenance section was instructed to create a vehicle with bucket-type seats for the commander's use in following tanks over the "scrub oak and sand of the Meade reservation." Called the 'puddle jumper,' Wallace described it as "the first Jeep." Apparently, more than one example was built since Wallace reported that "Sometime after 1931, an inspector from the War Department saw these vehicles, reported them as unauthorized and the regiment was ordered to get rid of them."

By the early thirties, with funding for the "Cross-Country" project terminated, Colonel Wallace recollected in his previously noted 1943 letter that "Washington said that if and when we ever went to war again we would have to be satisfied with whatever the automobile factories were turning out at the time."

Historians estimate that fewer than one hundred cross-country vehicles were constructed. Typically weighing in initially at just over one thousand pounds, performance rapidly deteriorated as machine guns, ammunition, tools and spare parts were added.

In his paper *The Development of the Jeep*, Captain Michael R Frost explained that "The final versions ... became so bloated with additional weight ... that they lost their original purpose of being light and easily maneuverable. The final versions could barely move their own weight."

This issue resurfaced years later when the Jeep's

designers, after shaving weight from early models, watched the pounds return as the military specified the use of heavier components and additional equipment. Compounding this matter was the tendency of troops in the field to seriously overload the Jeep.

After the cross-country era ended, several new initiatives moved to the forefront of research and development. Following the British Army's use of the Austin Seven and the Morris Minor for reconnaissance and radio communication, the US Army's Infantry Board, in the early thirties, tested the Austin Seven's American counterpart, the American Austin. In 1976, Roy Evans, who owned American Austin in the thirties, related to several Austin/Bantam enthusiasts that he loaned several stripped down American Austin cars to the Pennsylvania National Guard in 1933 ...

The Infantry Board equipped its American Austin with oversize tires and a rear compartment-mounted triple machine gun unit. Rifkind observed that this vehicle "while a far cry from the ultimate jeep, served the useful purpose of indicating to the Army what it might expect in the way of performance from a small car."

In 1936 Brigadier General Walter C Short, Assistant Commander of the Infantry School at Fort Benning, narrowed the gap between what existed and what the military needed by authorizing the construction of what became known as the 'Belly Flopper.' Included in Short's expectations was one that would later be a factor in blunting criticisms about the early Jeep's weight: that four men should be able to move the vehicle over or around small obstacles. Short additionally wanted the vehicle to make maximum use of existing components. This practical approach would also be evident in the future designs from Bantam, Ford, and Willys.

One of the project's leaders was Captain Robert G Howie, an infantry instructor in the school's tank section, with both enthusiasm for midget racing cars and experience as an infantryman prior to and during World War I. Aware of the need for rapid deployment of relatively heavy automatic weapons in offensive operations, he devised a low profile, self-propelled vehicle mounting a machine gun, carrying sufficient ammunition and operated by a two-man crew. Assisting Howie in the construction of the 'Belly Flopper' (officially labeled the 'Howie Machine-Gun Carrier') was Master Sergeant G L Rush. Master Sergeant Melvin Wiley joined them in completing the vehicle in April 1937.

Aware of the Army's testing of American Austins, in 1936 Howie shared his design with representatives from American Bantam and a Timkin-Detroit Axle Company field engineer; American Bantam responded by providing him with a new engine/transmission unit.

At approximately the same time Harry Miller, one of America's foremost race car engine designers, was serving a short stint as American Bantam's vice-president in charge of engineering. H O Creazzi, who was later associated with Miller and the Gulf-Miller racing car project, recalled in *Good Things Did Come In Small Packages, Automobile Quarterly, Vol 4, #14*, that Miller "was working on a four-wheel drive vehicle, had it running around on the second floor of a building up there in Butler."

The two-wheel drive Belly Flopper was depicted as "put together from junk parts" and resembling a "wheeled sled with a rear-mounted motor." Harold Rifkind noted that "Some salvaged Austin parts from the Fort Benning salvage pile – perhaps the very ones that composed the Austin purchased in 1932 – were used in the building of the machine." Richard Grace, writing in *Army Motors* (Number 93, Fall 2000) identified some of its components as those "salvaged from the remains of several American Austin automobiles that had been tested at Fort Benning in the early 1930s."

Positioned on standard military cot mattresses, the crew operated from prone positions. The driver used a tiller to steer the wheels with the gunner operating a 0.30 caliber machine gun. While the lack of a suspension system (the axles were bolted directly to the frame) made for some adventurous moments when traveling over rough terrain, the Belly Flopper's relatively wide tires and rear-mounted engine gave it excellent performance over sandy terrain.

In the Nov/Dec 1937 issue of *Infantry Journal* magazine, Captain Wendell G Johnson described the Belly Flopper as low, relatively fast, and highly maneuverable. It was able, he wrote, to "scoot from one firing position to another at five to ten miles per hour."

Although its low silhouette prompted Howie and others to refer to the Belly Flopper as "a snake in the

Belly Flopper specification	
Engine:	four-cylinder, in-line, L-head
Bore x stroke:	2.2in x 3.0in
Displacement:	45.6cu-in
Horsepower:	14.8 @ 3500rpm
Transmission:	3-speed, manual (chain drive to rear wheels
Height:	32.25in (Rifkind cited height as 33.25in)
Wheelbase	75in
Length:	124.0in
Ground clearance:	7.75in
Tires:	6.00 x 9in tractor tires
Weight:	1233lb (Rifkind reported its weight without machine gun and equipment as 1015lb)
Maximum speed:	28mph

grass," limited ground clearance and restricted mobility contributed to its rejection as a General Purpose Vehicle (GPV) after approximately 4000 miles of testing by the Infantry Board.

While recognizing the modified Austin convertible and the Belly Flopper as predecessors of the Jeep, Rifkind was less certain about according them Jeep prototype status: "The first was experimented with as a reconnaissance car substituting for the motorcycle, while the Howie machine was designed strictly as a light, low silhouette weapons carrier." The problem, Rifkind continued, "was to combine these two functions into a single vehicle."

By the late thirties the military had gained experience with a wide range of 4x4 vehicles, and in 1938 possessed lightweight versions of the standard 1½-ton 4x4 cargo trucks as well as ½-ton Ford pickups converted to four-wheel drive by Marmon-Herrington in 1936. The following year, Marmon-Herrington supplied to the Army a number of cab-over-engine 4x4 ½-ton Fords with 'roadster tops' for use as ambulances. The Ford trucks played a major role in the subsequent development of other 4x4 military vehicles, including the Dodge Command Car, but their relatively large size and high silhouette offset their all-terrain capability. Bantam also sold three chassis to the Quartermaster Corps in 1938 for testing. According to Rifkind, they did not prove successful.

By early 1940, support for adapting existing vehicles for military use had been nearly displaced by the realization that only a 'new-from-the-ground-up' vehicle would meet the modern Army's needs.

As noted by Rifkind, this new design would combine the best features of the Austin and the Howie Weapons Carrier, a blending not possible in the ultra low budget environment of earlier years. Events in Europe had brought this era to an end; furthermore, the sense of urgency surrounding America's preparation for war resulted in contracts with time restraints, which competitors could only hope to meet by making maximum use of readily available components.

Many of the "Light Vehicle Development" guidelines issued by the Chief of Infantry on June 6, 1940 – including a maximum height of 36 inches, and a weight of between 750 and 1000 pounds – appeared tailor-made for a Bantam-based vehicle. With interest in the old Belly Flopper and current Bantams high (Bantam's effort to attract the military's attention included hiring Charles H Payne, a retired and resourceful Navy commander, to promote its interests in Washington. Payne's efforts included providing Secretary of War Henry Stimson with the results of Bantam's study of automobile use by the European military), several members of an Army technical committee representing the Infantry, Cavalry, Ordnance and Quartermaster Corps arrived at the Butler, Pennsylvania, Bantam plant on June 19, 1940 to evaluate

The Holabird test course's reputation for being a 'torture test' was underscored by the observation of an Army officer that it "tortures a truck like an inquisitional rack, and if a truck has anything to confess, it confesses." (Author's collection)

and test the contemporary Bantams. This group Included Colonel Howie and William Beasley, then serving as the Ordnance Department's Chief Engineer.

Committee members drove several Bantams over hilly terrain and, with one admitting that they "did all kinds of stunts", apparently found them both fun to drive and good performers. The committee then assigned Beasley and two Army engineers, Bob Brown and Bill Burgan, to outline the primary requirements for an all-new military vehicle. On June 19, 1940, along with Major Howie and engineers from Bantam, they began work on what became the basis for a specification, released by the Quartermaster Corps on June 22, 1940, for an all-new military vehicle. Its specification those elements shown in the table below. Bantam appeared well positioned to be the principle producer of such a vehicle. Although virtually inactive, its Butler, Pennsylvania facilities were considered adequate for manufacture and it already possessed, courtesy of Colonel Howie, blueprints and specification relating to the committee's proposal.

– Four-wheel drive and a 2-speed transfer case allowing the front axle to be disengaged
– Bucket seats for three passengers
– Hydraulic brakes
– Folding windshield
– A rectangular-shaped body
– Full-floating front and rear axles
– Maximum weight of 1200 pounds
– Accommodation of a pedestal mount for a 0.30-caliber machine
– A lighting system incorporating blackout lights
– A speed range of 3-50mph
– A wheelbase of approximately 75in
– Maximum height of 36in
– 45° degree approach and 40° degree departure angles

In late June 1943, Colonel Howie issued a statement describing his activities at Bantam. He explained that, in June 1940, he was participating in maneuvers in Louisiana when he was ordered to travel to Bantam's Butler plant with drawings of the Howie Carrier. In Butler, he was informed by the Ordnance and Quartermaster Committee that Bantam was to construct 70 vehicles. and he was to "turn over" the drawings and remain at Butler to "formulate plans and specifications for the new vehicle." Further, he added, "This vehicle was to be based on the characteristics and engineering data of the 'Howie Carrier,' incorporating four-wheel drive, with a capacity of three passengers." Major Howie also recalled that he was

Speaking to Karl Probst, Major Herbert J Lawes, who, as purchasing and contracting officer at Camp Holabird, had tested the Bantam, said: "I have driven every unit the services have purchased for the past twenty years. I can judge them in fifteen minutes. This vehicle is going to be absolutely outstanding. I believe this unit will make history." (Author's collection)

asked by the committee to "form an opinion as to whether or not the Bantam Company was capable of building the vehicle if awarded a contract."

After Howie's arrival, the Board (Howie used this term to identify the committee) stayed at Butler one day. It made an inspection of the plant (which was not operating at that time), and held meetings with various Bantam officials including President Frank Fenn, Karl Probst (identified as Bantam's Chief Engineer), and Charles Payne. Howie noted that he was instructed to "remain at the Bantam plant as long as necessary to complete plans and specifications so that the Bantam Company could proceed if and when directed."

Assisting Howie for the next two days was Board member, Robert F Brown, a civilian engineer assigned to the Holabird Quartermaster Depot. In that period of time, Howie said "we discussed engineering features of the vehicle." After Brown's departure, Howie remained at Butler for approximately a week. "During that time," he recalled, "I turned over drawings, photos and other data of the Howie Carrier to the Bantam Company, and wrote and submitted specifications for the new vehicle."

A point of contention between Howie and Bantam was the use of Bantam components in the new vehicle. "During this period," Howie recollected, "it was the desire of the Bantam Company to use many of their standard production parts and unit assemblies, without change. It was not without some discussion that I was able to

ALL BRAND-NEW STORIES

Popeye
on Jeep Island

Long before the first Bantam 'Jeep' arrived at Fort Holabird in 1940, many items, real and imaginary, were identified as 'Jeeps.' One example was Eugene the Jeep, who first appeared in a 1936 Popeye comic strip. Eugene is seen here on the cover of a 1940s era Dell comic.
(Courtesy Marshall Rimland collection)

convince them that the vehicle must be engineered completely as a new vehicle and that the success of the job depended on the inclusion of those characteristics, such as flotation, power to weight ratio, angles of approach and departure, size of axles, wheels, tires, frame, wheelbase and power transmission, all in proper relation to each other, as were proven in the Howie Carrier and which gave it cross-country agility and stamina. These characteristics were incorporated into the specifications. During this period an engineer of the Spicer Corp. was called in, and a drawing of a front-wheel drive [vehicle], prepared by me and with the aid of Mr Albrecht, was given to him." Howie had completed that project in 1936 along with John Albrecht, who was then the Field Engineer for the Timken-Detroit Axle Company.

Even with this advantage, Bantam still faced a reality in which far larger companies – including Willys-Overland, Marmon-Herrington, and Minneapolis Moline – were aware of the Army's interest in a new reconnaissance car. After Willys' offer to supply one or two of its products for testing as either a machine gun or personnel carrier had been rebuffed by the Quartermaster Corps in 1938 (the QMC's response was that "no good purpose would be served by making the suggested tests"), Willys succeeded in having one of its passenger cars tested at Fort Knox.

Willys-Overland's ebb and flow history of successes and setbacks was reflected in its management. Willys originated in 1903 as the producer of the Overland Runabout. In 1907, John North Willys was operating an auto agency in Elmira, NY, when he learned of Overland's impending collapse. Having contracted for Overland's entire year's output, he responded by traveling to the Overland plant in Indianapolis and arranging for

The 1940 Willys Quad. Eventually this model was selected in preference to the proposals from Ford and Bantam as the basis for the mass produced Jeeps of World War II. Most Willys-Overland historians believe that five Quad models were built. This example was photographed in the early 1950s: some Jeep enthusiasts hold out hope that it might still survive. The first Quad was delivered to the US Army on November 11, 1940. (Author's collection)

finance to keep it operating. In 1908 Willys – president, treasurer, secretary and purchasing agent – reorganized it into the Willys-Overland Company. By 1910, having relocated Willys-Overland to Toledo, Ohio, Willys was overseeing the industry's second largest producer.

In 1929 Willys left Willys-Overland to become the US Ambassador to Poland but was soon back in Toledo in an effort to save Willys-Overland from the financial consequences of the stock market crash and the Depression. Willys-Overland survived some grim periods of receivership and reorganization to produce a new Willys car in 1936.

Discussions between the company's Board Chairman, Ward Canaday, and ranking military officials late in 1939 kept Willys-Overland informed of the military's interests. According to A Wade Wells, author of *Hail To The Jeep*, Willys, while also aware of relations between Bantam and the military, understood Bantam to be interested in developing a messenger-type vehicle. Canaday claimed that Willys was focusing on adaptations of its passenger car for use as a "combat car."

Attendance at a March 1940 demonstration of the Howie-Wiley Belly Flopper at Ft Benning, Georgia, by Willys-Overland Chief Engineer Delmar Roos and its President, Joseph W Frazer, was not the first contact between Willys-Overland and the US Army concerning Willys' participation in future military projects, but it was significant. Several years later, Frazer recalled that the Belly Flopper was "crude, terribly crude, but it stimulated thought. It was in reality the embryo of the jeep ... To serve as an effective scout car, it would have to be stronger, more durable, more powerful, yet light, fast and low."

Richard Grace, a Jeep historian familiar with the Belly Flopper, has concluded (*Army Motors* No 93, Fall 2000), that after studying the Belly Flopper "Roos was able to visualize the modifications and improvements that would be required to overcome its shortcomings, and the results appeared in the Willys Quad which was submitted to the Army for testing on November 13, 1940."

For his part, Roos, In a paper presented to the Society of Automotive Engineers on October 12, 1944, credited Arthur W Herrington, co-founder of Marmon-Herrington in 1931, with first relaying to Willys the Army's probable interest in a small vehicle.

Benefiting from Roos' skills, Willys would prove to be a formidable competitor. But for the moment, Bantam still had the inside track, as its engineers – working along with the Ordnance subcommittee – visited Camp Holabird, Maryland, where tests of wheeled military vehicles were conducted. They were also in contact with the Spicer Manufacturing Company of Toledo, Ohio, a leader in the development and production of 4-wheel drive systems.

By July 2, 1940, the QMC's specification for the new military vehicle had been revised. The maximum allowable weight was now 1275 pounds; maximum height increased to 40 inches, and the wheelbase was extended to 80 inches. In addition, these "Tentative Specifications, Truck, Motor Gasoline, Light Reconnaissance & Command Car (Four Wheels-Four Wheel Drive)" also called for a prohibition against the use of an aluminum cylinder head, and the requirement that at least eight of the seventy vehicles to be constructed had four-wheel steering.

Agreement, in mid-1940, between the military and Bantam that the Bantam engine wasn't powerful enough for the task at hand led to Bantam's use of a standard 45hp Continental BY-4112 engine for its proposal. More ominously, this change also highlighted the pivotal role played by the Willys 'Go-Devil' engine in the eventual dominance of the Willys proposal.

In a move that would have eliminated Willys, or any other company as prime competitor, Bantam offered to contract for a lot of seventy vehicles at a unit price of $2500. Although the argument that Bantam deserved this privilege due to its earlier contributions and interest was not without logic, the Quartermaster Corps maintained that the contract should be open to bids from other firms.

Consequently, the QMC invited 135 companies, including Bantam, Willys and Ford, to submit bids and plans no later than 9:00am, Monday July 22, 1940 for an initial $175,000 contract for 70 prototype vehicles (eight with four-wheel steering) to be delivered within 75 days. The first prototype model was to be delivered in seven weeks with the remaining 69 vehicles, incorporating changes requested by the Quartermaster Corps, to be delivered just 26 days after these changes were specified.

The only bids received came from Bantam and Willys, the latter's initial advantage as the lowest bidder quickly disappearing when its request for an extension of 120 days incurred a substantial penalty for every day it failed to meet the stipulated 75 day time limit. With Bantam declaring it would meet the specified delivery date, not surprisingly, its bid of $171,185 was accepted.

Aspects of the design of Bantam's pilot model, and the issue of where credit for the Jeep's design is most deserved are discussed in the next chapter. None of the subsequent controversy over the latter point mattered when the Bantam arrived at Camp Holabird 30 minutes ahead of the 9:00am contract deadline on September 23, 1940. It had been completed on September 21, 1940 and, after road testing and minor adjustments were made, had departed Butler for Holabird. Accompanying Bantam Plant Manager Harold Crist on this trip was Karl Probst. Gene Rice, Willys-Overland's representative in Washington DC, was present when the Bantam arrived at Camp Holabird, According to Karl Probst ("One Summer In Butler – Bantam Builds The Jeep" *Automobile Quarterly*, Fourth Quarter 1976 Vol 14, Number 4), the Bantam's performance convinced Rice that large orders would be forthcoming for such a vehicle. Rice informed Probst that he was going to advise Willys officials to quickly complete its pilot model under construction. Probst told Rice that Willys had plenty of time since the parts Bantam used were also available to Willys.

Regardless of the wide variety of published opinions about this Bantam, ranging from criticism for lacking power and the many 'bugs' in its construction, to praise for its overall performance, many historians recognize it as 'Jeep No 1' and 'Old Number One.'

The demand placed on a vehicle by test conditions at Holabird subject any negative comments about the Bantam to qualification. Rifkind, explaining that the Holabird test course enjoyed a reputation for being a "torture test," quoted one source as believing it was essentially the same as "rolling it [a truck] down the Grand Canyon." Even more graphic was this Army officer's comment: "That test course tortures a truck like an inquisitional rack, and if a truck has anything to confess, it confesses." Highlights of the 'Holabird Inquisition' included 5000 miles of highway operation with both full payload and towed loads; a 1000 mile cross-country trial (Rifkind reported the average speed over this section as in the 7-9mph vicinity), including passage through mud holes, runs over twisting hill passages and travel up grades as steep as 65 degrees. Then came another 1000 miles on what Rifkind called "a concentrated section of clay road." After an additional 500 miles on a "rolling sand course," with both full payload and towed load, came the grand finale: ten hours of operation over sandy terrain in low gear at speeds ranging from 1.5 to 2mph.

The Bantam's test report, dated October 23, 1940, was submitted by Lieut Col William B Johnson, Chief of the Engineering Branch of the Quartermaster Corps. It noted that the "operations test" began on September 27, 1940 and was completed on October 16, 1940. The accumulated mileage of 3410 miles was divided into these categories:

Highway operation: ....247 miles
Test track operation: ....1894 miles
Cross county operation:......................901 miles
Bad road operation: ....244 miles
Miscellaneous tests:...........................124 miles

Johnson identified a total of twenty "difficulties that developed during the operations test." Considering the scope and intensity of this evaluation, during which Captain Frost asserted that "repeated attempts to destroy the vehicle were made," damage to the Bantam was minor.

Although the Bantam's tire wear was depicted as "very excessive," Johnson noted that "This could have been due to operation on the test track which is very severe on tires."

When Probst and Crist left Butler for the trip to Camp Holabird, they had packed some stiffer springs as spares. Apparently they were not stiff enough to suit Johnson, since he noted: "No satisfactory springs were submitted for test. The last springs furnished were the best, but require more strength."

The cooling fan was identified as the reason why "considerable difficulty was experienced in grounding out the ignition system at any time the vehicle entered water above a foot and a half in depth." As Johnson explained "This is due to the fan turning the water and splashing it about the sparkplugs and distributor coil."

Johnson expressed dissatisfaction with the Bantam's carburetor which "became inoperative due to the entry of water and dirt." The problem, he said, was "due to an unnecessarily large hole where the accelerator plunger linkage enters the carburetor body."

A matter later successfully addressed by Ford when it submitted its prototype model, the Pygmy, for testing, concerned the Bantam's windshield. Johnson said it was "inadequately braced and failed early in the test." He also reported that the windshield wiper (a hand-operated, driver's side only unit) needed stops to prevent it from "being pulled off the windshield during operation."

A skid plate was brazed to the crankcase after it was

The Pygmy which was tested at Holabird in 1940 is currently owned by the Alabama Center for Military History, the only known survivor of the Bantam, Willys and Ford prototype Jeeps. Its existence offers Jeep enthusiasts an unparalleled window on the past and the opportunity to appreciate its contribution to the Jeep's design. Many aspects of the Pygmy – including location of its gas tank under the driver's seat, and two-piece windshield with tubular steel frame – found their way onto the MB and GPW models. (Courtesy Lawrence Wade/ Alabama Center of Military History, Huntsville, AL)

damaged by rocks and other obstructions on the course. Johnson noted that "a proper skid plate protecting the crank case is a necessity on this vehicle."

A number of body/chassis components came to grief during testing. These included the headlight bracket ("... broke loose from the fender ... must be braced more adequately ..."); the exhaust muffler ("... torn off during the test."); fenders and grille ("loosened during the test."), and headlights ("difficulty was experienced keeping the headlight lens in its frame due to loosening of the clamping screw").

The Bantam's testing concluded after the side frame rails gave way at the point of support for the rear motor mounts. "This was undoubtedly due," wrote Johnson, "to the combined weight of the operating personnel, the transfer case and the weight of the rear end of the motor, all of which is supported at that point. The frame must be reinforced to prevent this failure."

None of this dampened the military's enthusiasm for the Bantam; Johnson provided a view of the Bantam's prospects almost as an afterthought to comments about its emergency brake and wiring: "The emergency brake as furnished on the prototype model was not satisfactory in operation and it is understood that a new type of emergency brake will be furnished on production vehicles..." Several shorts developed in the electrical system. This may have been due to the fact that this was a hand built vehicle but care should be exercised in production vehicles to prevent chafing of the electrical system."

Although the Willys Quad's performance would

The Pygmy was equipped with a 60mph speedometer, with shifting point indicators, which was used by Ford's 4-cylinder pickups. (Courtesy Lawrence Wade/Alabama Center of Military History, Huntsville, AL)

decrease its significance, the final report on the Bantam was a tribute to its design, noting, for example, that "This vehicle demonstrated ample power." Major Herbert J Lawes, as the purchasing and contracting officer at Camp Holabird, had tested the Bantam, told Karl Probst that "I have driven every unit the services have purchased for the past twenty years. I can judge them in fifteen minutes. This vehicle is going to be absolutely outstanding. I believe this unit will make history." Nonetheless, the arrival of the Willys Quad at Camp Holabird in November 1940 was the beginning of the end for Bantam.

The Quad's performance at Holabird provided both its critics and supporters with plenty of points to bolster their positions. Donald Kenower, a Willys test driver, noted that in the cross-country runs the Quad's light springs and ability to ride "fairly well" enabled the test crew to drive it "about twice as fast as they did other similar vehicles ..." In contrast, Rifkind reported that "spring failure was encountered throughout the test."

Noting that the cross-country test area had become "a mud lake due to continuous rain," Kenower conceded that the Quad's oil bath cleaner had not been properly mounted, allowing dirt to enter the engine through the air inlet. "Before this was discovered," he explained, "the engine had been damaged, and in order to continue the test and avoid delay an engine was taken out of a Willys passenger car and installed in the pilot model."

For his part, Rifkind wrote that "like any other pilot model submitted for test the Willys jeep took quite a battering from the Holabird course." Referring to the

One of the most apparent Pygmy contributions to Jeep history was the integrated design of its grille and headlights. (Courtesy Lawrence Wade/Alabama Center of Military History, Huntsville, AL)

Quad's engine, he added that "... cylinders were badly worn after 5011 miles of operation, and the entire engine was replaced by a used motor taken from a Willys Americar, which also failed after 1316 additional miles."

Also cited as examples of what Rifkind depicted as the "extreme punishment to which pilot models were subjected" was the fracturing of the Willys frame after 5184 miles, and failure of the transfer case main shaft bearings at the 6190 mile mark. Rifkind also mentioned that "the steering pin mounted on the front axle went out after 1814 miles." Rifkind emphasized the point that these mechanical failures "were the rule, rather than the exception, for all pilot models subjected to the severe Holabird test."

In August 1941, when Lt Col Edwin S Van Duesen testified before the Truman Committee concerning awarding the Jeep contract to Willys-Overland, he said "I can't recall a single new production vehicle pilot model that has passed through these engineering tests that has not required some minor changes, and in some cases, comparatively major changes, in order to make the vehicle ... acceptable under the award."

In late 1940, as Bantam used the lessons learned from the Camp Holabird tests to improve the performance of the next batch of seventy models (designated the BRC-60 and often referred to as the Mark II model), the pace of activity leading to mass production of Jeeps accelerated. Even before Bantam had met the December 17, 1940 due date for the delivery of the BRC-60, it had received an additional order for 1500 additional units, identified as the BRC-40 model.

Paralleling these developments were others which

enabled Willys and Ford to present their proposals as alternatives to Bantam's. Ford's offering, the Pygmy, arrived at Camp Holabird on November 23, 1940. It performed well in the Holabird tests and was accepted on January 6, 1941.

Rifkind set out the general parameters of the battle between Bantam and the far larger Willys and Ford operations. "It seemed," he wrote, "as if everyone took sides." Initially Bantam had the support of the 'using arms' (the Infantry, Cavalry, and Field Artillery). Rifkind pointed out that the QMC, while willing to include Willys, inclined toward Ford as it was seen as the "largest and most dependable" producer.

The Ford and Willys representatives present for tests of Bantam's pilot model received copies of the Bantam blueprints (Willys' proposal of July 22, 1940 included what has been described as a "rough sketch."). The 'fairness' of this action has been a contentious issue for years. The Army asserted that since the Bantam was government

This view of the Pygmy shows its steering wheel, which Randy Windrow, Director of the Alabama Center of Military Museum, identifies as being from a 1940 Ford pickup or standard car. He explains that "in the factory photos they have a little three-spoke steering wheel and I understand that during testing, it broke and was replaced with this one." (Courtesy Alabama Center of Military History, Huntsville, AL)

The Pygmy was acquired by the Center in the early 1980s at a Hudson & Marshall auction of surplus vehicles owned by the Henry Ford Museum and Greenfield Village. The catalog, which included a reversed photo, described it as: "1940 Ford GP 'Pygmy,' Serial No 1. Very few produced. Not a production 'Jeep.' Condition good. Army Green. Length: 133in." (Courtesy Lawrence Wade/Alabama Center of Military History, Huntsville, AL)

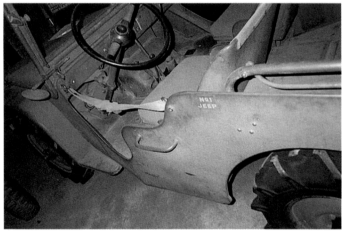

These two views of the Pygmy illustrate the 'No 1 Jeep' plaques attached to each side of its body. "During World War II," says Randy Windrow, "the Pygmy, depicted as 'Ford's Jeep Number 1,' was used for a variety of public relation and war bond rallies in the Detroit area. (Courtesy Alabama Center of Military History, Huntsville, AL)

property, it was under no obligation to regard its design as proprietary. Also cited as justifying this action was a growing consensus that the Bantam plant in Butler would be unable to fulfill a large order from the government. Thus, although Bantam had received an order from the Adjutant General for 1500 vehicles, the stage was set for another round of competition.

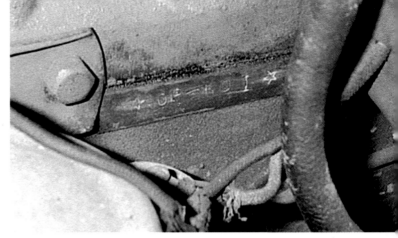

The Pygmy has a star symbol, the letters GP and No 1 stamped on its engine block. (Courtesy Alabama Center of Military History, Huntsville, AL)

Opposition to the plan for Bantam to build the 1500 vehicles came from the Motor Transport Subcommittee, which argued in an October 18, 1940 report for the contract to be divided into three equal parts: 500 each for Bantam, Ford, and Willys. "The subcommittee," explained Rifkind, "held that to allot the entire proposed order for 1500 jeeps to one manufacturer would 'limit the Army to the development of a single type of vehicle which may not be the most satisfactory of the three types offered'."

Rifkind added that representatives from Ford and Willys had been "called in" and "encouraged" to make major investments in the development of prototype models. The Subcommittee's proposal was rejected by both the Army's general staff and Secretary of War Henry Stimson, who received an emphatic letter from Charles Payne in October 1940 explaining why such an action was inappropriate.

Contrasting with Bantam's efforts in developing the Jeep, Payne noted that there had been "no other automobile manufacturer contributing one iota to its successful completion." Furthermore, whereas Bantam had virtually abandoned its commercial activities in order to work on the jeep, other companies had continued theirs unabated, whilst still securing military contracts.

Bantam may have had had no alternative but to seek a government contract if it hoped to continue to exist; for 1940, American Bantam sales amounted to just 800 units. The previous year, the figure had been just over 1225. Yet, as exemplified by an effort (albeit unsuccessful) to build small tractors for Sears and Roebuck, American Bantam's resourcefulness, in the face of continual disappointment, seemed boundless.

This degree of corporate energy, even if motivated by desperation, added substance to Payne's claim that Bantam's experience in the production and design of small cars was unequaled in the US, so thus merited status as sole supplier of the Jeep. Payne also called Stimson's attention to the relationship between problems Spicer was having in increasing its axle output and the logic of letting Ford and Willys share in the latest contract. Regardless of how many manufacturers were given a share of the Jeep orders, he maintained it would not significantly boost production until Spicier (or other suppliers) increased production levels of critical components. Therefore, he reasoned that until Bantam's production capacity had been fully utilized, there was no reason for the government to go shopping elsewhere for a source of Jeep output. As quoted by Rifkind, Payne told Stimson that if Bantam was unable to supply the required number of Jeeps, it would be "glad and willing to turn over all detail drawings and other help to other automobile manufacturers in the interest of national defense."

One of the most spirited arguments on Bantam's behalf came from the Infantry, whose representative asserted that in contrast to the vehicles from Ford and Willys which "had never been seen, much less tested," the Bantam model had been "engineered, thoroughly tested, and found satisfactory." He also argued that, unlike Bantam, which was portrayed as being extremely responsive to the needs of the military, "the past attitude of Ford and Willys has been one of indifference to the special requirements of the military service. It does not seem either in the interest of the government or consistent to fair play to discourage Bantam in such efforts by failing to give them the support to which their initiative and cooperative attitude entitle them."

Nonetheless, opposing views expressed by several key players in the contract process prevailed. The Quartermaster General, uncomfortable with Bantam's finances and the possible consequences of a total reliance upon Bantam in case of an unforeseen emergency, wrote that he "wishes to go on record that he did not consider the directed action [giving Bantam the 1500 vehicle order] in the best interest of the government." The National Advisory Commission, which had to approve the Bantam contract, also supported the concept of having more than one supplier for the new vehicle: "We believe the division between at least two sources desirable." Thus, approval was given on November 14, 1940 for the Quartermaster, in addition to the Bantam contract, to contract with Willys and Ford for 1500 vehicles, contingent on certification of their prototype models. Willys delivered its MA model to Camp Holabird on November 11. Ford's GP arrived on November 23, 1940.

On June 26, 1941, Bantam, Willys, and Ford – having each produced their 1500 vehicles – engaged in a showdown, officially designated the "Service-Test Finals," which took place at Ft Benning, Georgia. At that point the issue of who deserved the lion's share of praise for the Jeep's creation mattered little; what was on the line was a substantial government contract, whose eventual magnitude was unknown.

The relative merits of the Bantam BRC 40, Ford GP

The Ford Pygmy undergoing testing. The Pygmy engine was very closely related to the Ford 9N tractor engine, which had been introduced in June 1939. With a 3.19in bore and 3.75in stroke, it had a 119.7 cubic inch displacement. Since it was basically half of the 95 horsepower Mercury flathead V-8, many of its parts, including the pistons, rods, valves and lifters, interchanged with those of that engine. (Author's collection)

and Willys MA have been a topic of spirited discussion amongst Jeep enthusiasts and historians for many years. Both the Willys and Ford had external similarities to the Bantam model, but all three had unique specifications.

The Infantry Board's Test Section "Partial Report of Comparative Tests" between the three models, released on July 22, 1941, indicated the order of finish as Willys, Bantam, and Ford. Using Rifkind's summary of this report as a source, a ranking of the competitors on a first, second, third basis in a number of significant categories is detailed in the accompanying table.

Rifkind's summary of the "Partial Report" provided additional evidence of the overall superiority of the Willys compared with its competitors, whilst indicating that the Ford and Bantam models also had merit. The MA received praise for the torque output of its engine, the ease with which its transmission could be shifted, and the strength of its frame. Both its radiator and top were judged "better" than those of the competition. In the case of the GP, its top was considered difficult to put up. Whereas the panel praised the location of the Ford's gear shift, transfer case controls and hand brake, as well as its abundant leg room and overall driver comfort, it found little to like about the MA's driver accommodation which it judged

cramped and awkward. Specifically criticized was the location of the Willys accelerator and hand brake. The MA's steering column mounted gear shift lever, with its relatively involved linkage, was considered susceptible to breakdown. The Bantam had the edge in steering and braking performance.

In his article, "The Jeep In Action" (*Army Ordnance*, September 1944), Major E P Hogan explained that on the basis of testing the first Bantam, Willys, and Ford prototypes (described as "among the toughest ever carried out in this country"), and the subsequent evaluation of the MA, GP and BRC40 models, "the US Army made its choice in favor of Willys, whose Jeep came closest to meeting the specifications and the requirements of the

A pair of BRC-60 Bantams on maneuvers. Only 69 of these models were constructed. (Courtesy Marshall Rimland collection)

Army." Almost as an afterthought, he added: "Moreover, the price quoted by Willys was the lowest."

After completion of the 1941 tests, the process of eliminating Bantam – innovator and pioneer – as a contender for future Jeep contracts would be swift and complete. With the performance of the MA well documented, Willys-Overland had moved into the limelight. But in an environment in which America was to

The GP's engine was also used in this form in a number of Ford's 1941 light-duty trucks as a replacement for the 60hp V-8. (Courtesy Richard Stauffer)

Model:	Willys	Bantam	Ford
Category			
High gear acceleration:	1	2	3
Maximum speed[a]:	1	2	3
Grade climbing ability:	1	2	3
Fuel economy[b]:	3	1	2
Turning radius[c]:	2	3	1
Braking:	2	1	3
Hill Climbing[d]:	1	3	2

Notes
[a]The MA reached a level road maximum speed of 74mph. Respective figures for the BRC40 and GP were 64 and 59mph.
[b] The BRC40 averaged 23.3mpg over a speed range of 30-50mph. Respective figures for the GP and MA were 20.9 and 20.2mpg.
[c] The GP's turning radius was 17.5ft, the MA's 19.4ft, and the BRC's 20.4ft.
[d] All three vehicles, carrying the driver and a passenger, plus a load of sand, were driven up a 28 degree grade in low ratio second gear. The Willys crested at 10mph, with what was depicted as a "great reserve of available power." The Ford failed to complete the test; the Bantam was successful but with "no reserve power left."

become the "Arsenal of Democracy," Ford, by virtue of its massive production facilities, remained a force to be reckoned with.

Historians have used words such as "incredible" and "astonishing" when describing the decision by the QMC to award the next Jeep contract, for 16,000 units, to Ford because it was the "largest and most dependable" producer. Only action by the Office of Production Management prevented this from becoming a reality.

Instead, as Rifkind noted, "In accordance with its instructions from higher authority," the QMC proceeded to seek bids on an "all or none" basis for the 16,000 jeeps.

The lowest bidder, out of a foursome consisting of Willys-Overland, Ford, Bantam, and the Checker Cab Company, was Willys. Once again, though, it was Ford which emerged the apparent winner as the QMC, maintaining that the company was best positioned to meet the commitment, recommended to the Quartermaster General that the contract be awarded to Ford.

Testifying before the Truman Committee, John Biggers of the Office of Production Management explained why this decision was set aside by its Director General,

The Smithsonian Institute's 1940 Bantam BRC-60 is the only one of the 69 constructed known to exist. It was delivered to the Quartermasters Corps on November 29, 1940. After being comprehensively tested by the Army at Fort Knox, Kentucky, it became part of the Smithsonian collection in 1944. For many years it was displayed at the US Army transportation museum at Fort Eustis, Virginia. (Courtesy Smithsonian Institute)

William S Knudsen: "Mr Knudsen decided the question, and when the War Department recommended the award of this contract to Ford, at a $640,000 premium cost to the government, Mr Knudsen refused to approve it. He said that in his judgment as an automobile manufacturer the low bidder was a competent source of supply for that number of vehicles, and he wouldn't reject the bid."

Ford was to receive a sizable order for Jeeps, but the contract issued on November 10, 1941 was for 15,000 GPWs (General Purpose Willys) built according to Willys specification. Once World War II began, Ford, like virtually all American businesses, committed its resources to the quest for victory. In this case events of the recent past

The 4-cylinder engine of this 1941 Ford panel truck links it with the Ford GP. Regarding the 4-cylinder's performance, owner Richard Stauffer says that "the thing really surprises you when you drive it with the amount of torque it has and its pickup with the 4:55 rear end." (Courtesy Richard Stauffer)

mattered little. Eventually Ford did produce 277,896 GPWs.

In his *Army Ordnance* article Major Hogan described the meeting between Major General E B Gregory, the Quartermaster General, and Edsel Ford, the President of the Ford Motor Company, which led to this development: "Having learned that Mr Ford was in Washington the officers were on their way to see him when they met the industrialist in a corridor of the Social Security building. Accompanying General Gregory were Brig Gen H J Lawes and Col E S Van Deusen. General Gregory, in effect, said: 'Mr Ford, the Army wants to standardize this vehicle. We also want two sources of supply. You and your company can do the United States and our army an immeasurable service in this war if you will agree to manufacture this vehicle according to the Willys design with the Willys motor and every single part interchangeable.' The idea was revolutionary, but without hesitation Mr Ford replied: 'Gentlemen, the answer is yes'."

Joseph W Frazer, President and General Manager of Willys-Overland from January 1939 to early 1944, later explained Willys' role in this development: "We were asked to turn over our blueprints and specifications to the Ford Motor Company, and

This depiction of 'Jeeps on the warpath' has in the foreground a Bantam BRC-40. To its right is what appears to be a Bantam BRC-60. It's likely that the Jeep undergoing a tire change is also a BRC-40. (Courtesy Marshall Rimland collection)

This Ford GP was purchased by Fred Heine, Mayor of Lucas, Kansas, from Berg's Truck & Parts in Chicago in 1943. A story about Fred Heine and his Jeep, entitled 'US Civilians Buy Their First Jeeps,' was featured in the January 3, 1944 issue of Life *magazine. Fred Heine had a 2000 acre farm on which he put the Jeep to work.* Life *noted that Heine said the "Jeep was invaluable for reaching the inaccessible parts of the farm because it can climb hills, cross*

The interior of the Heine Ford GP. The instrumentation insert is from a contemporary production model Ford truck. (Courtesy Lawrence Wade/ Alabama Center of Military History, Huntsville, AL)

rivers, and travel indomitably over mud or snow." With it he planned to rope cattle, repair the fences, harrow his fields, haul farm machinery and trailers and even hunt wolves. (Courtesy Lawrence Wade/Alabama Center of Military History, Huntsville, AL)

The MA Jeep at the Willys-Overland Toledo, Ohio plant.
(Author's collection)

we were happy to comply with this request, without compensation, as one of our many contributions to the war effort."

Whether it was fair for Bantam to be eliminated from the Jeep program remains debatable. Bantam President Francis Fenn, appearing before the Truman Committee on August 6, 1941, reported that the Butler plant reached a peak output of 65-68 vehicles per day on an eight hour shift. Fenn claimed that this was achieved by utilizing only 60 per cent of Bantam's assembly line capacity. He asserted that without any additional tooling the plant, operating on three eight hour shifts daily, could turn out 275-300 Jeeps each day. Using the 275 total, this would mean a weekly output of over 1900 Bantams or approximately 100,000 each year.

In 1941 the view that Bantam lacked the necessary facilities for mass production still prevailed. As a result, after completing production

The Ford GP. At Ford, 'GP' was a Ford engineering term in which 'G' represented a government contract vehicle and 'P' denoted an 80 inch Reconnaissance Car.
(Author's collection)

Another view of the same MA as in the previous photo. It is likely that this is the first of the initial batch of 1500 built. It was driven up a series of steps to this location at the Willys-Overland administration building.
(Author's collection)

Barney Roos testing an MA. Unlike the MA seen in the previous photos, which had a single bow top, this example has the two-bow version that was used on the MB. (Author's collection)

Barney Roos obviously enjoying himself at the wheel of the MA. (Courtesy Notre Dame University)

of 2643 examples of the BRC-40, Bantam, rather than building Jeeps, received contracts for a variety of items for the military including trailers, torpedo motors, and aircraft landing gear.

This outcome, regardless of its positive impact upon the Butler economy, was a bitter ending to an episode in military history that, for a time, had centered around that western Pennsylvania community. In his congressional testimony Bantam President Fenn had also noted, with regard to Bantam's elimination from

Amidst civilians and military personnel, including two MPs, the Willys MA had a purposeful, no-nonsense appearance. (Author's collection)

A Ford GP of the 2nd Corps provisional anti-tank battalion pulling a 37mm anti-tank gun. (Courtesy Marshall Rimland collection)

A Willys MA Jeep. Along with Ford and Bantam, Willys was pleased when action shots of its Jeeps were released to the public. (Courtesy Marshall Rimland collection)

This MA Jeep was restored by Jeep historian Stirling Parkerson. With serial number 85504, it was built on September 23, 1941. It was part of an additional number of MAs with a serial number range of 85501-85550, built by Willys-Overland after it had completed an original order for 1500 examples. (Courtesy Lawrence Wade/ Alabama Center of Military History, Huntsville, AL)

By embossing 3in high 'WILLYS' lettering on the MA's front end, Willys-Overland made certain that no-one would mistake it for a Bantam or a Ford. (Courtesy Lawrence Wade/Alabama Center of Military History, Huntsville, AL)

the Jeep program, that "before either of the others had received orders, our cars were in Holabird, undergoing tests, and were subjected to the thorough scrutiny of competitive engineers. In brief, although this had been our idea for years, we shortly found ourselves completely out of the picture."

In response to a committee member's comment about "small concerns ... getting a little business," Fenn explained that "we are not very large, but we have been awfully sincere and honest in producing this car." This prompted Chairman Truman to interject: "It is your baby isn't it?" Fenn's reply said it all: "It is our baby, and building the first one in 49 days meant day and night for about 12 or 15 of us."

From that point Willys-Overland, emerging as the

During World War II, whilst Willys was manufacturing thousands of Jeeps as well as numerous other military items, Henry J Kaiser's shipyards were turning out hundreds of cargo ships and aircraft carriers. Less than ten years after the war ended Willys was acquired by Kaiser-Frazer.

This is a 1962 photo of Henry J Kaiser. (Courtesy Kaiser Aluminum)

The MA's single hand-operated windshield wiper mounted on the driver's side can be seen in this view. (Courtesy Lawrence Wade/Alabama Center of Military History, Huntsville, AL)

successful bidder for the contract awarded on July 23, 1941 for 16,000 vehicles designated the MB Jeep, went from strength to strength. In short order, the contract total was increased to 18,600 units at a price of $738.14 per vehicle. Mass production of the MB model and global association of Willys with the Jeep meant that the issue of its origin, whilst still controversial, was all but forgotten as the US economy mobilized to defeat the Axis powers. As Bantam slipped out of public awareness, Willys and Jeep became ever more synonymous. Even production of tens of thousands of GPWs by the Ford Motor Company did little to dilute Willys' stature during World War II. "Willys" and "Jeep" had become inseparable.

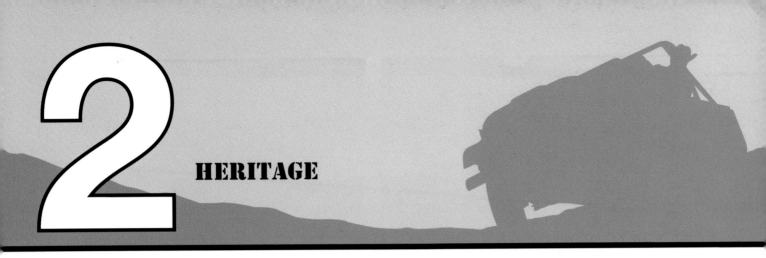

2

HERITAGE

If character is tested by adversity, then the Jeep's true nature was never in doubt during World War II. It was used by just about everyone and transported Presidents, Prime Ministers, Kings, Queens, Princes, Generals, and Privates. It was seen in all the war's theaters, performing every role imaginable in modern combat, in the process becoming one of the most recognized and most admired vehicles of all time.

Playing a key role in staking out the Jeep's place in military history was the late Ernie Pyle, whose down-to-

A 1941 Willys MB slat grille. The first 25,800 examples of the MB Jeep have this grille of welded iron bars. This is the 2224th example, assembled on December 3, 1941. (Courtesy Bob Parmerter/Tennessee Museum of Aviation, Sevierville, TN)

A group of slat-grilled MB Jeeps at Fort Devens, Massachusetts. (Courtesy Marshall Rimland collection)

earth accounts of American GIs and their equipment in the North African campaign earned him a Pulitzer Prize in 1944. "In the mechanical end of our African war," he wrote, "three American vehicles stand out above all others. They are the Jeep, the two-and-a-half-ton truck and the DC-3 cargo plane."

The DC-3, identified as the C-47 in its military form, was described by Pyle as the "workingest airplane in existence ... Almost any pilot will tell you it is the best airplane ever built." The "deuce-and-a-half" truck was portrayed as the DC-3's land-based alter ego "capable of hauling big loads, seldom gets stuck and able to take staggering amounts of punishment." Then came the Jeep's turn. "I don't think," wrote Pyle, "we could continue the war without the Jeep. It does everything. It goes everywhere. It's as faithful as a dog, as strong as a mule and as agile as a goat ... a divine instrument of wartime locomotion."

But even a Jeep advocate such as Pyle, who drove them thousands of miles during his wartime journalist career, had to admit the Jeep was not above criticism, albeit of a minor

nature. "If I were called upon to suggest changes for a new model," he wrote, "I could think of only one or two things. "One is a hand brake. It's perfectly useless – won't hold at all. They should either design one that works or else save metal by having none at all." Pyle also grumbled

This photo formed the basis of several Liberian postage stamps issued after the death of President Franklin D Roosevelt in 1945. It shows the President in an MB Jeep reviewing African-American troops of the 41st US Engineers stationed in Liberia in 1943. (Author's collection)

This Willys-Overland MB was photographed on October 9, 1943. Just visible is the blackout driving lamp mount on the MB's left fender: early MBs and Ford-built GPW Jeeps did not have this feature. The significance of this photo, as noted by early civilian Jeep historian, Fred Coldwell, is the X17 identification on the MB's front bumper, indicating its use by Willys-Overland in development of the postwar CJ-2A. (Author's collection)

A 1942 Ford GPW used by the US Navy shore patrol. (Courtesy Bob Parmerter/Tennessee Museum of Aviation, Sevierville, TN)

a bit about the Jeep's combat tread tires: "I wish they could somehow fix the Jeep so that at certain speeds the singing of those heavy tires wouldn't sound exactly like an approaching airplane. That little sound effect has caused me to jump out of my skin more than once."

But Pyle quickly assured his readers that the Jeep's reputation for reliability was factual: "Only once in my long and distinguished Jeep career have I ever had anything go wrong. That time the gears got all mixed up and the thing wouldn't come out of low."

Pyle's judgment of the Jeep was endorsed by the men at the top of the American military chain of command. George C Marshall called it "America's greatest contribution to modern warfare." General Eisenhower cited the Jeep, the Dakota C-47 transport airplane and the landing craft as "the three tools that won the war." Echoing these widely read remarks were words of praise, admiration and appreciation from countless Allied service men and women who owed their lives and those of personnel under their care to the Jeep's durability, reliability and versatility.

During the war, Americans weren't alone in recognizing the Jeep's extraordinary capabilities. For example, it took only one ride in a Jeep to convince British Field Marshall Sir John Dill that the Jeep "can do everything but bake a cake."

In 1943, after returning from a year's service in North Africa as an ambulance driver with British and French forces, John D Dun, former editor of the *Toledo Times*, shared some of his recollections of the Jeep in combat with Willys-Overland President, Joseph W Frazer. At Willys-Overland, Frazer was known as J W 'Jeeps' Frazer' and undoubtedly he enjoyed reading of Dun's experiences. After telling Frazer that he never felt he was completely away from home as long as he was able to drive a Jeep, he provided him with a graphic example of the Jeep's versatility. "The Jeep's ability to negotiate the desert terrain," he said, "far surpasses that of British vehicles, and it was not unusual for a Jeep to be called upon to rescue a three-ton truck stuck in the sand." Dun also shared some of what he saw of the Jeep's combat effectiveness with Frazer. "The British used their Jeeps," he explained, "in groups of fifty or sixty for sorties around the Rommel lines in raids which took the enemy completely by surprise. The Jeep caravans were able, because of their low silhouette,

Two views of a Ford GPW 'script body' Jeep. The Ford GPW script body was manufactured for only the first six months of production and abandoned after July 1942. (Author's collection)

An MB Jeep in what appears to be a staged pose. (Author's collection)

An MP checks the credentials of the Jeep's driver after his interest was piqued by its occupants. (Author's collection)

Exactly what has led five WWII Jeeps to this predicament is unknown. (Author's collection)

to hide behind the dunes and wadis, undetected by the enemy."

During the war years, it seemed that Jeeps were anywhere American service men and women were to be found. Major E P Hogan in his article "The Jeep In Action" (*Army Ordnance*, September-October 1944) related the famous story of the French sentry on duty at a crossroads in Tunisia during the North African campaign. Confronted in the darkness by several soldiers on foot claiming to be Americans, he responded by opening fire with his submachine gun. It was quickly determined that the soldiers were Germans dressed in US Army uniforms. When asked by his superior how he knew they were enemy soldiers, he replied: "That's easy sir, all Americans come in Jeeps!"

Hogan also noted that in the Pacific theater "the sight of Jeeps became as familiar to the native people as the sound of rifle shots." Jeeps were pressed into service for virtually every purpose; military, humanitarian, and spiritual. "In far countries, hot and cold," Hogan wrote, "Army chaplains have used Jeeps' flat hoods to support their altars, and Army nurses have washed their faces from 'tin hats' on Jeep hoods."

Few readers likely remained

An evocative photo of King George VI of England inspecting a Bantam BRC-40 from an airborne division at Bulford Camp in 1942. (Author's collection

dispassionate when Hogan quoted from Robert Sherrod's epic book, *Tarawa*. "Now at three minutes past six," wrote Sherrod, "the first two American Jeeps roll down the pier, towing 37mm guns. If a sign of certain victory were needed, this is it. The Jeeps have arrived." And, of course, Jeeps went ashore with Allied forces in the first wave of troops liberating France on June 6, 1944.

Perhaps the most famous cartoon to come out of World War II was penned by Bill Mauldin. First published in the *St Louis Dispatch* in 1944, it depicted a grieving cavalry sergeant standing with his back to his Jeep, one hand over his eyes and the other hand holding a 45 caliber pistol pointed at his beloved Jeep. The Jeep had sustained irreparable damage in combat and the sergeant was about to put it out of its misery. The cartoon carried no caption; none was needed because it was quite evident that Mauldin had captured on paper with a few strokes of his pen the true feeling of affection countless GIs had for the Jeep.

It's not likely, though, that many of the thousands of soldiers who spent time in a Jeep, either as driver or passenger or as a casualty being transported to a medical facility, envisioned a time when a Jeep would be displayed in an art museum. But, in 1951 when The Museum of Modern Art in New York City presented an exhibit entitled "8 Automobiles," it included a Willys-Overland MB Jeep from World War II.

A stylized rendition of a Bantam BRC-40 was used for this 1940s vintage postcard. (Courtesy Marshall Rimland collection)

Jeeps attached to the First Armored Division of the US Fifth Army in Vergata, Italy in April 1945. (Author's collection)

Above: This photo of General Joseph W Stillwell was reportedly taken on Easter Sunday 1944. It shows the General's Jeep leading several others as they cross a river in Northern Burma. The chains on his Jeep are clearly visible. (Author's collection)

The virtually universal affection that GIs had for the World War II MB Jeep is evident in this photograph. (Courtesy Marshall Rimland collection)

"Don't tell the General . . . but I helped put his army on synthetic rubber tires!"

"It all began back home before the war, with a road test that totaled 80,000,000 miles"

"Here's what I mean," said the P.F.C. "The tires I drove in the test were the *ancestors* of the ones on this buggy. The B. F. Goodrich Company wanted to prove that synthetic rubber would work in passenger tires. So they sold several thousand tires, and asked people to send in mileage reports. All together we rolled up 80,000,000 miles, and that's a lot of miles."

The passenger car tires used had more than 50% of their natural rubber replaced by our own synthetic—Ameripol. Today's all-synthetic passenger car tires are made with government synthetic—"GR-S." And 99% of the natural rubber has been replaced by it.

That pre-Pearl Harbor test gave us a 3-year head start. It gave us the "know how" that has already enabled us to produce a synthetic passenger car tire *almost* as good as the Silvertowns you used to get! It's easily the best synthetic tire you can buy today.

There are some synthetic tires today available to those who can qualify. But our fighting forces still need every ounce of rubber they can get. So do everything you can to make your present tires last—don't drive even one unnecessary mile.

The B. F. Goodrich Company, Akron, Ohio

In war or peace

B.F.Goodrich

FIRST IN RUBBER

Awards to 9 plants

During World War II many contributors to the war effort – such as B F Goodrich – made use of the Jeep in their institutional advertisements. (Courtesy Marshall Rimland collection)

Placed among the other automobiles on display (1938 Mercedes-Benz SS, 1949 Cisitalia, 1939 Bentley, 1939 Talbot, 1937 Cord, 1948 MG TC, and 1941 Lincoln Continental), the Jeep appeared out of its element. But the exhibit's catalog persuasively argued that its presence was both appropriate and relevant, encouraging Museum visitors to set aside, at least for a time, their existing notions of automobile design, and instead, consider automobiles from the perspective of their designers. Suggestions included viewing a vehicle as a "box on wheels," or as a "single envelope covering passengers and motors as well as accessory parts." Another approach offered for consideration was to recognize that "the designer may wish to maintain a distinction between separate parts, and yet choose to treat each section as a piece of sculpture."

Christopher Mount, then serving as Assistant Curator in the Museum's Department of Architecture and Design, wrote a short history of this exhibit in the spring 2000 issue of *Jeep News*. He explained that the Jeep's presence was justified "for the fact that its form really does follow its function ... It wasn't designed to look great or impress the neighbors. It was designed to transport soldiers from point A to point B. It was also extremely adaptable."

The original exhibit's catalog depicted the Jeep as an example of 'Machine Art,' an expression, which Mount noted, identified "something not necessarily meant to be esthetically pleasing. Its purpose was to function, and to work properly." In that context, he continued, people looked at machines as "beautiful and rational."

The catalog also suggested that the Jeep's attraction went well beyond this mechanistic perspective: "The admirable Jeep seems to have the combined appearance of an intelligent dog and a perfect gadget. It is an appeal so vast that this wonderful tool for transportation has won approval for much more than its practicality, although the engineers who perfected it worked without the concern for style with which other automobiles are designed."

After offering the simile that "The Jeep looks like a tray, or perhaps a sturdy sardine can, on wheels," the writer, focusing in on some of its primary features, noted that "large wheels dominate the design, and insist rather than suggest that the Jeep's primary purpose is transportation.

"One of the most striking illustrations of its direct design is the front fender. It is composed of two rectangular platforms placed at the best angle for preventing mud splash. The two sections are connected by an overlap, left plainly visible, and the lower section is joined to a small step. The sidewalls are low enough for passengers to step in, thus eliminating mechanically troublesome doors. Even refinements of contour grow out of practical considerations: the fenders have rounded corners to avoid cutting passengers as they get in.

"With its wheels removed and windshield folded flat, the Jeep fits into a shipping case. Uncrated and on the road it can maneuver its way through spaces blocked to larger vehicles. It can be stood on end and pushed through narrow passages; it has on occasion been dismantled and carried, piece by piece, over unmanageable terrain, and with suitable equipment, it can be driven under water. Bolts visible on the wheels and the body facilitate either the removal of parts or periodic tightening.

"Those who have used the Jeep will recall certain limitations of comfort. Yet there are few automobiles which give their drivers so exhilarating a sense of speed and control. The Jeep substitutes for a deliberate esthetic program, the formative principles of construction; its design is unified by the economy (disdaining the merely decorative) with which each part is fitted for its purpose. It is one of the few genuine expressions of machine art."

The benefits of functionality serving as the basis of industrial design had been previously expressed on October 15, 1947 by Delmar Roos, Willys-Overland Vice President of Engineering. Addressing over 450 business leaders attending Willys-Overland's second annual 'Institutional Day,' he noted that Willys-Overland had designed its utility vehicles around the Jeep face. "It isn't the most beautiful in the world," he continued, "but it is sturdy, simple and practical."

Not every automotive historian would agree with Willys' depiction of Roos as "the designer of the world-famous military Jeep." Nor, for that matter did the Federal Trade Commission (FTC) in 1948 when it concluded that "in truth and in fact the idea of creating the Jeep was originated by the American Bantam Car Company in collaboration with certain officers of the United States Army and the same was developed by the American Bantam Company in collaboration with said officers and not by the respondent, Willys-Overland Motors, Inc."

The FTC's consideration of this issue began in 1943, as a deceptive trade practice suit concerning Willys-Overland advertisements asserting that Willys played a direct role in the Jeep's creation. One example of this claim, challenged by both Bantam and Minneapolis-Moline, was found in an advertisement in the May 30, 1942 issue of *The Saturday Evening Post*. Its headline read: "The Jeep calls them Daddy ... THE QUARTERMASTER CORPS OF THE US ARMY AND THE CIVILIAN ENGINEERS OF WILLYS-OVERLAND." The accompanying color artwork showed a group of military men and civilians (including one displaying a scale model of the Jeep), gathered around a blueprint. At that time *The Saturday Evening Post* was among America's most widely circulated magazines and undoubtedly this ad was seen and likely read by millions of readers.

As Willys-Overland's President, Joseph W Frazer had no qualms about giving Willys much – but not all – of the credit for the Jeep's creation. In 1943, referring to the Jeep's versatility he wrote "neither we nor the Army officers who worked with us in designing it ever visualized

Before and after views of an MB Willys Jeep (serial number 127955), restored by Ray Abbott of Kalispell, Montana. Ray was awaiting seat cushions to complete his restoration. (Courtesy Ray Abbott)

Little is known of the origin of this Jeep board game, but it is believed to have been produced during the Second World War. (Courtesy Marshall Rimland collection)

The MB was equipped with Kelsey-Hayes split rim wheels. The two parts were secured by eight lug-type bolts. They were also identified as combat wheels and, by preventing the tire from coming off the rim, enabled the Jeep to be driven for short distances with flat tires. (Courtesy William Fredette)

the thousand and one jobs it would do in this war."

Since the FTC acknowledged the role Willys did play in the Jeep's development, advertisements noting that "Willys Builds the Mighty Jeep" and that "the sole source of Jeep power, Jeep speed, Jeep flexibility, and fuel economy, is the Willys 'Go-Devil' Jeep Engine, designed and perfected by Willys-Overland, Inc., Builders of the Mighty Jeep" were permissible.

In 1950, after a lengthy legal process, Willys-Overland obtained a United States trademark registration for the 'Jeep' name, thus establishing its sole ownership of a name with worldwide recognition. When Chrysler acquired Jeep via the purchase of American Motors in 1987, there had been over 1100 registrations worldwide for the Jeep trademark.

Willys-Overland enthusiasts have cited the Willys Go-Devil's powerful engine as the main reason for its ability to outperform its Bantam and Ford competitors. Unlike the discord over the matter of who deserved credit for the Jeep's origin, the evidence is overwhelming that Barney Roos was the key player in the development of the Willys Jeep engine.

Throughout Roos' career (which began in the early days of the auto industry, matured in its golden age and continued into modern times), his ability to envision unconventional, yet practical solutions to contemporary problems was evident. His nickname of 'Barney' from high school days (he was born in New York City on October 11, 1887) linked him with one of the influences on his life, the great racing driver, Barney Oldfield.

Roos' engineering career began in 1911 at General Electric's Lynn, Massachusetts facility where he worked on centrifugal compressors and steam turbines. The following year he joined the Locomobile Company in Bridgeport, Connecticut. Under chief engineer Andrew Riker he participated in the development of electrical starting lighting for automobiles, the Riker truck, which was used in the First World War, the Army's Mark 8 tank, and its Liberty engine. He was also involved in the construction of what have been depicted as "bulletproof 100-mile-an-hour staff cars" for General Pershing.

After Locomobile went into receivership in 1920, Roos spent about eight months in Europe studying its postwar automotive industry before joining Pierce-Arrow as its Chief Engineer. In 1922 he returned to Locomobile, then controlled by William C Durant, to develop the Locomobile Junior Eight. In 1925 he became Marmon's chief engineer. Although the 1927 'Little Marmon' is credited to him, Roos had, in fact, left Marmon before it went on sale. He joined Studebaker in 1926, first as Assistant Chief Engineer, progressing to Chief Engineer. By 1937 Roos was Studebaker's Vice President in charge of Engineering.

Studebaker historian William A Cannon, noted in *Studebaker: The Complete History* that Studebaker's engineering staff was in a state of steady decline before Roos' arrival. One of Roos' first attempts to reverse this trend was to move the department from Detroit to a new state-of-the art facility in South Bend, Indiana. Led by Roos, the team developed Studebaker's first straight-eight engine, the 100 horsepower Studebaker Eight which debuted in 1928. Roos also devised Studebaker's Planar

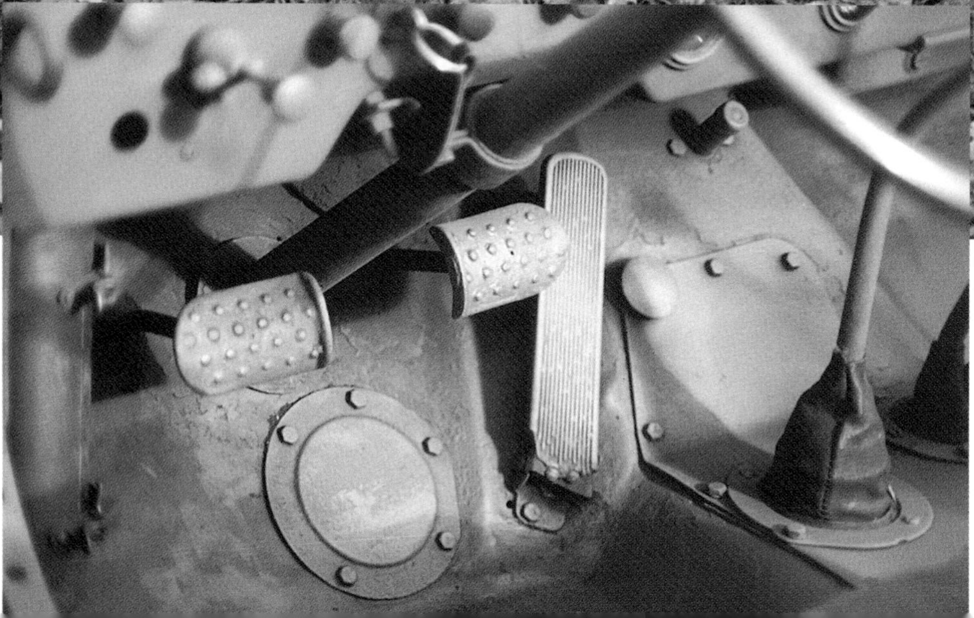

Get a grip! The no-nonsense design of the MB's clutch, brake and accelerator pedals. The fire extinguisher mounted to the left of the clutch pedal was standard issue. The MB's starting button is seen to the right of the accelerator. A small circular pad was provided to position the driver's heel when the starter was operated. (Courtesy William Fredette)

Main picture: The straps holding the MB's axe and shovel (also identified as 'pioneer tools') securely in place were quickly released when the tools were needed. (Courtesy William Fredette)

Top: A view of the MB's left-side rear bumperette. (Courtesy William Fredette)

Above: The heart and soul of the MB Jeep was its Go-Devil engine. Seen at the lower right is the in-line fuel filter added by the owner of this MB. (Courtesy William Fredette)

Left: These corner handles, located on each rear corner of the MB body, were used by soldiers when it was necessary to employ manpower, instead of horsepower, to move the Jeep. (Courtesy William Fredette)

independent front suspension for its 1935 President models.

Roos left Studebaker in 1937 and worked in England as a consultant for the Rootes Group, manufacturer of Sunbeam, Hillman, Talbot and Humber cars, and Commer trucks. He returned to the US in 1938 to become Willys-Overland's Vice President in charge of Engineering, One of his first tasks was to upgrade the Willys 48hp automotive engine, an engine which dated back to 1926 when the Whippet, often depicted as "America's first compact," was introduced.

Whippet historian and author, Paul Young, author of *The Whippet Encyclopedia,* a definitive Whippet history, traces the origin and development of this engine, which played a pivotal role in Jeep history, back to 1923 when John North Willys, ostensibly heeding his physician's advice to spend some time away from his office, sailed to Europe. "However," explains Mr Young, "it was not in his nature to take life easy and he took the opportunity to closely study the European automobile market in which small, economical and relatively powerful (for their size) cars were predominant."

Willys Overland had, three years earlier, established a European subsidiary, Willys Overland Crossley, and North was interested in developing a product that would improve its sales. Toward this goal, North had a half dozen small French and British cars shipped back to the Willys Overland plant in Toledo, where, writes Paul Young, "They were extensively road tested, dismantled and analyzed."

American critics regarded these cars as having several undesirable features, including a narrow tread, low maximum speed, limited performance in mountainous regions and, by American standards, a cramped interior. But, says Mr Young, "certain attributes, such as low center of gravity and economy, were found desirable and it was decided that a new car would be developed around the European Light Car concept." The end result, named the Whippet, was designed to compete in both American and overseas markets, though its relatively wide tread, and roomy body were intended to attract American customers.

To take advantage of England's RAC horsepower (tax) rating, which penalized owners of cars with large bore engines, the Whippet engine combined a small bore with a long stroke. This made for an interesting comparison with the engines of the 1927 Model T Ford; its successor, the 1928 Model A, and the 1927 Series AA Chevrolet (see table below).

Paul Young sums up the Whippet's attributes relative to the Model T and Series AA Chevrolet in this way: "The Whippet was smaller and faster but more expensive ..." In 1927 it established two impressive records. Early in the year a stock sedan completed a 620 mile round trip between Philadelphia and Pittsburgh in just over 19 hours (over eight hours less than the previous record for cars in its class). Averaging 31mph, the Whippet remained in high gear for the entire run. Fuel consumption was 29.5mpg. In the autumn a standard Whippet roadster completed a non-stop run of 12,008 miles over public roads in northern Pennsylvania and New York State. The climax of this effort took place at Ithaca, New York, where the Whippet completed ten laps over a half-mile track in six-and-a-half minutes. In an AAA sanctioned run from Kansas City to St Louis, another Whippet averaged 54mph.

Historians have much debated the merits of the Whippet engine. What one, Ken Gross, has depicted as "an unenvied reputation for unreliability;" another, the late Arch Brown, termed a "reputation, only partly deserved of being fragile."

"As a Whippet owner, and as someone who has driven in the equivalent day Ford and Chevys,"_explains Paul Young, "I can verify the reliability of the original design. The Whippet engine in its day was described as a 'Small Bore, High Speed Engine.' In comparison with contemporary Chevys and Fords the engine was high revving and therefore noisy and vibrating as it was mounted directly on the chassis without any rubber mounting. It was unkindly dubbed 'The Toledo Vibrator,' yet, its performance was described as 'peppy.' In the right hands and with regular oil changes, it would be long lived, but in the wrong hands it could be over revved, and without regular oil changes would wear out relatively quickly. The slower revving Fords and Chevs, with slower piston speeds and less piston travel, could probably stand a bit more abuse and less frequent oil changes."

Mr Young offers this summary of the Whippet's engine's evolution up to the time of Barney Roos' arrival at Willys: "The Whippet Model 96 engine was revamped for

Model	Whippet*	Model T	Model A	Chevrolet
Displ. (cu-in)	134.2	176.7	200.5	171
Bore (in)	3.125	3.75	3.875	3.687
Stroke (in)	4.375	4.0	4.25	4.0
Horsepower	32@2800rpm	20@1600rpm	40@2200rpm	26@2000rpm

This engine's displacement was the smallest of any American 4-cylinder unit. The Whippet also produced more horsepower per cubic inch than any other American 4-cylinder engine.

Top left: Most MB Jeeps were fitted with manually operated windshield wipers for both driver and passenger. Starting in March 1945, a manual vacuum wiper system was used. This MB has a tandem manual unit. Individually operated manual units were also used on the MB. (Courtesy William Fredette)

Above: The MB's Olive Drab, plastic 3-spoke steering wheel with metal spokes had a small horn button at its center. Early MB Jeeps had black solid rubber wheels with larger center rings, similar in appearance to wheels on prewar passenger cars. (Courtesy William Fredette)

Left: During WWII, the MB's rear bumperettes identified the unit to which it was assigned. Thus, '83/329-I' on the left unit signifies 83 Infantry Division, 329 Regimental Combat Team. At the right, E/4 indicates E Company, vehicle #4. (Courtesy William Fredette)

From every angle the MB Jeep's appearance reflected its creator's uncompromising commitment to the form-following-function design philosophy. (Courtesy William Fredette)

These louvers, located in the MB's left front fender wells, extracted heat from the engine compartment. The right front fender well was configured to accommodate the battery in the engine compartment. (Courtesy William Fredette)

The MB was equipped with full-time running front hubs which it was not possible to disengage. (Courtesy William Fredette)

The MB's front leaf springs had different load ratings. As seen here, a torque reaction spring was attached to the driver side spring to stabilize it under extremely rough operating conditions. (Courtesy William Fredette)

the 1929 Whippet Model 96A ... with stroke increased by 0.375in and now using Invar strut aluminum alloy pistons. The increased capacity of 145.7cu-in (up from 134.2), increased compression ratio of 5.1:1 (up from 4.4:1), larger by 1/16in intake valves and redesigned valve timing gave the engine 40bhp@3200rpm ... By 1933 the engine powered the Willys 77 but with stroke back to 4.375in and 48bhp@3200rpm with a downdraft Tillotson carburetor. A few more changes and the engine went on to power

This view of the MB shows its two-bolt spare tire carrier and spare tire rest. Earlier models used a three-bolt design without the rest, which put excessive stress on the rear body section. (Courtesy William Fredette)

the 1938 Willys 38 with 48hp@3400rpm. Unfortunately, at that speed the engine had a maximum life of two to four hours."

At this point, Paul Young notes the arrival of Barney Roos at Willys-Overland: "A sustained development program was undertaken over the next two years, under the direction of Bronx born, hard-driving Delmar (Barney) Roos."

Roos began his work of enabling the Whippet to run at higher rpms for extended periods without failure by conducting a series of tests that proved of short duration as pistons collapsed, blocks cracked, and cylinder heads failed. His eventual success was based on a careful study of the stress level of the engine's cylinder head, the effect of flywheel mass and crankshaft counterweight upon engine operation, and an examination of main bearing loads. Additional items scrutinized included cam design, bearings lubrication, and the adequacy of the coolant system.

This undertaking was depicted by Roos as weeks of "day-and-night painstaking work". Mr Young details the results: "This intensive development effort saw improved alloys, closer tolerances, counterweights added to crankshaft, the replacement of the semi-steel pistons with aluminum alloy, more effective piston rings, addition of exhaust valve inserts, use of thin wall insert main and big end bearing steels, a one-degree Carter carburetor with increased diameter manifold and ports, a reduction in flywheel weight from 57 to 37 pounds, the curing of head gasket and water pump leaks and elimination of pre-ignition troubles. The compression ratio was raised

The MB's World War II Olive Drab finish blends beautifully with the autumnal woods of upstate New York. (Courtesy William Fredette)

from 5.7 to 6.3; 61bhp was achieved at only 3600rpm and torque was improved by six percent."

As used for the Willys Jeep, the revitalized Willys engine with a 6.48:1 compression ratio developed 63hp@3800rpm and had a peak torque output of 108lb/ft@1800rpm. It was capable of running at 4440rpm for 100 hours without failing, a level of endurance far beyond the capability of the original engine.

During WWII that data was the benchmark for engines used in the Willys MB Jeep. To ascertain its maintenance, the same tests were conducted approximately every ten days with engines randomly selected from the assembly line.

Recalling both his youth and combat experiences from World War II, military Jeep historian Stirling Parkerson told the author that "as a kid, I had a neighbor who bought a second-hand Whippet roadster. I can remember looking at that engine and thinking, 'Oh! That has a long stroke.' That's why those engines wore out so quickly." But then, he continues, "they beefed the engine up and kept the basic design."

Ross was extremely talented, but no miracle worker. Whilst he created an engine that enabled the Jeep to be the great workhorse of the war, there were limits to its survivability. Mindful of its long stroke, Stirling Parkerson notes, "Of course Jeeps didn't stand up on the highways. They didn't because the engine revved so high at 60mph that you would wear them out in a hurry."

Nonetheless, the Willys engine, in its element, was an outstanding performer, earning respect and admiration from friend and foe alike. Parkerson considered the engine the decisive factor in the selection of the Willys Jeep design for mass production; not without reason was it known as the 'Go-Devil' engine ...

Barney Roos died of a heart attack on February 13, 1960 at age 72. His obituaries, noting his accomplishments, included acknowledgment of his work on the Jeep. For better or worse, most gave him the lion's share of the credit for its creation. *The Detroit Free Press* wrote that "He designed the Jeep at government request during World War II." *The Detroit News* expanded on this point, reporting that "Roos designed the jeep at the request of the government when he was vice president in charge of engineering at Willys-Overland, now Willys Motors Inc." Yet another obituary, portraying him as "The father of the Jeep," added that US Army officers "reportedly said 'Barney, make it tough,' early in World War II, when they asked him to design a rugged vehicle for the mechanized forces."

At war's end when Jeep production totaled 646,930 units (Bantam: 2643, Ford: 281,446, Willys: 362,841), it mattered little to the general public if Bantam and Ford had received their just desserts. In 1945 with Bantam fading into obscurity and Ford engaged in a major effort to restructure its operation, it was Willys that was uniquely

These two views illustrate the MB's trailer socket receptacle. It used an electrical cable from the trailer to operate the trailer's tail and stop lights. (Courtesy William Fredette)

Two perspectives of the Jeep's pintle hook used for towing various pieces of equipment such as ¼-ton trailers and light field artillery pieces. Pintle hooks of various designs and origins were installed on Jeeps during the war. The pintle hook on William Fredette's MB is a Ford unit. (Courtesy William Fredette)

The MB's rear foot rest. A different design was used on the Ford GPW. To its left can be seen the guard behind the driver's seat which protects the fuel tank. (Courtesy William Fredette)

positioned to begin producing a version of a military vehicle for the civilian market.

The introduction of the first Willys-Overland civilian Jeep, the CJ-2A, heralded a new era in transportation history and history in general. In the public's view, "the sun never set on the mighty Willys Jeep" and at war's end Willys was ready to elevate its domain to 'universal' stature.

The area at the back of the MB was shared by the spare tire, a 5 gallon fuel can, and a collapsible canvas water bag. Fuel cans of various designs were used. (Courtesy William Fredette)

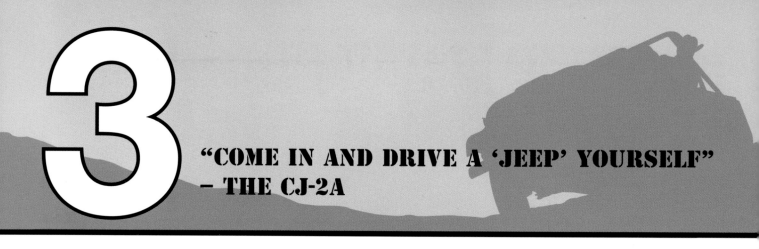

During the war years Jeeps – driven by men and women of all nationalities and cultures – were seen all over the globe; carrying loads of all shapes, sizes and descriptions, crossing all sorts of terrains in all types of weather conditions. *Fortune* magazine called the Jeep "an international byword during the war." Willys was content to advertise in July 1945 that "To millions of people all over the world 'JEEP' means WILLYS."

The Jeep's worldwide reputation for durability, reliability and versatility was well founded, unrivaled and unprecedented. Arthur W Harrington, co-founder of the Marmon-Harrington company, knowing a few things about four-wheel drive vehicles described it as "the most remarkable vehicular development in 50 years of automotive history."

Continuing its assessment of the Jeep's future, *Fortune* magazine noted that "with all the world engaged in a barefaced love affair with the US Army Jeep it would have been unusual if Willys-Overland failed to give some thought to a postwar civilian adaptation of the vehicle."

Preceding these comments, and beginning in 1942, military Jeeps had undergone testing by the US government to evaluate their suitability

The war was over and the GIs were coming home: it was time to have a hoot and do some joy-riding in a Jeep! (Courtesy Marshall Rimland collection)

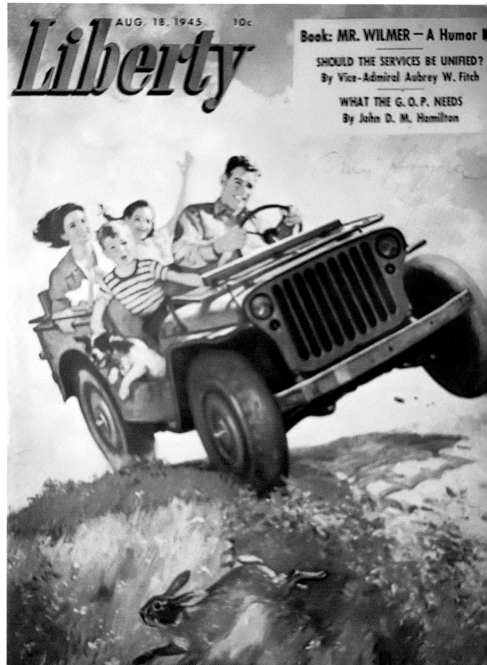

AUG. 18, 1945   10c

Liberty

Book: MR. WILMER – A Humor

SHOULD THE SERVICES BE UNIFIED?
By Vice-Admiral Aubrey W. Fitch

WHAT THE G.O.P. NEEDS
By John D. M. Hamilton

The Universal 'Jeep' Will Work and Save

AROUND THE CLOCK

AROUND THE YEAR

AROUND THE WORLD

In 1945 Willys-Overland wasn't bashful about announcing its global ambitions for the CJ-2A. (Author's collection)

as civilian farm vehicles. The following year the results were released by R B Grayson, head of the US Department of Agriculture's Farm and Equipment and Research Division. The studies took place at the Bureau of Agricultural Chemistry and Engineering Tillage Machinery Laboratory at Auburn, Indiana, as well as at additional agricultural stations around the country. Grayson's conclusion, that the Jeep was "highly useful in plowing, harrowing and other field work" added credibility to the notion, subsequently promoted by Willys in its postwar Jeep advertisements, that the Jeep could substitute light trucks, tractors and passenger cars on the farms.

Interest in the Jeep's adaptability to civilian use, stimulated by accounts of the Auburn tests in publications such as *Country Gentleman* (June 1942) and *Popular Science* (January 1943), grew rapidly. *Modern Industry* (April 15 1943), reported that a "flood of inquiries testifies that garages want jeeps for tow cars and railroads seek them as vehicles for track maintenance workers; logging camps, hunting camps, lawn mowing machines, snow plowing, and countless other postwar uses present themselves as possibilities."

Aware that cessation of automotive production for the civilian market in February 1942 virtually guaranteed an unmet demand for new vehicles at war's end, the disposition of surplus military equipment – including Jeeps – concerned several members of Congress. One representative, Alabama Congressman Carter Monasco, asked Willys-Overland Vice President and General

This Jeep has been identified by pre-production civilian Jeep historian Fred Coldwell as X27, one of the CJ-2 late pre-production versions of the CJ-2A. (Author's collection)

Fred Coldwell has also determined that this Jeep, seen here with rear PTO operating a buzz saw, is also X27. (Author's collection)

This heavily retouched photo of two CJ-2 Jeeps was used in several Jeep brochures for the CJ-2A. Fred Coldwell's research turned up the original photo which differs in numerous ways from this version. In 1945, no-one knew any better, nor probably cared, as Jeep penned this caption: "One 'Jeep' pulls an ensilage harvester, powering it from the spline shaft of the special rear end power take-off. The other pulls the trailer." (Author's collection)

Counsel George W Ritter to testify in regard to this matter. The transcript of this committee's hearings, often referred to as the 'Monasco Report,' contains sixteen pages of Ritter's December 9, 1943 testimony, detailing his view that numerous modifications would be needed to make military Jeeps suitable for commercial and agricultural use.

In New York State, a favorable report by Robert B Cooper, research director of the Grange League Federation's (GLF) farm supplies Division, spurred interest in the Jeep amongst New York's farmers and those in neighboring states. "We have tested the Jeep over a period of several months in a variety of jobs from plowing

Fred Coldwell
identified this
CJ-2 Jeep as
X28. He dates
the photo as late
1944. (Author's
collection)

to sawing lumber," Cooper said, "and in all operations it illustrated a great postwar potential.

"Because of its fourfold function of tractor, light truck, mobile power unit and passenger car, we believe that on the basis of our tests, it will relieve farmers of many back-breaking jobs."

The GLF, which served farmers in New York, New Jersey and Pennsylvania, said its tests were held on farms in those states as well as Maryland, Virginia, and West Virginia. Since Cooper said he could not reveal the details of the farm Jeep's design and performance, it is probable that these tests were conducted with preproduction versions of the CJ-2A. Cooper did, however, give specifics of the nature of the test jobs which the jeep had completed, which included plowing snow, drawing logs to a saw mill, powering a saw mill, rescuing a 'mud-bound' truck, shelling corn, mowing and chopping corn, pulling tree stumps out of a field, blowing green hay into a mow, and herding milk cows from pasture to barn.

Little of this was lost on early postwar Jeep dealers, particularly those located in rural areas. One of the first Jeep dealers in upstate New York was J Gill and Sons, Willys Sales and Service, of Oneonta, New York. In the mid-forties, Oneonta, located in Otsego County, was the trading center of a major agricultural section of the state. Oneonta and surrounding area had a population of approximately 20,000. Otsego County's dairy cows numbered over 47,000. In neighboring Delaware county there were over 72,000. In this environment, explained Jim Gill, "the market for Jeeps is a major one as its main use as a light truck or tractor is very valuable to the farmer."

During the war, Delmar Roos spoke on numerous occasions about the Jeep's place in a peacetime America. In early 1943 when he was publicly depicted as engaged in developing a Willys postwar car, Roos regarded the Jeep as "a pure combat vehicle, designed with simplicity, with no concession to art and damn little to comfort." He was slightly more appreciative of the Jeep's postwar potentialities in an article appearing in the February 14, 1943 issue of *The New York Times*. While recognizing that the Jeep "has great possibilities in agriculture, where a small farm is concerned," he dismissed it as a viable competitor in the passenger car market. "Certainly the jeep is not going to affect the passenger car," he said, "because no one wants a four-wheel drive passenger car that has big tires and is a hog on gasoline. It would eat up tires and gasoline and would be expensive."

Additional evidence of Roos' swing in support of the Jeep as a prominent player in Willys-Overland's postwar business can be found in his October 1944 Society of Automotive Engineers (SAE) paper on the Jeep's development. Writing that it would have many postwar applications, Roos also mentioned that an intensive study was under way of modifications required to make it more adaptable for farm and civilian use. Here, Roos was referring to the development of the CJ-2A based on the use of modified MB models, identified as CJ-1 and CJ-2. Frederic Coldwell in his book *Preproduction Civilian Jeeps: 1944-1945: Models CJ-1 and CJ-2* (published by Vintimage Inc, Denver, Colorado, ISBN 803220-0127), describes these vehicles as "the first purpose-built civilian jeeps designed from the ground up expressly for postwar civilian tasks."

Preceding the CJ-2A Jeep's July 18, 1945 introduction, many publications carried Willys-Overland advertising conveying Willys Chairman Ward Canaday's belief that the postwar Jeep was intended "mainly for the farm market ... where it would take care of the numerous tasks that abound down on the farm." These ads were illustrated by paintings by artist James Sessions of Jeeps in peacetime surroundings. One advertisement, headlined "Jeep-Planning," appearing in the *Country Gentleman* of May 1945, depicted a Jeep parked outside the local general store. Amidst the crowd gathering around the Jeep was its owner, busy answering a multitude of questions: "Will she pull a plow ... What's her draw-bar horse power ... Bet she'd be great stuff on a hay loader or a hay hook! ... Can she do 60 on the highway? ... How about pulling

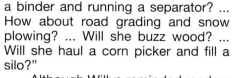

Another CJ-2 Jeep, with the production model's removal tailgate as well as numerous other features seen on the CJ-2A. (Author's collection)

A purposeful view of the CJ-2. (Author's collection)

a binder and running a separator? ... How about road grading and snow plowing? ... Will she buzz wood? ... Will she haul a corn picker and fill a silo?"

Although Willys reminded readers that "On every battle front and in every country touched by this war both soldiers and civilians link together the names 'Jeep' and Willys," the general theme of the advertisement's text was peacetime marketing of the Jeep. A Michigan farmer was quoted as saying "From where I sit, the tough Jeep, with its great war record, has already set a standard for postwar transportation and work. This 'Jeep' is new, modern – the kind of equipment that can be made to serve both farm and city at work or at play. Willys has done an historic job."

A more direct example of Willys' plans for the Jeep's future was a 1945 advertisement entitled "'JEEP' INVADES MIDWEST FARM, demonstrates Post-War Possibilities," which contained enthusiastic quotes (apparently from one individual) who had participated in a wartime test of the Jeep's agricultural potential: "Yes," he said, "we had a real, genuine 'Jeep' at our farm for a few days. It was the biggest event that ever occurred in our section, in my opinion ... We hooked the 'Jeep' up to the reaper and when we gave her the gas she walked right away with it ... Close as I can figure, we saved the best part of a day on the cutting of our grain – and that means a lot with conditions what they are ... The 'Jeep' gives you a nice, steady, smooth pull and moves right along, hour after hour ... We hauled feed over to a neighbor's. We hooked it up to a manure spreader. Then we drove out to the pasture to round up the cows – and the 'Jeep' made nothing of it ... On the highway she went like a scared Jack Rabbit. Talk about fast! I certainly will try to have a 'Jeep' if they are

available after the war. Willys has done a great job."

Prior to the start of civilian Jeep production in July 1945, Willys published a large brochure, "Jeep Planning," with the same Sessions artwork as used in the "Jeep-Planning" advertisement on its cover that was aimed squarely at the farmer as a potential Jeep customer. "For some time after peace comes to the world," it began, "the world will continue to look to America's farmers for food.

"You will be asked to produce more record-breaking crops. You'll be called upon for more cattle, hogs, sheep, milk, eggs, poultry, etc, to feed the war-starved peoples of Europe as well as our own people. You will want to do your peace work with less physical strain than was necessary during wartime. You'll want to do it more easily and better and in fewer working hours. You'll want more time for rest and pleasure.

"To do this you'll need the newest and best in power equipment, at a cost you can afford. And that means one thing today – the Universal Peace 'Jeep' from Willys-Overland."

Noting that "The Universal Jeep is a 4-in-1 motor vehicle which will carry record-breaking Jeep performance into many peace jobs," Willys obliquely referred to the

Fred Coldwell identified that these two CJ-2 Jeeps are painted in the first two colors offered for the CJ-2A. The Jeep in the foreground is colored Harvest Tan whilst the second Jeep had a Pasture Green finish. (Author's collection)

pre-CJ-2A models by explaining that "the civilian model Jeep has been fitted by Willys engineers to met the needs of farmers, industries, businesses and individuals in the busy postwar era."

At the same time Willys assured potential buyers that it hadn't compromised the Jeep's fundamental design. "The Universal Jeep is the famous military Jeep in all basic features," it noted. "It looks very much like the military Jeep. It has the world-tested Willys Jeep engine, proved in billions of miles of Jeep military service. It has four-wheel drive. It has Jeep dependability and Jeep versatility." Illustrating these assertions were numerous photos some heavily retouched, of pre-CJ-2A Jeeps performing a variety of agricultural tasks.

Included in this brochure was a mail-in coupon for farmers to send to Willys for the "earliest possible information about the Universal Jeep." Implying that new Jeeps might be in short supply, readers were told by Willys that "many farmers, from all over the country, have already registered with us their interest in a Universal 'Jeep' after the war. If you have not sent your name and address to

us, do so right away. Orders are being carefully recorded with our dealers. Letters asking for first-hand information are being answered as promptly as possible. Sending in your inquiry now means that you will be among the first to get all the facts about the Jeep."

Thanks partly to this promotion, Willys had a large inventory of potential agricultural buyers on hand after the first CJ-2A civilian Jeep was produced at the Toledo, Ohio, Willys-Overland plant on July 17, 1945. Charles Sorensen, who had succeeded Joseph Frazer as Willys President in 1944, hosted a 2-day media affair at "Cesor," his 2000 acre farm, in New Hudson, Michigan. Jeeps were already familiar sights on Sorensen's farm since he had been keeping a small cadre of them busy plowing fields, cultivating threshing, digging post holes, spraying orchards, and operating as mobile power sources.

Shortly after the CJ-2A debuted, *The New York Times*, in a July 28, 1945 editorial, assessed the Jeep's role in peacetime America: "The Jeep is no limousine for long hauls, but it will carry the farmer and his family to market and the movies, or a hundred-and-one errands speedily and with reasonable comfort. It will also serve as a useful workhorse for many specialized applications as well, in field or barn yard. The unusual degree of traction developed by its 4-wheel drive makes it one of the most interesting motor vehicles to appear in many years."

Charles Sorensen had earlier predicted that in addition to farmers, the Jeep would appeal to hunters, fishermen, contractors, and oil well drillers. He also saw the Jeep quickly proving itself as a useful vehicle in road construction, as well as enabling various types of maintenance work to be performed in isolated areas.

Examples of how the Jeep's versatility had captured public imagination were found among the top 400 entries in a contest sponsored by *Popular Science* magazine for the best postwar uses for the Jeep. Although the winner

Three views of an early CJ-2A with a column shift in three stages of weather protection. (Author's collection)

This early CJ-2A is positioned by a DC-3 operated by Trans World Airways. It was delivered to TWA on December 22, 1937. During the Second World War, about half of the domestic airline's fleet of DC-3s was requisitioned by the military. The remaining aircraft, such as this DC-3 with its patriotic 'Victory is in the Air – BUY BONDS' message, remained in civilian operation. (Author's collection)

Universal 'Jee

This Jeep can be identified as a CJ-2A by its side body fuel filler cap and high-back seats. (Author's collection)

' does many jobs for industry

The Universal
'Jeep'
for the
Peacetime World

Willys used this retouched photo of one of the pre-production CJ-2 models (X-32) to let customers know about the recreational opportunities that CJ-2A ownership would offer. Fred Coldwell's diligent research unearthed the original photo. (Author's collection)

was selected from the agricultural applications that dominated the list, included in an article entitled "1001 Postwar Jobs For The Jeep." (*Popular Science*, February 1944), the second place entry recognized the Jeep's value as a recreational vehicle.

The public's recognition of the Jeep's versatility was shared by Willys-Overland management. With the war over, Willys' expectations for the Jeep were frequently expressed, both in public and behind closed corporate doors. For example, an internal memo from late 1946 noted "The Jeep of the future is still evolving and will continue to evolve as new uses are found for it. The Jeep is an ever-changing functional vehicle. Its development differs from that of the conventional transportation vehicle in that it does not stop with transportation alone."

The following year, a promotional brochure "A New Concept Of Automotive Production," noted that "The Universal 'Jeep' is an adaptation of the world-famous military 'Jeep' which was an expression of motor transportation in fundamental terms, functional in every detail. The blunt front end, square fenders and stark simplicity of the 'Jeep' exactly fulfill this purpose. And with its Willys Overland 'Jeep' engine and selective 2 and 4 wheel drive, the Universal 'Jeep' is making a place for itself in industry and agriculture. Its functional efficiency was something the world needed – as evidenced by its reception – although that need had never been consciously expressed."

Barely discernible in the CJ-2A's depiction as a farm-to-town vehicle was the genesis of a gradual shift in emphasis away from its merits as a purely utilitarian vehicle, toward an image expanded to include Jeeps as versatile, fun-to-drive, fun-to-be-in vehicles An early example of the Jeep's ability to be almost all things to nearly all men was when it went on sale at Hearn's Department Store in New York City. The Bronx was far removed from the rigors of rural farm life, but when Hearn's displayed two Jeeps in early October 1945 with price tags of $1195.59, their cushioned seats, column-mounted shift levers, and Pasture Green and Harvest Tan paint schemes attracted considerable attention from urban dwellers.

This early CJ-2A has column shift, side body fuel filler, and side body tool indents. Fred Coldwell has identified the non-standard ivory color of its shift knob. (Author's collection)

As civilian Jeep production began in mid-July 1945, Willys-Overland was sanguine about the immediate future: "The plan we have evolved for the manufacture of the civilian Jeep and other motor vehicles is designed to keep our employment at a high level through the reconversion, and into the postwar period as the curtailment of military production makes civilian material available. We plan to furnish our dealers with the vehicles which we know will be greeted by a large waiting market."

This proved difficult: although initial production plans for 1945 called for the output of approximately 20,000 civilian Jeeps, Willys-Overland managed to produce just 1824 units with a serial range of 10001 to 11824. Nonetheless, Willys-Overland finished its fiscal year on September 30, 1945 with a net profit of $2,711,332. By June 1, 1946 Willys had sold around 28,000 Jeeps in spite of plant shutdowns totaling 83 days due to strikes in supplier plants.

A view of the Willys-Overland plant in Toledo, Ohio as it appeared in 1946. (Author's collection)

Priced initially at $1090 FOB Toledo, the CJ-2A was available with both soft top and removable hardtop. Referring to the changes which made the Jeep more appropriate for the civilian market, *Fortune* magazine noted that "most engineers will concede that the Universal Jeep is sturdier, more usable, and generally superior to the Army Jeep," a view similarly expressed by *Motor Age* magazine, which noted that "The civilian Jeep resembles its military counterparts and shares many of the same design features. However, it does embody numerous changes in the interest of

The Jeep on the left is a legitimate CJ-2A. The airbrushed nature of the CJ-2 Jeep alongside is easy to detect and not sufficient to disguise its MB-type windshield. (Author's collection)

9 REASONS WHY THE 'Jeep' CAN DO ALL IT DOES!

1 **THE 4-CYLINDER, 60-H.P. WILLYS-OVERLAND 'JEEP' ENGINE** ... which powered the military "Jeep" over billions of miles in all parts of the world has been improved for even greater economy and more versatile performance on the farm. Its long life under the pressure of round-the-clock, round-the-calendar farm usage proves its ability to take it.

2 **TRANSMISSION** ... 3 speeds forward, 1 reverse in 2-wheel-drive for economical highway travel.

3 **TRANSFER CASE** ... an auxiliary gear unit, attached to the rear of the transmission, engages front-drive axle for 4-wheel-drive, used for pulling farm implements and trailed loads. Shift lever to driver's right. Transfer gear ratios, in conjunction with transmission gear ratios, give the "Jeep" 6 speeds forward and 2 reverse.

4 **REAR DRIVE AXLE** ... drives the "Jeep" at 60 m.p.h. in 2-wheel-drive.

5 **FRONT-DRIVE AXLE** ... teams with rear axle in 4-wheel-drive for tractor work; hard pulling in mud, sand or snow; towing highway trailed loads.

6 **SPRINGS AND SHOCK ABSORBERS** ... newly engineered for easier riding on the road or across the field.

7 **REAR POWER TAKE-OFF** ... furnishes power from spline-shaft drive for power mowers, sprayers, binders, post hole augers, etc.; for pulley-drive for threshers, corn shellers, ensilage cutters, buzz saws, etc.

8 **CENTER POWER TAKE-OFF** ... powers insecticide blowers, compressors, generators and other V-belt-drive equipment.

9 **DRAW BAR** ... provides 9 horizontal positions and 2 heights for proper tracking of towed implements. Braced, welded iron construction gives maximum strength.

providing adequate capacity and life for heavy-duty jobs." The initially concurrent production of the CJ-2A with the MB (output of the MB continued, explains CJ-2A historian Harold West, through September with approximately 9000 produced), and the economic advantages of using existing stocks of interchangeable MB parts meant that the transformation from military to pure civilian Jeep was not instantaneous. The eclectic nature of the CJ-2A Jeeps produced under those conditions has prompted Jeep historians to identify early models with serial numbers up to 34530 as 'Very Early Civilian' (VEC); and those built to mid-1947, when stocks of MB parts began to be exhausted as 'Early Civilian' (EC).

Some of the more prominent examples of this process illustrate the degree to which Willys utilized its stock of MB parts for the early years of CJ-2A production. Early models up to serial number 13453 had the same Spicer model 23-2 (full-floating) rear axle as the MB, except for a 5.38:1 ratio in place of the MB's 4.88:1. The purpose of the higher numerical axle ratio was to increase the Jeep's low end power; important for the intended use of the CJ-2A in agriculture and industry. After serial number 13453 the CJ-2A's Dana/Spicer 25 full-floating front axle was replaced with a stronger, semi-floating Dana/Spicer 41-2 unit. CJ-2A Jeeps up to serial number 15304 used the same windshield adjusting arms as found on the MB that utilized a long, flat, thin slotted bracket which slid on a stud. When the windshield was opened to the desired point, the operator tightened a knurled thumb nut against the bracket to secure it in place. As Harold West explains: "Since it

Willys used this worm's-eye view of the CJ-2A to illustrate its virtues to prospective owners. (Author's collection)

This CJ-2A, listed as a 1945 model, was equipped with driver's seat only. (Courtesy DaimlerChrysler Media Services)

much torque on the thumb nut. If the windshield was in any other position except closed or straight out, it would slip out of position due to the pounding the Jeep took over rough roads." The updated CJ-2A arrangement used a larger star washer and a winged thumb screw. "This did a much better job," says Harold West, "of holding the windshield in the half-way open position."

The CJ-2A began production with the 1944 version MB exhaust system which routed the exhaust pipe to a muffler exiting in front of the right rear wheel. At serial number 18638 it was replaced by a arrangement which routed the pipe straight back, up over the transmission cross member and the rear axle where a 90 degree turn was made. At this point (just past the axle) a short round muffler was installed between the rear braces for the draw bar. The tailpipe exited behind the right rear wheel.

Like the MB, the tie rods on early CJ-2A Jeeps bolted to arms that formed part of the top king pin. This arrangement was replaced at serial number 22972 by a setup which had the arm cast with the steering knuckle.

Beginning at serial number 24196 the transmissions and transfer cases were drilled to provide oil circulation between the two units.

One of the most memorable features of the military Jeeps which was also found on the early CJ-2As were the tool indentations on the driver's side body panel. Not all Jeep owners and historians agree exactly when Willys stopped using these panels for the CJ-2A. Some believe that it

had very little surface area, you couldn't get

occurred around serial number 29500: CJ Jeep owner and researcher Todd Kerzic notes: "I have serial number 27992 and there is no sign of them. The body of this CJ-2A was in poor condition and when I removed it from the frame, it still had the original pal nuts Willys used on the body bolts. These are similar to a locknut or a jam nut. They run a washer up to the nut and jam it in, creating a lock. They came from the factory like this and if a person removed the body and replaced it with a non-indent body, I highly doubt they would use the pal nuts over since they are half the thickness of a conventional nut and would most likely have been lost or discarded." Todd believes that the tool indents ended around serial number 27500, and suggests that the confusion has arisen from the original handwritten Willys paperwork concerning production in which the "7" looks like a "9."

Harold West, who maintains a database of surviving CJ-2A Jeeps, says "Todd may be correct. However, my database indicates a pattern of some 2As having and some not having the tool indents. This leads me to believe that one reason for this is that the new panels could have been

This illustration of an early CJ-2A, without a steering column mounting shift lever, was included in a Willys-Overland marketing brochure entitled A New Concept of Automotive Production and Distribution. The CJ-2A was described as "an adaptation of the world-famous military 'Jeep' which was an expression of motor transportation in fundamental terms, functional in every detail. The Universal 'Jeep' is making a place for itself in industry and agriculture. Its functional efficiency was something the world needed – as evidenced by its reception – although that need had never been consciously expressed." (Author's collection)

These two views of early CJ-2A Jeeps towing fully-loaded dollies were intended to demonstrate their utility to operators of large industrial facilities. (Author's collection)

stacked on top of the old panels, and, as the newer units were used, the older models were once again utilized until either the supply was finally exhausted or a run of new models was available."

Further complicating this issue is the matter of color choice for the CJ-2A. Noting that only Pasture Green and Harvest Tan were initially offered, and that on the production line "so many were painted green and then so many were painted tan," Harold West believes that "if they needed green bodies, they may have used up bodies with the old panels before finishing the run with bodies with the new panels. Then, if they went back to producing Jeeps with tan bodies, they may have started with bodies with the old panels.

"The bodies, like the engines, were not installed in exact serial number order. The workers just went and got one from the pile: from the middle/on the end/left side/right side – it didn't matter. The only thing that mattered was which color they needed! We are the ones trying to nail down when this change took place. It didn't matter to or concern Willys!"

Prior to serial number 38221 the CJ-2A had a column shift. Although not a carry over from the MB, this was a shortlived return to the original design for the MA. After that point, a cane-type floor shifter was used.

Until serial number 38687 the headlight rims were body color (then limited, as previously noted, to either Harvest Tan or Pasture Green). Beginning with this serial number they were chromed.

At approximately serial number 45723, the rear tail lamp door (a metal part securing the red lenses) was changed from black to chrome. The tail light housing remained gloss black.

At approximately serial number 67921 the rear reflector housings were changed from black to chrome. Also occurring at this point was replacement of the 2A's solid disc wheels with wheels containing four ventilating slots.

A new front grille with flush parking lights mounts was

A CJ-2A, posing with an early 1946 Model 463 Willys Station Wagon at the Willys plant in Toledo. (Author's collection)

Early postwar advertising of the CJ-2A promoted it as a versatile [vehi]cle for use on the farm. (Courtesy Marshall Rimland collection)

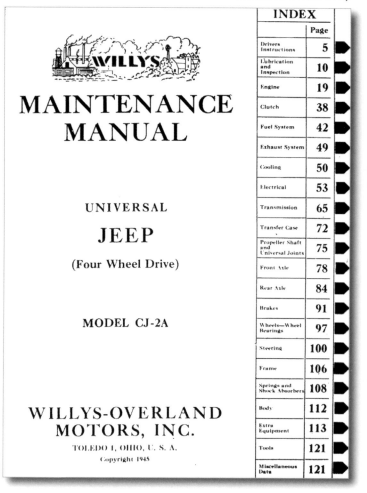

Early CJ-2A models of 1945 were delivered with this maintenance manual. (Courtesy Marshall Rimland collection)

WILLYS

MAINTENANCE MANUAL

UNIVERSAL

JEEP

(Four Wheel Drive)

MODEL CJ-2A

WILLYS-OVERLAND
MOTORS, INC.

TOLEDO 1, OHIO, U. S. A.
Copyright 1945

introduced from serial number 148458. The early grille had a cut-out for the parking lights, and a small panel spot welded behind the grille on which the light assembly was mounted. Its replacement exemplified Willys' attention to detail, making owner-maintenance of the CJ-2A relatively straightforward. The parking light bulb was inserted in a small hole stamped with two notches. The bulb locked into the socket in the usual fashion, but the entire socket assembly also twisted and locked into the grille body at the notches, making it possible to remove the socket and bulb as a unit through the grille back.

The ease with which this arrangement allowed replacement of the parking light bulb was explained by Harold West: "You could reach behind the grille, twist and unplug the light assembly, and bring it up where you could see it and work on it. You could then twist and unplug the light bulb for replacement. This was a small bulb and it was possible for it to pass through the hole in the grille. You could then refit the assembly back into the grille without having to remove the front lenses."

CJ-2A Jeeps in the 176062-185769 serial number range had a driver's side spare tire mount. This arrangement was intended to improve visibility over the driver's right shoulder and, as Harold West notes, "to minimize getting small trees caught between the spare tire and the body, and thus the possibility of ripping the spare tire off the Jeep. Since it actually impaired rather than improved rear visibility on the driver's side, it was soon abandoned." Todd Kerzic agrees, noting, "The spare was moved in response to all the complaints Willys was getting ... People backing out of a garage would hit the passenger side spare against the side of the building ...

In tight spaces the spare would also be hit. Willys did not give much thought to the consequences of moving the spare to the driver's side since it now obstructed vision in the side-mounted rearview mirror. So this change was shortlived and the spare was soon put back on the passenger's side."

Commencing with serial number 199079 a new steering bell crank and mounting (a support welded to the front cross member) entered production. The new bell crank pin was much sturdier than its predecessor.

Although minor, there were some differences between the physical dimensions of the CJ-2A and the MB, as the following table shows.

The CJ-2A engine was nearly identical to that of the MB. Whereas a Carter WO-539S carburetor was used

Model	MB	CJ-2A
Wheelbase:	80.0in	80in
Tread:	49in	48.25in
Height:	69.75in	69in
Length:	132.25in	130.125in*
Width:	62in*	59in
Ground clearance:	8.75in	8.75in

*The positioning of the CJ-2A's spare tire mount on the passenger's side, rather then at the back as on the MB, accounted for these differences.

Weight and capacity differences were also minor:

Model	MB	CJ-2A
Curb weight:	2453lb	2215lb
Gross weight:	3253lb	3500lb
Capacities:		
Fuel tank:	15gal	10.5gal
Cooling system:	11qt (with heater)	12qt (with heater)

OPERATION AND CARE

UNIVERSAL JEEP
MODEL CJ-2A

FIRST EDITION

WILLYS-OVERLAND MOTORS, INC.
TOLEDO, OHIO, U.S.A.

COPYRIGHT 1946

CJ-2A owners were provided with this operation and care manual in 1946. (Courtesy Marshall Rimland collection)

for the MB, the CJ-2A was equipped with the WO-596S model. Although most of them were minor, numerous changes occurred in the L-head engine specification during its long production life. Early models up to serial number 44417 had a chain driven cam; the silent type chain was non-adjustable and was subsequently changed to a gear drive setup consisting of helical cut gears, a steel gear mounted on

Willys wasn't bashful about promoting the CJ-2A's ability to handle a wide variety of tasks. "Built more sturdily than even its famous military progenitor," it said, "the Universal 'Jeep' combines the basic functions of a small truck, light tractor, mobile power unit and personnel carrier." (Author's collection)

the crankshaft, and a pressed fiber gear on the camshaft.

Major specifications of the CJ-2A engine were as per the following table.

Whereas the military Jeep had a 7.875in diameter driven clutch plate with a capacity of 132lb/ft, the

Engine	
Type:	L-head, 4-cylinder, cylinder block and crankcase cast integrally
Bore x stroke:	3.125 x 4.375in (79.37mm x 111.12mm)
Displacement:	134.2cu in (2199cc)
Compression ratio:	6.48:1
Horsepower:	60 @ 4000rpm
Torque:	105lb/ft @ 2000rpm
Crankshaft:	Fully counterbalanced
Main bearings:	Three
Valves	
Intake head dia:	1.531in
Exhaust head dia:	1.47in
Valve lift:	0.351in
Valve duration:	239 degrees
Crankshaft:	Forged steel (SAE 1040)
Camshaft:	Alloy cast iron, with four support points in the cylinder block
Pistons:	Aluminum alloy
Connecting rods:	Forged Steel (SAE 1141)
Fuel pump:	AC model 153886
Carburetor:	Single barrel downdraft, Carter model 596S
Flange:	1.0in
Primary venturi:	0.03475in
Main venturi:	1.0in
Air cleaner:	Oakes-Donaldson model 613300-E653, oil bath, 1.25pt capacity
Radiator:	Jamestown model J-161 with 4-blade fan
Clutch:	Auburn, single dry plate
Clutch area:	72sq in
Pressure plate:	Driven plate; Borg & Beck, 144lb/ft torque capacity
Wheels:	16 x 4.50E, Kelsey-Hayes, steel disc
Tires:	6.00 x 16in, 4-ply rating*

Inflation pressure:	Front: 26psi; rear: 28psi

*The CJ-2A was equipped with military non-directional (NDT) tread tires. In the words of one contemporary CJ owner, "an NDT tire just bounces all over the road. So, most of us who drive CJs on the road have put on a flatter, wider snow-type tire."

Frame:	Ladder, double-drop design with four steel channel intermediate cross members, front bumper bar and rear K member
Overall length:	122.656in (333.54cm)
Front/rear width:	29.25 x 29.25in
Section modulus:	1.493cu in

Model	MB	CJ-2A
Transmission	Warner Gear T84J	Warner Gear T-90a
Ratios:		
First:	2.665:1	2.798:1
Second:	1.564:1	1.551:1
Third:	1.0:1	1.0:1
Reverse:	3.554:1	3.798:1

Model	MB	CJ-2A
Ratios:		
High:	1.97	2.43
Low:	1.0:1	1.0:1

CJ-2A had a 8.5in diameter unit with a torque capacity of 175lb/ft.

The CJ-2A transmission was a different model, larger than that used for the MB (see middle table).

The CJ-2A transmission also had several new design features including larger bearings, the addition of an oil scoop in the front section to provide pressurized oil for the main shaft pilot bearing, an improved rear bearing oil seal, mounting of the counter shaft on needle bearings, and the addition of a breather and breather baffle for the transmission case. Transmission oil capacity was also increased from 1.5pts to 3pts.

Although the two Jeeps were fitted with the same Spicer model 18 transfer case, different ratios were used for the CJ-2A (bottom table).

The CJ-2A's transfer case had a lubricant capacity of 4 pints; the MB's 3 pints. Both models used the same Ross T-12 cam and twin pin lever steering with a variable steering ratio of 14-12-14 to I. As the following chart indicates. MB and CJ-2A suspensions differed in many of their specifications.

The CJ-2A and the MB shared the same foot brake system but differed in the setup of their hand brakes.

Front suspension	MB	CJ-2A
Type:	Semi-elliptic leaf springs	
Length x width:	36.25in x 1.75in	36.25in x 1.75in
Number of leaves:	8	10
Rear suspension		
Type:	Semi-elliptic leaf springs	
Length x width:	42in x 1.75in	36.25in x 1.75in
Number of leaves:	9	9 (optional: 11)
Shock absorbers:	Hydraulic, double action*	
Length (compressed/extended):		
Front:	10.3125in/16.9375in	10.75in/17.5in
Rear:	11.3125/18.3125in	10.75in/17.5in

*The CJ-2A's rear shock absorbers were mounted on the outside of the frame side rails. The MB's shocks were positioned inside the frame.

"The 'Jeep' will get you through – regardless!," promised Willys. "Here, it explained, the 'Jeep' forges through the soft ground of spring, climbing a steep woodland hill with three hefty lumbermen as passengers. In 4-wheel drive, the 'Jeep' can go most anywhere." (Author's collection)

Undoubtedly hoping the CJ-2A would 'measure up' to customer expectations, an enterprising Jeep dealer offered showroom visitors this ruler embossed with the image of a CJ-2A. Just to make sure that the message about the Jeep's usefulness wasn't missed, he added a listing of some equipment he offered for the Jeep. (Courtesy Marshall Rimland collection)

Chrysler Corporation included this photo of a 1946 CJ-2A in a special "Jeep – The First Fifty Years" media package in 1991. (Author's collection via Chrysler Corporation)

This CJ-2A earned its keep by pulling a train full of tourists enjoying the sights at Africa USA, a Florida theme park. (Courtesy Marshall Rimland collection)

This 1946 CJ-2A, minus its spare tire, served as a mobile power source for this jack-hammer operator. (Author's collection

These unique Willys collectibles date from at least 1948 when the Jeepster was introduced. (Courtesy Marshall Rimland collection)

GENERAL USE OIL

WILLYS-OVERLAND MOTOR

GLASS CLEANER

WILLYS-OVERLAND MOTOR

The MB's actuated an external contracting brake band positioned at the rear of the transfer case; the CJ-2A brake operated on the rear propeller shaft.

Not found on the MB was the CJ's radiator shroud, added to improve engine cooling at low speeds. A wider steel panel between the cowl and the base of the windshield glass raised the top of the CJ-2A's windshield 2.5in above that of the MB. Whereas most MB Jeeps were fitted with manually-operated windshield wipers for both driver and passenger (beginning in March 1945, MB Jeeps had been equipped with dual vacuum wipers), the CJ-2A had a standard, driver's side, vacuum-powered wiper. The wiper for the passenger remained a manual unit. When it came time to fill up, most CJ-2A owners were pleased that Willys had repositioned the fuel filler cap from directly under the driver's seat on the MB to a location on the CJ's left body side, behind the driver's seat and just ahead of the rear wheel cutout. The fuel tank remained located beneath the driver's seat. Embossed 'WILLYS' lettering was positioned on the CJ-2A's side hood panels, tailgate, and on the cowl panel below the windshield. The CJ-2A windshield and frame could be lowered to rest upon its hood by unlatching retaining catches located on the cowl just above the instrument panel. Willys-Overland cautioned owners to ensure the windshield was secured by a strap mounted on top of the radiator guard.

Use of a chain-supported tailgate on the CJ-2A provided a load area of ten square feet when the rear seat was removed. Incorporating a tailgate into the CJ-2A design also made it possible to install a Monroe hydraulic implement lift, with a three-point attachment system via which many pieces of mechanized farm equipment could be operated.

Readily apparent was the CJ-2A's flush-mounted, seven-inch, Corcoran-Brown headlights with stainless steel nacelles, and a seven-slot grille with concave outer units to accommodate the larger headlamps. This setup contrasted with the military Jeep's much smaller 5in, Mazda No 2400 sealed beam headlights which recessed within the nine-bar grille. These were mounted on hinged brackets and, when a securing wing nut was loosened, could be used as a engine compartment trouble light. Standard for the CJ-2A was a single tail light mounted on the driver's side.

In place of the MB's rear fender-installed tool boxes, a small tool compartment was located under the CJ-2A's front passenger seat. The grab handles located on the

Seen here pulling a two-bottom plow, this 1946 CJ-2A was described by Willys-Overland as having a draw bar pull sufficient for most farm implements. (Author's collection)

rear sides of the MB were not used on the CJ-2A.

Compared to the seats used on military Jeeps, the CJ-2A's – with higher seat backs – were described by the British weekly, *The Motor* (August 8th, 1945) as "vastly more comfortable." Replacing the MB's one-piece, fold-down top bows was a three-piece bow assembly.

Three power take-off (PTO) points were optional. The front unit operated directly from the front end of the engine's crankshaft and provided power for capstan or drum winches, suction or booster pumps. The center unit, available as Willys-Overland Kit No 640725, was offered with a belt pulley drive (Willys-Overland Kit No 643883) that could be installed behind the transmission, either alone or in connection with the rear PTO unit. Operated at engine speed or through a 1.55 or 2.80 transmission reduction, this unit transmitted a maximum of 33 horsepower. The belt drive accommodated from one to four pulleys and could power equipment such as an air compressor, electric welder, and generator.

The rear PTO was mounted on the frame rear cross member and provided an SAE standard 1.375in, six-splined shaft for driving a power-operated implement behind the CJ-2A. For belt-driven equipment, a pulley-drive governor controlled unit was bolted to the unit and fitted with an 8.0in diameter pulley with speeds ranging from 255 to 2674rpm. When ordered with the center PTO,

this unit was identified as Willys-Overland Kit No 640726. When the pulley drive was included it was offered as Kit No 646452. If only the pulley drive was desired, Willys-Overland Kit No 644193 was specified.

To operate these accessory drives and PTOs, the CJ-2A could be equipped with a King-Seeley centrifugal-type, variable-speed governor providing controlled constant speed operation. It was operated by an instrument panel-mounted control handle. The governor was belt-driven from the inner groove of a crankshaft-mounted double pulley. The outer groove was for the accessory drive. One of the governor's many useful features was accessibility of major working parts and non-interference with other Jeep accessories, such as the PTO and tow bar hitch.

Two optional canvas tops, constructed of 10oz soldenized mildew-resistant duck with double-sewn seams, were offered for the CJ-2A, Kit No 667888, and enclosed the front cab region, whilst Kit No 667826 (which could not be ordered separately) enclosed the rest of the body.

A CJ-2A operating in two-wheel drive, high gear on a level paved road, with a 3250 pound gross weight and tires inflated to 28psi, could average 19.8mpg at a speed of 30mph. As speed increased, fuel consumption reflected the gearing: for example, at its maximum speed of 60mph, the Jeep averaged 8.8mpg.

As shipped from the factory, the CJ-2A was not actually capable of a speed of 60mph. When owners took delivery of their new Jeeps they were advised that "at assembly a restrictor is placed between the intake manifold and the carburetor to limit the road speed to approximately 42mph. To protect the vehicle, leave the restrictor in position for the first 500 miles of road travel, or equivalent in industrial operation, after which remove and discard it."

When the CJ-2A was first introduced, the only two paint schemes offered were those shown in the accompanying table.

The pinstriping on CJ-2A wheels was 0.25in wide, positioned just past the roll of the center part of the wheel.

Joining the two introductory CJ-2A colors by mid-1946

Body	Wheels	Pinstriping
Pasture Green	Autumn Yellow	Pasture Green
Harvest Tan	Sunset Red[1]	American Black

[1]Contemporary newspaper accounts describe this color as "orange." Harold West describes it as a "bright pumpkin orange."

An all-original unrestored 1948 CJ-2A owned by Rick and Melanie West, seen here with a 1946 Bantam trailer. (Courtesy Rick & Melanie West/Bob Christy)

The hydraulic power lift developed for the new CJ-2A enabled it to operate many farm implements, including this tandem disc-harrow. (Author's collection)

(beginning with serial number 38221), were these four color combinations:

In 1947 the Harvard Red body color was dropped and two new combinations offered:

One additional color combination was offered in 1948:

Body	Wheels	Pinstriping
Princeton Black[2]	Harvard Red or Sunset Red	American Black
Normandy Blue	Autumn Yellow	Normandy Blue[3]
	Sunset Red	Normandy Blue[3]
Michigan Yellow	Pasture Green	Michigan Yellow
	American Black	Wake Ivory
	Sunset Red	American Black
Harvard Red	Autumn Yellow	Harvard Red
	American Black	Wake Ivory

[2]Harold West notes that this color, "which is sometimes mentioned as American Black, is such a rare color that not much is known about its wheel color." He reports that contemporary color ads show wheels that are the colors listed above.
[3]Or American Black

For the production model CJ-2A, Willys-Overland decide to stamp 'WILLYS' on its hood instead of 'JEEP.' Would it have mattered to Jeep customers? (Courtesy Rick & Melanie West/Bob Christy)

This matchbook cover, showing a CJ-2A plowing snow, was from Turner Motors, an Allentown, Pennsylvania Jeep distributor. (Courtesy Marshall Rimland collection)

For the final year of CJ-2A production in 1949, three colors – Picket Gray, Normandy Blue and Michigan Yellow – were dropped. A new Emerald Green color was offered,

Body	Wheels	Pinstriping
Picket Gray	Harvard Red	Americar Black
Luzon Red	Universal Beige	Luzon Red

but, according to Harold West, no definite CJ-2A wheel color has been established.

Body	Wheels	Pinstriping
Potomac Gray	Harvard Red	Americar Black
	Americar Black	Wake Ivory

One additional color offered in the early years (1946-1947) of CJ-2A production was Olive Drab. Specifics on its use are elusive but Harold West notes that "It is assumed by many that this color was used on models for military export ... A couple of foreign countries ordered CJ-2As for use in their military. Their use by South Africa and Switzerland militaries has been documented."

In its assessment of the Universal Jeep in 1946, *Fortune* magazine hadn't been optimistic about its longevity, depicting it as "a unique vehicle that deserves longer life than it probably will enjoy. As a fad it is selling, even in passenger-car markets now, though by such standards it is uncomfortable and expensive."

This opinion of the Jeep's future was based on the Jeep's basic design and the sales quality of the Willys-Overland dealership network. "Generically," said *Fortune*, "it is a piece of machinery and has to be sold as such. In the long run, Willys Jeep sales (except for export), will

An attractive Willys-Overland match book cover featuring the classic W-O logo. (Courtesy Marshall Rimland collection)

THE UNIVERSAL Jeep'
BY WILLYS-OVERLAND

AROUND THE CLOCK
AROUND THE YEAR
AROUND THE WORLD

This CJ-2A Jeep cut-out model was a Kelloggs cereal box top premium. (Courtesy Marshall Rimland collection)

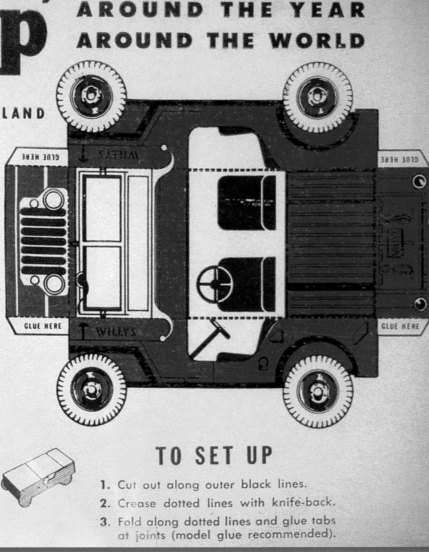

ally, when you get a p", you get the services our machines: A Tractor Truck...A Mobile Power t...and a highly man-erable and economical about.

unmatched versatility of military "Jeep" was ed on the battlefields of It has been redesigned to to work at hundreds of an jobs where it can save hard work, and money. destiny of the "Jeep" is to h in civilian life its world-military reputation.

he best-loved piece of pment in the hands of ighting men, the "Jeep" signed by Willys, now e's its bow to you, to all rica, to all the world... asks for work to do

TO SET UP

1. Cut out along outer black lines.
2. Crease dotted lines with knife-back.
3. Fold along dotted lines and glue tabs at joints (model glue recommended).

brochure entitled "What we mean when we say ... America's Most Useful Vehicles," it explained that "Bodies for the Universal Jeep, which had been purchased outside during the first three years of postwar production, will be made in this press shop starting early in 1949." Based on his research Harold West believes this switch was made sometime earlier, most likely late in 1948.

Most CJ-2A owners had little or no awareness of the origin of the body of their Jeep. What mattered to them was its versatility,

depend largely on the ability of its dealers to develop the techniques that sell tractors and machinery. Unless automobile salesmen have changed a lot, the Jeep is a worthy piece of business that may pass away by default."

When Willys-Overland began producing its own Jeep bodies late in the CJ-2A production run, it ended a phase of Jeep history dating back to early 1944. Until then, the Willys MB Jeep had used a body produced by the American Central Manufacturing (ACM) Corporation of Connersville, Indiana. Bodies for the GPW Jeep were built in-house by Ford. In order to enable the Ford body plant to fulfill other military obligations, all parties involved agreed that the MB and GPW should share a common, or 'composite' body built by ACM. The Ford and Willys Jeeps began using this body in January 1944.

Producing Jeep bodies in its body press shop was part of Willys-Overland's self-sufficiency program. In a

dependability, and go-anywhere, do-anything personality. But there was some owners who, after purchasing a new CJ-2A, drove it very sparingly and did not subject it to the rigors of the farm or construction site. The result, a handful of low-mileage, original VEC Jeeps, is exemplified by "Harold the Jeep," today owned by Marshall Rimland of East Stroudburg, Pennsylvania. With serial number 10284, the 284th CJ-2A built (all its engine, frame and dash numbers match and are clear and legible), this Jeep is one of the most remarkable CJ-2As in existence. "Harold the Jeep" was originally purchased by Harold Sterling Vanderbilt in 1945 for use on his farm, Mt Airy, in Mt Valley, Pennsylvania. Mr Vanderbilt (1884-1970) was the great grandson of railroad magnate Commodore Cornelius Vanderbilt. His older brother, William Kissam Vanderbilt II, donated the trophy for the Vanderbilt Cup auto races held on Long Island from 1904-1916. Both brothers were avid

A sample of employee identification badges worn by employees at Willys-Overland's Toledo plant. (Courtesy Marshall Rimland collection)

These sew-on Jeep emblems were probably provided to employees by Willys-Overland dealers. (Courtesy Marshall Rimland collection)

sailing enthusiasts, and Harold successfully defended the America's Cup in 1930, 1934 and 1940. (The 1930 race debuted large J-class boats.) Vanderbilt's victorious racer, the Enterprise, was 80 feet in length and had a 165 foot tall mast. Vanderbilt was pictured aboard the Enterprise on the cover of the September 15, 1930 issue of *Time Magazine*.

Marshal Rimland suggests it was this activity, rather than his invention of Contract Bridge, that influenced Harold's driving habits. One story from the mid-fifties, he explains, concerns Mr Vanderbilt driving his 1956 Thunderbird from New York to his Pennsylvania farm in such a way that his staff thereafter preferred to make the

trip in a separate car ... Once at the farm, James Hiner, a son of one of the farm's managers, recalls that Harold would take the CJ-2A out for a ride around the property, occasionally deciding to abandon the Jeep and walk back and sending his chauffeur to retrieve the Jeep and return it to the garage. On one occasion, Mr Hiner remembers that it took staff two days to locate the Jeep!

Having been well maintained, almost always garaged, (its mileage is less than 11,066), never damaged and free from any sort of physical deterioration, this CJ-2A is not only in outstanding condition but, with a few identifiable exceptions, is as it was when it left Willys' Toledo factory in 1945. Marshall Rimland identifies these items as being non-original:

Marshall Rimland's 1945 CJ-2A 'Harold the Jeep,' the 284th CJ-2A produced. Marshall Rimland had plans for the two Jeep trucks seen slumbering in the background. (Courtesy Marshall Rimland collection)

With regard to the CJ-2's 6-volt electric system, Marshall Rimland notes "I agree with modern thought that a 12 volt system is better. But somehow the Jeep made it through its wartime years in extreme climates. On the coldest day, I can start Harold with the choke all the way out without touching the gas pedal. It never takes more than five or six very slow revolutions of the engine before it fires up." (Courtesy Marshall Rimland collection)

– Aftermarket top
– Body color slightly lighter than the original Harvest Tan finish
– Slotted wheels which were used on later CJ-2As in place of the original equipment solid disc wheels
– A non-original, aftermarket temperature gauge
– Re-upholstered driver and front passenger seats. (The rear seat still has its original Military Olive Drab upholstery.)

But the importance of this CJ-2A in Jeep history far exceeds the sum of its parts, or an analysis of its mixture of military and civilian Jeep components. Once behind the wheel of an early CJ-2A of this condition and originality, issues such as who deserves credit for its creation, or precise details about the Jeep's evolution, fade into insignificance, replaced by an appreciation for the integrity of the Jeep's design and its ability to perform as promised.

Initially, to some owners of contemporary SUVs the CJ-2A may seem anachronistic, old-fashioned, and woefully out of step with the pace of modern times. But, as Marshall Rimland explains, the CJ-2A sets its own cadence and rhythm: "There is a certain joy in driving at just a couple of miles an hour. That tiny four cylinder engine with only sixty horsepower can produce enormous working force using its transfer case in low gear. With a slow moving vehicle, you don't have to pay that much attention to your surroundings.

"It's safe enough that you can concentrate on the various mechanical units with their distinct sounds and

With the exception of an aftermarket temperature gauge, the Rimland CJ-2A's instrumentation is original. (Courtesy Marshall Rimland collection)

Marshall Rimland's CJ-2A has been well maintained, nearly always garaged, never damaged, and is free from any sort of physical deterioration. Its current color is slightly lighter than the original Harvest Tan finish, and the original equipment solid disc wheels were replaced by the previous owner with slotted wheels used on later CJ-2As. The driver and front passenger seats have been upholstered. The rear seat still has its original Military Olive Drab (OD) upholstery. (Courtesy Marshall Rimland collection)

The Willys-Overland body serial number plate located under the hood on the passenger side firewall and just under the Willys serial number. Serial number, body number and frame numbers all matched up to late 1948. Serial numbers started at 10,001, making this CJ-2A the 284th off the assembly line. The bodies were manufactured by American Central Manufacturing (ACM) and they had their own serial numbers starting at number 1. Note the original air filter bracket bolt head marking of EC. (Courtesy Marshall Rimland collection)

Marshall Rimland, speaking of his CJ-2A: "Rather than built around beauty, it was constructed for practicality, and it was perfect for its purpose." (Courtesy Marshall Rimland collection)

actions. The old Jeeps are simple enough to enable the driver to conjure up images of their various parts as they go about their business – some sliding, others rotating and meshing together. Modern vehicles are too mysterious and fast to enjoy in that way.

"The Jeep is a low speed vehicle – not a highway cruiser. It was designed for heavy-duty work. There have been countless adaptions, making it akin to the Swiss Army knife. It started out as a military fighting machine with a very small profile with the windshield down. It could squeeze into tight places, and was easily assembled, disassembled and repaired in the field.

"Rather than built around beauty, it was constructed for practicality, and was perfect for its purpose. Due to its low weight you could build a tramway and easily lift it across a ravine; you could float a Jeep in a pontoon boat or a raft. The Jeep was small enough to hide in hard-to-find nooks and crannies.

"For military use a top and doors were sometimes a disadvantage – better to wear heavy clothing and leave the top and doors off so you could leap out quickly under fire.

"My Jeep was built and first operated at a time when the world was finally finished with a fearful and devastating war. All the world was yearning for peace and the Jeep became an appropriate symbol of a 'sword beat into a plowshare.' The very same machine that made so much

"Harold's design is basically crude, a far cry from modern vehicles built for style and comfort," says Marshall Rimland . "Crude, but very functional, strong, durable and adaptable." (Courtesy Marshall Rimland collection)

war made it successful in peacetime. It was strong and durable, light in weight and reliable.

"I enjoy driving Harold slow. I have other vehicles in which I can travel at high speeds in comfort but I enjoy driving Harold slowly along small country roads, sometimes at only 10-15 miles an hour with that trusty little engine purring smoothly, never missing a beat. With the windshield down and the top and doors off, there's always a refreshing breeze, even on the hottest summer's day. Sixty years after it was assembled, the transmission still slides easily from gear to gear with assurance and confidence.

"There are no unnecessary elements on the Jeep. When I'm driving it, I sense that every part of it is there for a purpose, each one a well proportioned contributor to a medley of sights and sounds unique to the Jeep.

"I have the honor of being the caretaker of this modest, but strong hero."

The CJ-2A moved the Jeep into a new era in its history. In 1945 it was a hero of World War II. By 1948 it had become a unique part of postwar America's rekindled love affair with automobiles. On or off the road, the Jeep was in a class by itself.

The CJ-2A remained in production into 1949, essentially unchanged from its 1946 form. Total production of the CJ-2A was 214,292 units.

of a contribution in combat could now be enjoyed and utilized in peacetime.

"After the war the Jeep was put into service for agricultural use. With its four-wheel drive it could function as a tractor and was used as a source of mobile power for a multitude of tasks. It could run generators, compressors, and welders; it could dig ditches, and fence posts, haul farm supplies and pull agricultural implements. A farmer could drive it into distant fields to repair equipment or to lay cable or wire in remote areas. At day's end, it was ready to serve as a means to go to town.

"Harold's design is basically crude, a far cry from modern vehicles built for style and comfort. Crude but very functional, strong, durable and adaptable.

"This machine's beauty was not in its appearance, but in its utility. The same attributes that made it great in

Visit Veloce on the web: www.velocebooks.com

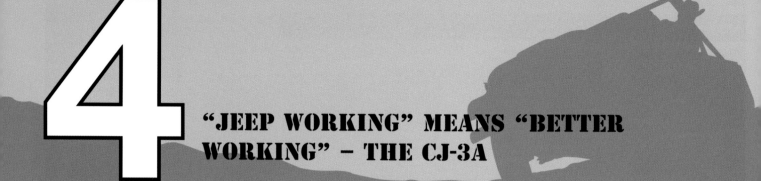

4 "JEEP WORKING" MEANS "BETTER WORKING" – THE CJ-3A

Introduced in late 1948, the CJ-3A entered a market where conditions were tilting in favor of the buyer. In January 1949, Willys-Overland Board Chairman and President James Mooney told a Cincinnati, Ohio audience that, within six months, car buyers would be able to enter an automobile showroom and order any model they wanted. "We've switched," he asserted, "to a buyer's market." Aside from discussing the ramifications of this long-anticipated development, Mooney also expressed concern over the prices of new vehicles that, he said, were "shrinking the use of motorcars." Recognizing that "a lot of rocks have been thrown at management and labor because of the high prices of motor cars," Mooney was not willing to accept full responsibility for price increases. In his view they were a result of the "lower purchasing power of the dollar for all manufacturers because of our devaluation of the dollar" and the fact that "The present cost of motor cars is heavily loaded with direct and indirect taxes amounting to several hundred dollars per vehicle."

Although 1949 calendar production of all Jeep vehicles fell to 83,250 (including 31,491 CJ-3As) from 136,648 in 1948, matters might have been worse if Willys hadn't reduced prices in March. In reporting this development, *Business Week* (March 26th, 1949) noted: "Willys-Overland Motors finally took a step last week it has long been considering: it cut prices on its entire line of cars ... The cuts ranged from $25 on the Jeep to $270 on the Jeepster models. The factory list price of the Jeep is now $1195 fob Toledo ... Willys cut prices because its sales have been slipping. The recent blizzards in the Midwest slashed Jeep sales so sharply that the company closed down its plant in February, finally reopening it last week ... Throughout the winter, however, sales have been slowing down."

At first glance, the CJ-3A appeared very similar to the CJ-2A, but there were numerous differences, including many with regard to physical dimensions, as the accompanying table shows.

In place of the CJ-2A's model 596S Carter carburetor,

This illustration answers one of the burning questions of the day: "What could be more useful down on the farm than one CJ-3A ?" (Author's collection)

70

Model	CJ-2A	CJ-3A
Front overhang:	20.75in	20.59in
Rear overhang:	22.31in	22.31in
Ground line to lower body edge:	17.375in	17.4375in
Ground to upper edge of rear body:	37.375in	37.6875in
Ground to lower edge of rear body:	19.25in	19.71875in
Passenger compartment length:	68.5in	68.31in
Tailgate height:	19.25in	19.71in
Cargo bed length:	35.62in	32.0in
Overall body length*:	123.12in	123.0in
Steering wheel to seat back distance:	14.0in	15.12in
Steering wheel to seat distance:	7.0in	7.37in

*When spare tire overhang was included these dimensions were 130.125in and 129.75in respectively.
Willys also reported that the CJ-3A's shipping weight and curb weight were at 2110 and 2205 pounds respectively, ten pounds less than those of the CJ-2A.

the 2A. Later models had radiators mounted to the grille, not the frame.

Replacing the CJ-2A's Jamestown J-161 radiator was a Harrison unit. Cooling system capacity remained eleven quarts without heater and twelve quarts with heater. The thermostat on early CJ-3A Jeeps went unchanged from that used on the CJ-2A. It began to open at 150 degrees F and was fully open at 180 degrees F. Subsequent models used a thermostat with respective temperature levels of 180 degrees F and 202 degrees F. The fan-to-crankshaft ratio of the early CJ-3A was 1.83:1, which then

These two schematics illustrate many of the dimensional differences between the CJ-2A and the CJ-3A. (Author's collection)

the CJ-3A used a model 636SA. Both were of the same basic design and shared many components, however.

Physically, the domestic model CJ-3A was identified by its one-piece windshield (a two-piece windshield was available for export) and dual windshield wipers positioned on the windshield base. When the windshield was mounted in its upright position, a hinged ventilator, set in the center of a panel between two indented sections, provided air flow to the Jeep's occupants.

As with the early CJ-2A, Willys saw no good reason to throw out existing stock of CJ-2A parts which were suitable for use on the CJ-3A. As Todd Kerzic notes: "So here we go again with the old Willys game of using up leftover parts on new models before completely changing things over." Some results of Willys "waste not, want not" philosophy included early 3As with their radiators mounted to the frame as on

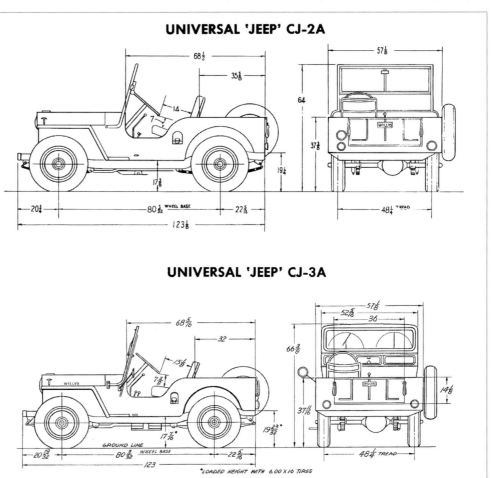

This CJ-3A was equipped with a removable steel cab. (Author's collection)

reverted to the 1.19:1 ratio used on the CJ-2A. The length of the engine drive belt used on the CJ-3A was 44 inches as compared to the 42.34 inch length belt installed on the CJ-2A. The angle of the belt 'V' also differed between the two models: the CJ-2A's had a 42 degree angle; the CJ-3A's a 45 degree angle.

Additional mechanical revisions for the CJ-3A included a change in piston clearance to 0.003in from 0.004in, and a valve tappet clearance of 0.016in instead of 0.014in.

Both Auburn and Rockford clutches were specified for the CJ-3A. Their specification – along with the CJ-2A's – was as per the table.

	CJ-2A Auburn	CJ-3A Auburn	CJ-3A Rockford
Spring pressure:	180-195lb	220-230lb	170-180lb
Torque capacity:	144lb/ft	165lb/ft	140lb/ft

An Auburn heavy-duty clutch with a spring pressure of 160-170lb and a 145lb/ft rated torque capacity was optional for the CJ-3A.

Most CJ-3As had a Spicer Model 44-2 semi-floating rear axle in place of the CJ-2A's Spicer Model 41-2, which had a standard 4.27:1 axle ratio with optional 5.38:1 ratio. Road clearance, at 8.0in, was slightly less than the 8.75in of the CJ-2A's axle.

Lower king pin bearing shims were eliminated by increasing the king pin boss on the steering knuckles. Adjustments were now made by using shims at the top bearing cap only. Flanged bushings were adopted to control end float of front axle shafts.

The canvas top offered as a factory option for the CJ-3A was constructed of 10oz soldenized duck, treated to resist mildew. All seams were double-sewn for improved wear. Willys claimed the top could be assembled or removed in "a few minutes by one person." (Author's collection)

During the CJ-3A's production run, which ended in 1953, a number of additional changes were made in its mechanical make-up. Effective with serial number 30973 a 4.5in

These two views of a CJ-3A at work in winter and summer are graphic examples of its off-road capability. Willys reported that "with all four wheels pulling, the 'Jeep' can move loads of 2½ tons." (Author's collection)

push-button type starter switch located to the right of the accelerator treadle – also used on MB and CJ-2A models – was replaced by a switch activated by turning the ignition key to its extreme right position. When the key was in a vertical position, the electrical system was off; turning the key to the left energized the instrument panel and instruments, including the radio and heater.

A specialized version of the CJ-3A, the Farm Jeep, fitted with a standard power take-off, was introduced in 1951 and remained available until 1953.

As the CJ-3A's list price – as well as the cost of several of its popular options – indicates, being able to buy it remained within reach of many prospective owners (see table).

By the early 1950s, Willys, having

Factory advertised delivered price:	$1290.00
Front top:	$59.94
Rear top:	$34.99
Rear seat:	$25.53
Front seat:	$19.56

expanded its product range to include 4-wheel drive Station Wagons and trucks, was eager to improve the ability of its dealers to compete in the new postwar buyers' market. In order to overcome resistance from dealers satisfied with the volume of their business, who tended to be resentful of corporate pressure to alter their business model, Willys-Overland followed a policy of gentle persuasion in a paper, *Market Research and Analysis*, sent to its dealers. It began with a favorable depiction of the Willys dealer and his products: "The Willys Jeep and Commercial Car Dealer is unique among automotive merchants. He is fortunate in that he alone has an exclusive product and an exclusive market.

"Commercial Car and Truck Dealers generally in a given community are in direct competition, one with the other for each and every potential sale in the market area. This is true because there is little difference in the products which they have to offer – they are similar in design, appearance, function and purpose. There is little that one has to offer that the other does not, and since styling and appearance are not factors of such importance in the case of commercial transportation equipment, as with passenger cars, the selling approach generally boils down to price, trading allowance, prestige of the manufacturer, the standing of the dealer in the community and the service he renders, etc.

starting motor was used which incorporated a new starting switch and flywheel drive. Unlike the starting motor used on the early CJ-3A, which was equipped with a overrunning clutch type drive, the new motor's Bendix 'Folo-Thru' type drive was intended to prevent the drive pinion from prematurely de-meshing from the flywheel ring gear until a predetermined engine speed was reached.

Commencing with serial number 37549, a front axle design was used in which the axle shaft's outer splined end 'floated' in the wheel driving flange (previously it had been retained by a nut and lock washer). This change eliminated the need to install shims between the driving flange and the wheel hub to provide the correct end float of the axle shaft universal joint.

Late in CJ-3A production, the foot-operated,

This CJ-3A was used by the Philadelphia Police Department in traffic control. (Author's collection)

A key fob from Colove Jeep-Pontiac-Cadillac, a dealership located in Robesconia, Pennsylvania. (Courtesy Marshall Rimland collection)

"The Willys Dealer, on the other hand, has a combination of versatile utility vehicles in the Jeep, and 4-Wheel Drive Station Wagon and Trucks which no other dealer can offer. He has a product which can perform all of the functions performed by competitive vehicles in the same GVW classification, plus a multitude of others which conventional commercial vehicles cannot approach. His market, therefore, is an exclusive, specialized market calling for careful approach and analysis to ascertain its true potential, to be followed by intelligently planned follow-through sales activity pointing in the direction of that specialized market."

Then came an effort to present the concept of market research and analysis in a positive light. "There might be an inclination," dealers were told, "to shy away from the term 'market analysis.' It smacks somewhat of the research laboratory, it has something of a scientific ring to it. That, perhaps, was in the mind of the successful rural market dealer when he said, 'I know every commercial car and truck owner in my community. I know the make and model of truck he uses. I know how old his vehicles are, and what chances there are of selling him a new truck. Why, then, should I waste my good time putting their names on cards and juggling them around?'" Willys had no argument with a dealer running his business in that fashion, except that it prevented both the Jeep dealer and corporation from maximizing sales. "Generally," it responded, "with that kind of intimate knowledge and familiarity with his market, there would be no reason in the world, assuming the dealer is handling a conventional line of vehicles. His market was

small enough and simple enough to carry in his head – at least he thought it was and as has been pointed out, our jobs are the product of our thinking.

"For you – the Willys dealers – however, there is a vast difference. You have a different set of conditions. You have a different market and potential. You have a broader opportunity requiring an even more intimate knowledge of your market."

Driving this point right into the dealer's pocket book, Willys asserted that "every community has commercial vehicle operators who do not even know that they need a Willys Jeep or 4-Wheel Drive Truck."

In order to help dealers identify these hidden markets Willys encouraged them to submit 'Retail Delivery Cards' which included information about the customer's occupation, the make and year of the vehicle traded in, trade-in prices and the purpose for which the vehicle was purchased. Explaining in common everyday terms that this information was one of the core elements of market analysis, and that the individual dealers played a key role in its collection, helped to sweep away many of the abstractions of market analysis and replace them with concepts easily understood by Willys dealers. For example, citing the widely held view that 4x4 sales were seasonal in nature, it asserted that "Registration figures show that there is no general 'Off Season' for the sale of 4-Wheel Drive Vehicles. The steady, year round trend of sales is made up of the snow season, rainy season, spring season and harvest season."

Analyzing the information from over 2500 Retail

Delivery Record Cards (Willys-Overland did not specify the years covered but anecdotal comments found in its text suggest it primarily dealt with sales of the CJ-3A), Willys provided its dealers with the accompanying chart of Jeep sales in nearly two dozen occupation categories:

Using a larger base of just over 5800 Jeep buyers, Willys computed this information concerning vehicles traded in for Jeeps (see table).

Finally, the same base of Jeep buyers, when analyzed by the type of vehicle they traded in on their new Jeeps, took this form in this table.

By any measure, be it market analysis or just plain good business etiquette, one of the most impressive examples of a Jeep dealer making every possible effort to ensure customer satisfaction is that of Wiley Bros & Lewis, a Packard-Willys dealer in West Chester, Pennsylvania, from whom Mr and Mrs Arthor Knorr purchased a 1951

Rank	Owner's occupation	Number of Jeeps purchased/%
1	Farmer	842/21.44
2	Extractive industry	389/9.91
3	Ranching	229/5.84
4	Merchant	287/7.30
5	Miscellaneous	236/6.01
6	Contractor	224/5.70
7	Garage and service stations	215/5.47
8	Skilled worker	191/4.86
9	Mail carrier	175/4.46
10	Public utility	152/3.87
11	Manufacturing	147/3.74
12	Laborer	115/2.93
12	Hauling and delivery	115/2.93
13	Service company	102/2.59
14	Government	86/2.19
15	Professional (excluding physicians)	68/1.73
16	Office worker	62/1.58
17	Retired	49/1.25
18	Salesperson	44/1.13
19	Transportation	37/0.94
20	Surveyor or engineer	37/0.94
21	Business executive	25/0.64
22	Domestic	24/0.61
23	Willys distributor or dealer	17/0.44

Make traded in	Number of Jeeps purchased/%
Willys	2634/45.2
No trade-in	2505/42.9
Ford	192/3.6
Chevrolet	151/3.6
Dodge	57/1.0
Studebaker	36/0.5
Plymouth	31/0.6
GMC	25/0.4
International	24/0.4
Buick	23/0.4
Pontiac	15/0.2
Oldsmobile	14/0.2
Hudson	11/0.2
Mercury	11/0.2
Packard	10/0.2
Kaiser	10/0.2
Crosley	8/0.1
Nash	7/0.1
DeSoto	6/0.1
Chrysler	6/0.1
Frazer	4/*
Lincoln	3/*
Cadillac	3/*
Others	38/0.6
Two or more trade-in vehicles	8/0.1

*less than 0.1 per cent

The Knorr CJ-3A Jeep as it is today.
(Courtesy Joe Caprio)

Body style	Number of Jeeps purchased/%
Pickup truck (including Jeep)	2743/47.0
No trade-in	2505/43.0
Four-door Sedan	169/2.9
Station Wagon	115/2.0
Two-door Sedan	109/1.8
Coupé	55/0.9
Convertible	41/0.7
Panel-Sedan delivery	22/0.4
Special bodies	20/0.4
Stake	14/0.2
Not stated	38/0.7

Completely equipped Universal Jeep:	$1588.88
Power take-off front and rear:	$130.50
Pulley and pulley drive:	$59.56
Governor-belt driven:	$29.63
Six-foot snow plow with power pack unit:	$325.00
Wood cutter (buzz saw):	$85.00*
Heater:	$31.85
Two-bottom, 12in general purpose mouldboard plow:	$174.00*
Two-26in disc plow:	$210.00*
Single bottom 16in mouldboard plow:	$145.00*
Bush and bog harrow:	$199.55*
Tandem disc harrow 5ft, 5in blade:	$165.00*
8.5in springtooth harrow:	$183.75*
6ft field and pasture cultivator:	$137.50*
6ft farm mower:	$235.00*
Terracing blade:	$330.00*
Hydro-grader and terracer:	$330.00*
60 CFM compressor:	$862.95*
105 CFM compressor:	$1795.00*
123.5 KVA generator:	$1153.64*
300amp DC arc welder:	$813.04*

*FOB factory

CJ-3A. The Knorrs lived in New York City, where Ruth Gray Knorr had enjoyed a distinguished show business career. Mr Knorr had successfully transitioned from theater to television and his production of the top-rated Milton Berle show placed him at the forefront of his profession.

Interested in purchasing a Jeep for use on her parents' Pennsylvania farm, Mrs Knorr initially requested, by phone, pricing information from Willys-Overland Distributors, Inc, which had its sales room at 1920 Broadway. In response, tCJ-3A prices shown in the table (right) – as well as many additional items (indicating that the Knorr's were familiar with the Jeep's reputation for versatility) – were supplied to the Knorrs.

Several Jeep historians, including Joe Caprio, this Jeep's present owner, believe the Knorrs were concerned about the consequences of the Korean war or a possible nuclear war, and wanted the Jeep to fit into a self-sufficient life on the farm. Acquiring the Jeep for this purpose would have been an expensive proposition since the cost of the equipment they specified for the CJ- 3A totaled $7395.97, more than 4.5 times the CJ-3A's base price.

The Knorrs did not purchase their Jeep from the New York distributor, but instead decided to do business with Wiley Bros and Lewis, a Packard-Willys dealer in West Chester, Pennsylvania, which was closest to the Gray family farm outside State Farm, Pennsylvania. The transaction began with a phone conversation between Mrs Knorr and M L Lewis, followed by a letter from Mr Lewis to Mrs Knorr, dated January 25, 1951, in which he reviewed the details of Mrs Knorr's order and discussed the possibility of securing a Jeep in Gray, the color preferred by Mrs Knorr. Mr and Mrrs Knorr ordered their Jeep after Mr Lewis demonstrated considerable knowledge about his product and a willingness to meet his clients' expectations. Regarding the color of the CJ-3A, Mr Lewis explained,

"We have been able to obtain two Jeeps which, except for color, are just what you ordered. The seats are gray. We can get no definite assurance that the gray color will be available in the near future. The next group expected to arrive may be gray or green. We are trying to get the gray for you but at this time we are holding the red so you can be sure of having a Jeep."

To assist Mrs Knorr in making her decision Mr Lewis then provided her with the following questionnaire:
If we can't obtain the gray soon, will you take red?
Yes ( ) No ( )
If green comes through instead of gray, would you prefer that to red?
Yes ( ) No ( )
Do you want us to have the red painted gray for you for $40.00 additional (our cost)?
Yes ( ) No ( )
Do you want me to wait a week or so to see if another

comes in, or go ahead and have the equipment installed on the red?
Yes ( ) No ( )

Mr Lewis assured Mrs Knorr that "Your interests down here are in good hands." After Mrs Knorr decided to accept one of the gray Jeeps with red seats, Mr Lewis continued to make extraordinary efforts to ensure it was equipped in the manner she preferred.

Eventually, On February 3, 1951, he submitted an invoice to Mrs Knorr for $2317.69 for a CJ-3A equipped with front and rear tops, rear seat, a ¾-ton Dump Trailer, Schenecker Snow Plow and a Newton 6ft power mower.

Mrs Knorr also wanted her Jeep fitted with a hood lock. "There is no patented hood lock for Jeeps on the market as far as I can find out," Mr Lewis explained, "however, I got a cost price of $8.00 from a local body and fender man for a paddock and strap arrangement. This should do the job quite well."

Over nearly five decades this Jeep was seldom used, and when it was sold at an estate auction in 1999, following the death of Mrs Knorr (Mr Knorr died in 1960), its odometer registered just 1650 miles ...

Production of the CJ-3A overlapped both that of its predecessor, the CJ-2A, and its successor, the CJ-3B. It also continued after the acquisition of Willys-Overland by Kaiser in 1953 and the creation of Kaiser-Willys. A variety of sources have compiled differing production totals for the CJ-3A. Most Jeep enthusiasts regard the production figures recorded by Norton Young, who worked at the Toledo plant, as the most accurate. Jeep historian Charlie Weaver worked with Norton Young's handwritten records and transformed them into electronic form, making them available to Jeep hobbyists worldwide.

Year	Production
1949	27,749
1950	26,034
1951	44,158
1952	29,652 (plus 13 stripped chassis models)
1953	10,617
Total	**138,210**

The Knorr Jeep was equipped with a Monroe hydraulic lift. Its tailgate has never been used. (Courtesy Joe Caprio)

5

"A REAL GO ANYWHERE, DO ANYTHING PERFORMER" – THE CJ-3B

On January 28, 1953, Willys-Overland introduced the CJ-3B. Just a month later, on February 28, 1953, public disclosure was made concerning negotiations between Willys and Kaiser-Frazer involving a possible merger. W-O Chairman Ward Canaday's office released a statement in which he disclosed that "various individuals and groups, including Kaiser-Frazer, have approached us in the past few years for discussion of merger possibilities. At this time there is no proposal before us and no action has been taken." But after several more weeks of negotiation, and the creation of the Kaiser Manufacturing Corporation as a subsidiary of Kaiser-Frazer to serve as the purchasing agent, an announcement was made on March 24, 1953 that Kaiser-Frazer was acquiring Willys-Overland for $62,300,000.

The President of Kaiser-Frazer, Edgar F Kaiser, reported that the combined companies, with assets of over $200,000,000 and a consolidated net capital

Willys' sales literature for the CJ-3B linked it to both the World War II models and the previous CJ Jeeps. (Author's collection)

in excess of $60,000,000, would be the world's fourth largest automobile manufacturer, exceeded in size only by General Motors, Ford, and Chrysler. At the time this also ranked as the largest merger in automotive history.

After Willys-Overland stockholders accepted the plan at a special stockholder's meeting on April 24 with 2,110,823 of the 2,795,713 outstanding shares voted in favor of the sale, Willys-Overland became Willys Motors, Inc. Nearly ten years later, in March 1963, this name was changed to Kaiser Jeep Corporation. This action was taken, explained a corporate spokesperson to "more closely identify the company as one of the growing Kaiser family of industries and to associate the corporate name with the famous 'Jeep' trademark."

When it announced the CJ-3B, Willys-Overland wanted to allay any fears that it was not worthy of the Jeep's military and civilian heritage. "In little more than a decade", it noted, "the fame of the 'Jeep' has reached round the world. With the reputation of the military 'Jeep' firmly established, the civilian Universal 'Jeep' added fantastic totals of mileage under the most rugged conditions of service in all corners of the globe. Today the Universal 'Jeep' is known far and wide as one of the world's most useful vehicles.

"Now the Universal 'Jeep' is powered with the famous Willys Hurricane F-head engine. This 4-cylinder power plant, already proven through millions of miles of service, gives the 'Jeep' 20 percent more horsepower. With the Hurricane engine, there is a marked increase in operating economy with outstanding performance."

Identification of the F-head engine followed the industry's traditional fashion of typing engines by the pattern the fuel mixture made as it traveled from the intake valve to the exhaust valve. The Hurricane engine combined intake valves located in the cylinder head above

Willys used this illustration of a CJ-3B to demonstrate its ability to get its operators where they were needed and, when the day's work was done, back home again. (Author's collection)

"In all sorts of weather ... on roads, trails or open country," Willys promised CJ-3B owners, "your Universal Jeep will prove itself time and again ... taking you through rough spots you'd call impassable without the power and traction of 4-wheel drive and the Hurricane F-head engine." (Author's collection)

the cylinder with exhaust valves positioned in the block at the side of the cylinder below the intake valves. Thus, the fuel mixture entered the cylinder chamber at the top, traveled down the length of the chamber and then back up and out through the exhaust valve, forming a pattern which resembled the letter "F".

The F-head design was not new. From 1919 until 1923 the Essex was powered by an F-head engine. The Hudson Super Six engines of 1928 and 1929 were F-head designs, and the winner of the 1908 Vanderbilt Cup Race, the legendary 'Old 16' Locomobile, had an F-head engine. In England, both Rolls-Royce and Rover equipped their cars with F-head engines.

Willys-Overland's primary reason for adopting the F-head arrangement was not to invite comparison between its Jeeps and "The Best Car In The World." Rather, it was a matter of market driven motives tempered by financial reality. Competition in the postwar market made a higher compression, more powerful engine for Willys imperative. In this context, Willys noted that "from the customer's point of view, power and economy are the most important factors considered in an automobile engine. Other features are of lesser importance."

With the L-head Hurricane engine still in production, Willys took care not to suggest the F-head relegated it to the scrap heap. "The Hurricane," said Willys, "stands as one of the most highly developed and perfected four-cylinder engines in the automobile industry ... Since its wartime introduction its performance has been steadily improved, vibration cut down, and horsepower increased."

Nonetheless, with Roos telling a *Popular Science* reporter (November 1950) that "When we started on this engine, we had no idea how good it was going to be," the F-head was a major advancement for the CJ. Always pragmatic in approaching a challenge, Roos' updating of the L-head involved minimal change and expense. Like the other small American manufacturers, the retooling costs associated with an all-new engine would have placed a severe strain on Willys' economic resources.

The new cylinder head used a revised camshaft with two sets of lobes. Engine bore and stroke were the same as the L-head's. Since the F-head design positioned the exhaust valves further away from the intake valves, it was possible to use larger exhaust valves. Their diameter was increased from 1.53in to 2.0in, resulting in a faster, more efficient ejection of burned gases. Relative to engine bore, these exhaust valves were the largest found on any US passenger car engine.

Incorporated into the F-head's design were valve rotators on the valve stems. With each stroke the valve turned slightly, resulting in uniform heating and longer valve life. This feature also removed any foreign matter lodged on the valve seat. The valve springs were wound more tightly at the top and bottom than in the center, thereby reducing vibrations which caused erratic valve action. The sparkplug was centrally located in the upper face of the combustion chamber for uniform combustion. Since the intake and exhaust valves were in opposite surfaces, the combustion chamber was small and compact, contributing to a 6.9:1 compression ratio. An optional high altitude head had a 7.4:1 compression ratio. Willys recommended its use "when the engine is used at elevations above 5000 feet and a good grade of gasoline is available."

Casting the intake manifold into the cylinder head resulted in a very short intake passage with few flow-hindering corners. In contrast to the industry's common practice of using exhaust heat to vaporize the gasoline in the intake manifold, the F-head's intake manifold was fully jacketed with thermostatically controlled water, thus preheating the fuel mixture for more efficient combustion and increased power. As a result, there was no requirement for the exhaust heat manifold control valve used on the L-head engine.

Dealers were reminded of this aspect of the F-head's design in an April 30, 1956 service bulletin concerning problems with a flat sport on acceleration and low speed "stumble" that owners of Jeeps with the F-head engine were experiencing. "It must be ... taken into consideration," explained General Service Manager, W V Kershow, "that the Willys 'F' head engine employs a water heated intake manifold. Proper vaporization of the atomized fuel is

Edgar F Kaiser was President of Kaiser-Frazer when the CJ-3B was introduced. (Courtesy Kaiser Aluminum)

dependent upon correct intake manifold temperature."

Although the L-head and F-head engines – with the exception of cylinder heads – shared most of their

WILLYS
One Of The Growing
Kaiser Industries

Any respectable Jeep dealer, in this case in business after Willys-Overland was acquired by Kaiser-Frazer, was happy to have prospective customers take home a complimentary pen as a reminder that the dealer was ready to take their order for a new 4x4.
(Courtesy Marshall Rimland collection)

Two badges of the security plant when the by Willys-Overland. became Willys Motors, Inc. A decade later, its name was changed to Kaiser Jeep Corporation.
(Courtesy Marshall Rimland collection)

worn by members force at the Toledo facility was owned In 1953 Willys-Overland

components, the use of overhead intake valves resulted in different valve specifications (see table).

Maximum horsepower of the Jeep engine was increased to 72 at 4000rpm. Peak torque output was 114lb/ft at 2000rpm. With the optional 7.4:1 compression ratio, horsepower moved up to 75@4000rpm. Torque remained at 114 lb/ft @ 2000rpm.

Although exceptions abound, engines with the standard compression ratio were to have blue cylinder heads and the high compression engines were to be identified by black cylinder heads.

Full throttle tests of the F-head engine revealed that, unlike many engines which experienced a power loss in excess of five per cent after one hundred hours of operation,

Engine	L-head	F-head
Tappet clearance (cold)		
Intake & exhaust (in):	0.016	0.018
Intake valve length (in):	5.797	4.781
Intake head diameter (in):	1.531	2.0
Intake valve lift (in):	0.351	0.260
Intake valve springs:		
Free length (in):	2.5	1.97
Standard pressure @ length:		
Valve closed:	53lb@2.109in	73lb@1.66in
Valve opened:	120lb@1.750in	153lb@1.40in
Service minimum:		
Valve closed:	47lb@2.109in	66lb@1.66in
Valve opened:	110lb@1.75in	140lb@1.40in

This 1953 CJ-3B was completely restored by its owner, Bob Christy. (Courtesy Bob Christy)

the F-head's output remained virtually undiminished.

The practically unanimous enthusiasm that greeted the use of the F-head in the CJ has persisted over the years. Long-time CJ-3B owner Steve Perialas calls it "one of the sweetest engines ever developed."

In that context, he recalls that, prior to owning a CJ-3B, "I had a couple of CJ-2As and the neatest thing about them was their very simple engine. But I don't know how many times anybody who had a CJ-2A probably changed the head gasket – maybe three or four times at least, in a year." The reason for this frequency, he explains, was simple: "because they were designed to go very slow – 45mph at maximum speed – and how many teenagers or anybody are going to run a vehicle at 40 or 45mph if they can boost it up to 50? So, you were always changing head gaskets on those things. You always had a supply of two or three in the garage."

In contrast to the CJ-2A's limited top speed, Steve Perialas notes: "the CJ-3B with overdrive will run at 65mph if you choose to do so. And that's moving with a Jeep. And it runs and it runs and it runs."

Jeep restorer and enthusiast Bob Christy concurs: "It's a great engine. I like it. It's a very tall engine. It's a very heavy engine. But they do seem to run forever."

The F-head engine's height, significantly greater than the L-head's, makes identification of a CJ-3B easy since its hood line was four inches higher than the CJ-3A's. On each side of the hood large 'WILLYS' lettering was positioned. A one-piece windshield was carried over from the CJ-3A but the CJ-3B did not have the high-mounted air ventilator of the CJ-3A. In addition to its new engine, the CJ-3B was equipped with a new, quieter transfer case.

For a time production of the CJ-3A continued, but it was the CJ-3B with its revised appearance and more powerful engine which attracted the most interest. In 1953

This view of the CJ-3B owned by Lawrence Wade illustrates why it is affectionately known as the 'High Hood'. (Courtesy Lawrence Wade)

and 1954 Willys offered a special Farm Jeep version of the CJ-3B, priced at $1439. The base CJ-3B was priced at $1377. Although the Jeep had been well received by farmers, the Farm Jeep generated limited interest and Jeep historians believe that only 77 were produced.

Tom McCahill, who seemed to have a soft spot for the Jeep, liked the CJ-3B he tested for *Mechanix Illustrated* so much that he ended up buying one for himself! McCahill reported that the CJ-3B was "undoubtedly one of the greatest vehicles ever conceived by man." Willys was content to settle for describing the CJ-3B as "one of the world's most useful vehicles."

As did other automotive manufacturers, Willys periodically issued Service Bulletins outlining and revising procedures for dealing with customer issues. Dealers were encouraged by Willys to pay close attention to customer concerns: "The majority of customer complaints received at the factory can be handled

The CJ-3B was true to the old Shaker belief that form-follows-function. (Courtesy Lawrence Wade)

CJ-3B sales literature invariably showed it being driven in a purposeful, responsible manner. (Author's collection)

to a satisfactory conclusion by Zones, Distributors and Dealers. Complaints handled at the Zone-Distributor-Dealer level tend to build goodwill for the retailer as well as build the customer's confidence in his vehicle."

If a customer wrote to the factory regarding a particular problem, the letter was acknowledged and a 'Request for Service' form issued to record and handle the complaint. After the Zones, Distributors and Dealers received these forms they were expected to promptly contact the customer by phone or mail and do whatever necessary to bring the complaint to a satisfactory conclusion as soon as possible.

In reaction to customer concerns, Willys made numerous changes in the CJ-3B's design. Responding to complaints that when a CJ-3B was required to stop on a steep grade, carburetor flooding resulted, Willys released a "steep grade carburetor field kit," Willys Motors Part Number WM 94481, on February 12, 1954, which appreciably increased the degree of slope at which satisfactory idle operation could be obtained.

On June 18, 1954, Willys made available a heavy-duty clutch assembly for Jeeps operating under extreme conditions. While Willys maintained that "the clutch assembly provided as original equipment is entirely

satisfactory for normal use," dealers were advised that "if clutch overhaul becomes necessary in a vehicle known to be frequently subjected to extreme operating conditions, it may be advisable to install heavy-duty clutch components." The heavy-duty clutch assembly (not including the driven disc) was assigned Willys Motors Part Number 906467. The part numbers for the heavy-duty driven discs were WM 906514 or 905589.

On May 3, 1955, both the CJ-3B and its successor, the CJ-5, were included in a Service Bulletin applicable to all 1955 Willys passenger cars and utility vehicles, which advised dealers about the possibility of a fire hazard involving the stop light switch. Dealers were informed that "it is of the utmost importance that all 1955 model Willys vehicles be brought in immediately" for the purpose of checking and replacing the stop light switch.

Willys shipped the fabric tops for the CJ-3B, as well as those for other CJ models, in a special heavy kraft bag that it claimed could "withstand considerable abuse and moisture." Nonetheless, problems arose with the top arriving at the dealership in satisfactory condition, as well as its proper treatment by owners. On January 22, 1957 dealers were advised that "If the package becomes water soaked in transit, or if condensation forms inside due to rapid and extreme temperature changes, the moisture can lead to damage from deterioration and mildew." In order to avoid this situation, Willys stressed that "It is imperative

Well, almost always ... (Author's collection)

that fabric tops be removed from their protective covering immediately after they are received and then stored in a dry, clean, airy place. If the material is wet, or appears to be damp, the top should be installed on the vehicle immediately. If there is any sign of mildew, we recommend washing with a mild soap and a quick, thorough rinsing. Owners should be advised of the proper way to care for the top so that it is not removed and stored when wet or dirty."

With a 72hp rating, the CJ-3B's F-head engine developed 0.537 horsepower per cubic inch of displacement, an excellent output for the time. By 1962, the originally optional 7.4:1 compression ratio was standard, increasing horsepower to 75. The 6.9:1 compression remained available. (Author's collection)

Early production CJ-3B models were equipped with the instrument panel-mounted oil pressure and ammeter gauges used on the CJ-2A and CJ-3A. These was eliminated on later model CJ-3B Jeeps which, along with the subsequent CJ-5, CJ-6 and DJ-3A (two-wheel drive) models, had a single large instrument cluster containing the speedometer, fuel and temperature gauges, indicator lights for the battery charge and oil pressure, and a red telltale lamp controlled by the

Mitsubishi built this version of the CJ-3B under license from Willys. (Author's collection)

in those days." He also explains that, today, "the Jeep has almost vanished from our roads and only a few are left. I think I see a car like a Ferrari more often than a Jeep."

When he learned of a Jeep being auctioned by the forest service, he says: "I saw my chance to become the owner of a Jeep so I took the opportunity and bought it." Readily conceding that emotion had overruled cold logic, he admits, "it was the first car I couldn't drive before restoration so I didn't know what came over me."

The CJ-3B that Erik van de Peppel acquired was originally imported by the Dutch government in 1954 for use by Rotterdam police. "The Jeep was put in service," Erik notes, "at the 'Mastunnel' in Rotterdam to push disabled cars off the road." The CJ-3B performed this task for many years until the widespread use of plastic body elements on modern cars made this type of removal impractical. After several more years of service in the Dutch Forest Association, the CJ was, in Erik's words, "in very bad shape, covered with rust and missing several parts ... The rust had taken the floor away."

ignition switch which lit when there was inadequate oil pressure.

CJ-3B historians currently place the number of CJ-3Bs built in the 1953-1968 time span at just over 155,000.

For many Jeep enthusiasts, the unique features and heritage of the CJ-3B Jeep are reason enough for them to undertake its restoration and preservation. Erik van de Peppel, who has restored a CJ-3B, explains that in his native Holland, as elsewhere in Europe, the Jeep's accomplishments in WWII earned it a legendary reputation for reliability. The Jeeps that were left after the end of WWII were purchased by the Dutch government, he explains, and were used for many different tasks, mainly related to rebuilding the nation. Most of the civilian models (including the CJ-3B) were purchased by the government since, as Erik notes, "most people living in Holland couldn't afford a car

It's not possible to determine all of the colors available for the CJ-3B in any one year. This brochure suggests that Orange was available in 1959. (Author's collection)

From this perspective, the lines of Erik van de Peppel's CJ-3B seem even more compact than its 81in wheelbase and 129.75in length would indicate.
(Courtesy Erik van de Peppel)

These 'before and after' photos of Erik van de Peppel's CJ-3B show how lowering its windshield dramatically altered its appearance.
(Courtesy Erik van de Peppel)

"The Jeep is a car that everyone admires," says Erik van de Peppel of his CJ-3B. (Courtesy Erik van de Peppel)

As this bucolic scene of the CJ-3B in The Netherlands suggests, the Jeep's functional design makes it 'at home' around the world. (Courtesy Erik van de Peppel)

The classic Jeep design provided the CJ-3B with plenty of space in the front fender for wheel travel, the installation of chains, if needed, and easy access to front suspension components for maintenance and repair. (Courtesy Erik van de Peppel)

Recalling these factors, he adds, "the Jeep is quite a simple vehicle and if you can find one in good condition, I say go for it. If the Jeep is in poor condition as the one I bought, it's another story because Jeep parts are hard to find and you have to purchase inch-sized tools. You will find that the restoration of such a Jeep can be quite expensive. It also takes a lot of time and it is almost impossible to do the restoration alone." None of this deterred Erik, however, who enlisted the help of his brother-in-law; "if one of us didn't know how to proceed, the other one usually had a suggestion that helped us continue." In addition, by contacting experienced Jeep restorers and utilizing the internet, he was able to overcome both the expected and unexpected challenges not uncommon to the restoration process.

Having decided to totally disassemble the Jeep, Erik began the process with the seats, followed by the electrical system, and finally the 3B's body.

"After removing the body, Erik notes, "we could see that the chassis was in poor condition also. We then removed both axles, the engine, transmission, brakes, suspension, and exhaust system in order to have the badly rusted chassis cleaned."

The refurbished chassis, finished in a rust-protecting paint, became the starting point of the Jeep's restoration. The axles were reinstalled, along with the completely overhauled gearbox and engine. The body's poor condition necessitated replacement of many parts in order to ensure that original structural integrity was retained. This was the most difficult part of the 3B's restoration since Eric admits "we didn't have any knowledge about bodywork at all." But after "some disappointments," the necessary welding was completed and the body was primed with a gray, zinc-based, rust-preventing paint.

"After reinstalling the wiring, the reupholstered seat, a new cylinder head, tail lights, instruments, and the license plate (we were able to get the original license number), it was time," says Eric, "for the first test drive. Following a few adjustments the Jeep was running smoothly." After the final coat of exterior paint was applied the Jeep was ready for Holland's annual vehicle inspection, which is conducted at special garages and must be completed before a vehicle is allowed to operate on the public roads. As Eric notes: "The Jeep passed the test the first time, so I think we did a very good job!

"The Jeep is a car that everyone admires, and when I'm driving mine, people always try to get a look at it. Almost always when I stop, someone comes over and wants to have a chat with me about the Jeep. People recognize the Jeep from the war and want to know everything about it. In fact my CJ-3B is so popular that it has been used for exhibitions and as part of product displays in stores."

The restoration experiences of American Jeep enthusiast Bob Christy, with his CJ-3B, are similar to those of Eric van de Peppel. Although he drove his CJ-3B for nearly six months before beginning its restoration, Bob had purchased it with restoration in mind.

His description of its original condition is graphic and succinct: "Everything on it was rusty and nasty-looking. It was real bad. The tailgate was really bad as the bottom was all rusted out. Since I didn't want to buy a reproduction tailgate that did not say 'WILLYS' on it, I found another one with a top that was in poor condition, but with a good bottom. So, I welded them together. Since I now had a spare 'WILLYS' logo, I sent it to someone who needed it for their Jeep restoration project."

Bob Christy agrees with Eric van de Peppel's perception that the CJ's basic simplicity is one of its most appealing attributes as a restoration project. "It's pretty straightforward," he says, "especially when you have the bare frame sitting there; you can work on everything."

Like Erik, Bob reminds would-be Jeep restorers that the early CJ's primary function as a work vehicle can make the restoration process quite eventful. "For the most part, Jeeps were outdoor vehicles, and over time they took a lot of abuse." One consequence of this was breakage of vulnerable exterior components such as the side steps mounted just below the passenger and driver seats, and the Jeep's original rearview mirrors. "They sat outdoors constantly," he continues. "Most of them didn't have tops, or what we would consider decent tops." When this treatment occurred in areas of the US where road salt was used extensively in the winter, deterioration of the frame, as well as key body and suspension components, due to rust can be a serious problem. "You need to be aware," he cautions, "that people did not take care of them." If a Jeep was used for plowing, he suggests that the buyer should make sure the front axles have not twisted as a result.

Explaining that the tendency of channels, located under the floor's surface, to retain water and mud makes the floor especially susceptible to rust, he adds, "on my CJ most of the floor was gone. I'm surprised it actually held together during the six months I drove it before I restored it."

Like Erik van de Peppel's CJ-3B, the frame of Bob Christy's CJ-3B was severely rusted. Since he "doesn't want this Jeep to rust out for the next fifty years," the frame was liberally coated with rustproofer.

Bob's first job in the restoration of his Jeep's body (tub) was an attempt to combine its salvageable parts with a CJ-3B body that had been stored for a number of years. "It wasn't in the greatest shape," he recalls, "but I thought I would be able to make something out of the two of them. So I spent about a month tearing the donor body apart, learning how it was built in the process, and doing all the spot welding and getting it down to the bare essentials. Then I pulled mine in the garage and started taking it apart. I soon realized that I needed a new body. Mine was so far beyond repair and the cost of replacement panels was prohibitive."

Using the internet Christy contacted a Californian entrepreneur who, as he explains, "looks everywhere he can for 3Bs, any Jeep thing. He had posted a message on a Jeep bulletin board that he had found a CJ-3B body that was going to be crushed by the California State Police." After a number of e-mails the two parties agreed on a price and, even after shipping expenses from California to Ohio were added, Christy says the total cost was far less than that of a new reproduction body.

Christy has reservations about using reproduction CJ bodies: "I don't think they look the same. There are so many grades of them that you have to spend quite a bit to get a good one and if you look at them there are subtle differences. For example, on the original body there is a transmission cover that is removable. To make it simpler to produce, some reproduction companies have made that opening smaller so its appearance is not correct." In some cases, he explains that the manufacturer has made the 3B cowl a two-piece affair, rather than a single unit as found on original 3B bodies. Christy does add that the body he acquired wasn't perfect." I had to do quite a bit of welding to close holes that previous owners had drilled and cut, but in every case, I used metal from the same areas from my old body, so I can say its sheet metal is all Willys."

Of course some CJ-3Bs, having lived a charmed life almost totally devoid of hard, daily use, require only minimal restoration to return them to prime condition. One such example is 'Cherry Red' (its factory color is Luzerne Red), a 1958 CJ-3B owned by Steve Perialas of Big Rapids, Michigan. One of the first vehicles that Steve owned was a Luzerne Red 1958 CJ-3B. Originally it had belonged to a young lady Steve was dating, the daughter of a Kaiser-Jeep dealer. As he recalls: "I must have fallen in love with her 3B [his first 'Cherry Red'] instead of her; who knows? Our love affair didn't last beyond eight months. However, my love affair with 3Bs has lasted beyond forty years and is still going strong."

No surprise, then, that when he saw an illustrated ad in the May 1998 Hemmings Motor News for a Luzerne Red 1958 CJ-3B with 35,000 miles registering on its odometer, the old 3B flame was rekindled. Acquiring this CJ-3B wasn't a case of simply agreeing on a price with the owner and then taking possession, since its owner insisted on selling the 3B only to a Jeep enthusiast who would also agree to purchase his 1946 and 1947 CJ-2A Jeeps! Steve Perialas hadn't waited nearly 40 years to allow the acquisition of two pristine CJ-2A Jeeps stand in his way of once again owning a CJ-3B, and with the encouragement and support of his wife, became the owner of a trio of classic Jeeps.

These views of Steve Perialas' 1958 CJ-3B epitomize the honest, down-to-earth form that makes it a timeless classic. Seen here at a cabin located north of Barryton, Michigan (built by a father and son team of Amish craftsmen, the CJ-3B was the ideal vehicle for a weekend of exploring old trails in the woods. And, come Monday morning, the Jeep was ready and able to get its owner back on the job. (Courtesy Steve Perialas/Carol Lynne Photography)

Except for the roll bar and perhaps the 'Cherry Red' heart-throb lettering on the CJ-3B's hood, this could be a scene from the lazy, hazy days of summer 1958. The Old Pioneer Store and Emporium has been been pleasing customers in downtown Grand Rapids, Michigan since the 1930s. (Courtesy Steve Perialas/Carol Lynne Photography)

"Anybody need their boat towed out of Chippewa Lake for the season?" Bob Perialas, son of the CJ-3B's owner, Steve Perialas, at the 3B's helm. (Courtesy Steve Perialas/ Carol Lynne Photography)

... and it runs as good as it looks! (Courtesy Steve Perialas/Carol Lynne Photography)

And how many of those burgers have been served to drivers of CJ-3B Jeeps? (Courtesy of Steve Perialas and Carol Lynne Photography)

As he explains, the owner "made me a deal I could not refuse ... now all I had to do was to convince my wife, the true love of my life, that I HAD to buy all three to get the one I wanted."

Steve relates the history of his second 'Cherry Red,' in this fashion: "It was bought in Michigan by the owner of a large apple orchard. It was only used during the apple picking time to drive around the orchards. In the mid-1970s it was sold to a family member whose daughter was going to high school and wanted a Jeep." Although well intended, this was destined to be a mismatch, since as he explains, "the daughter's desire for a Jeep was for a CJ-5 not an old 3B." As a result the Jeep sat unused in a garage until the mid-1980s when it was acquired by an avid Jeep collector in Grand Rapids, Michigan. "He had it completely – I wouldn't say restored – but refurbished, because everything was original. It had no rust. It just needed a new paint job and replacement of those items such as hoses, tires, etc,that dry up during extended periods of storage."

Shortly thereafter, the CJ-3B was used by the Danbury Mint as a reference for the development of its DJ-3B

Far left: A thing of [functional] beauty is a joy [to drive] forever. (Courtesy Steve Perialas/Carol Lynne Photography)

Left: Tom McCahill called it "Undoubtedly one of the greatest vehicles ever conceived by man." Steve Perialas, a more humble man, is content to say "My love affair with 3Bs has lasted beyond forty-five years and is still going strong." (Courtesy Steve Perialas/Carol Lynne Photography)

Below: "Take it easy, Dad! I believed you when you said Cherry Red can do 65 without even breaking into a sweat!" (Courtesy Steve Perialas/Carol Lynne Photography)

mail truck die-cast model. Of course, the DJ-3B was a two-wheel drive model with righthand steering but, says Perialas, "They photographed all the engineering features of Cherry Red. They measured and did this and did that, everything you could possibly think of, and then created their die-cast model from that. So that's kind of a neat part of Cherry Red's history."

For Steve Perialas, this is nothing compared to owning a Jeep that takes him back to his first CJ-3B: as he says, "that's all that really counts in my perspective."

The appeal of the CJ-3B – as with all CJ Jeeps – is timeless, and extends from generation to generation of Jeep enthusiasts. (Courtesy Steve Perialas/Carol Lynne Photography)

Who needs a drive-in when you own a CJ-3B and it's the right moment? (Courtesy Steve Perialas/Carol Lynne Photography)

Below & opposite, top: Appearances can be deceptive: this barn, built 35 years ago, is a good deal younger than the CJ-3B. Its owner, wanting it to appear "old," never covered it with paint or stain. (Courtesy Steve Perialas/ Carol Lynne Photography

How many roads such as this have beckoned to CJ-3B owners over the past half century? (Courtesy Steve Perialas/Carol Lynne Photography)

Steve and Kyu Hui Parialas and their two grandsons. Steve explains that the two boys are the "future generation of Cherry Red lovers. When I pass, Cherry Red will go to their dad, Bob, and then to them." (Courtesy Steve Perialas/Carol Lynne Photography)

6

"A COMPLETELY NEW UNIVERSAL JEEP" & "THE BIGGEST JEEP UNIVERSAL" – THE CJ-5 & CJ-6 JEEPS: 1955-1970

The announcement of a new Jeep model was not an annual event, so introduction of the CJ-5 on October 11, 1954 generated a great deal of public attention. Prospective customers were advised to "Take a good look at the new Jeep. Although it seemed impossible to build a more rugged Jeep ... Willys has done it and the new Jeep proves it with increased stamina reflected in every detail. Scores of new features ... tested and found worthy in exacting military [the MD-M381A was its forerunner] and civilian use ... all yours in the magnificent new Universal 'Jeep'."

Although the CJ-3B retained a loyal following, Willys made it clear that the CJ-5 represented a new era in Jeep, explaining to its dealers that "This is a wider 'Jeep,' longer' Jeep,' and roomier 'Jeep.' It's a better looking vehicle all round. It can carry more passengers, providing softer, more comfortable seats in front and rear. Easier riding front and rear suspension provides greater stability on the roads, more comfort and even longer life for the vehicle." Skeptics, fearful that these superlatives masked a betrayal of Jeep heritage, were assured by Willys that "like its predecessors, it will carry personnel, move machinery, dig trenches, shunt railroad cars, mow grass, work as a wrecker, fight fires, snake logs, pull mine cars, transport materials, load airplanes, drill wells, and power pneumatic tools."

A comparison with the CJ-3B highlights the areas in which the CJ-5 differed significantly from its predecessor (see table).

The CJ-5's cargo bed measured 36in x 39in with the

Dimensions	CJ-5	CJ-3B
Wheelbase;	81in	80in
Length:	131.625in	129.0in
Width:	59.875in	57.09in
Height:	67.125in	67.875in
Cargo bed length:	38in	39.75in
Turning diameter (curb-to-curb):	40ft, 10.5in	39ft, 3in
Tread (front and rear):	48.43in	48.25in
Shipping weight*:	2164lb	2134lb
GVW:	3750lb	3500lb
Standard tires:	6.00 x16in	6.40 x 16in

*Over the years, various shipping weights were listed for both models. For example, in 1959 Willys Motors cited 2132lb for the CJ-3B and 2163lb for CJ-5 respectively.

The CJ-5 was derived from the military M38A1 Jeep which Willys began producing in 1952. (Author's collection)

Additional specifications of the CJ-5 were as follows:			
Curb weight:	2274lb		
Maximum payload:	1476lb		
Road clearance: front/rear:	8.875in/8.0in		
Tread: front/rear:	48.437in		
Tire size:	6.00 x 16 4-ply		
Type:	All service non-directional tread		
Optional:	7.00 x15 4 ply, all service non-directional tread		
Wheels:	Five-stud, 16 x 4.5in		
Optional:	Five-stud, 15 x 4.5in		
Cargo area (tailgate down):	14sq ft		
Chassis specification:			
Clutch:	Single plate dry disc		
Lining material:	Moulded woven asbestos		
Lining area:	72sq in		
Torque capacity:	165lb/ft		
Transmission:	3-speed synchromesh		
	Speeds		
Ratios:		*High range*	*Low range*
First: 2.798:1		12.9mph	4.6mph
Second: 1.55:1		20.2mph	8.2mph
Third: 1.00:1		31.2mph	11.2mph
Reverse: 3.798:1		8.2mph	3.4mph

Transfer case:	2-speed with neutral for PTO work
Ratios:	
High range:	1.00:1 (for use in 2WD or 4WD)
Low range:	2.46:1 (for use in 4WD only)
Rear axle:	Semi-floating, hypoid gears
Capacity:	2500lb
Ratio:	5.38:1
Front axle:	Full-floating, hypoid gears
Capacity:	2000lb
Ratio:	5.38:1
Front and rear springs:	Semi-elliptic
Shock absorbers:	Double-acting, airplane-type
Brakes:	Bendix hydraulic with expanding shoes
Drum dimensions:	9.0 x 1.75in
Drum material:	Alloy cast iron
Lining area:	117.8sq in
Steering:	Cam and twin pin lever
Ratio:	Variable: 14-12-14
Turning radius:	20.5ft
Electrical system:	Six-volt,15-plate, 100-amp/hr capacity battery with 45 amp generator
Fuel tank:	10.5gal (39.75 liters)
Serial number location:	Under hood on right side of dash panel

This side-by-side comparison of the new CJ-5 with the CJ-3B (which remained in production), illustrates the physical differences between the two models. (Author's collection)

CJ-3B

CJ-5

This CJ-5 was equipped with an optional hardtop. It was also fitted with a rear draw bar. Willys explained that "the versatility and utility of the Universal 'Jeep' CJ-5 is greatly expanded by the development of this metal enclosure ... The addition of the metal enclosure and plastic roof provides full protection from the weather, and permits use of the vehicle every day of the year." (Courtesy DaimlerChrysler Media Services)

The rear door panel of the full cab was self-supporting in the open position, making for ease of loading and unloading the Jeep. (Author's collection)

Another perspective of the CJ-5 with the full metal cab. This one is set up for snow plowing. No alteration of the 'Jeep' body was required to install the cab. All the windows were of non-shattering safety glass. (Author's collection)

The two-door types available with the metal enclosure. Both had sliding door panel windows and locking doors. The hinged door version was offered as an aftermarket and factory-installed option. The sliding door model was available as a factory installation only. (Author's collection)

This 1955 CJ-5 is owned by Jack Leiser of Dover, Ohio. (Courtesy Bob Christy)

tailgate closed and 36in x 49in when open. Overall, the CJ-5 had two square feet more floor load area than the CJ-3B.

Identifying a CJ-5 was easy. Willys described its appearance as "Streamlined ... [a] modern design [that] brings better appearance to the NEW 'Jeep.'" Aside from 'Jeep' lettering just ahead of the door cutout, the CJ-5 had a newly-designed hood, body and fenders, which were flanged and overlapped for added strength. Both front fenders and hood had rounded surfaces, and the body section behind the driver had a deep Vee dip. Willys noted that this "new design not only creates a pleasing appearance, but offers tremendous resistance to damage."

A stationary windshield was standard. A divided,

opening windshield was optional for domestic models and standard for the CJ-5 export version. Both types had more glass area than did the CJ-3B's. The area of the stationary unit was increased by 92sq in for a total glass area of just over 682sq in. The ventilating windshield's area measured over 607sq in. A new, built-in defrosting chamber was provided.

It's likely that Willys' claim that the driver could see the road 5.5ft "nearer the bumper than in the previous model," was welcomed by some CJ-3B owners. Dean Thiem, a modern day CJ-3B owner/enthusiast, notes that "What everybody says about poor off-road visibility is true. When off-roading in hilly country, going over a crest of a hill is an adventure. You can't see down the hill until you are most of the way down."

The CJ-5's windshield wipers relocated to the top of the windshield, as on the CJ-2A. Other changes included a new back lit instrument cluster and a passenger-car type hand brake with improved grip. It was moved from the dash center to the driver's left side, just below the dash panel, and controlled an internal expanding drum on the

Model	CJ-3B	CJ-5
Front springs		
Length:	36.25in	39.625in
Width:	1.75in	1.75in
Spring rate:	260lb/in	240lb/in
Load capacity:	650lb	550lb
Number of leaves:	10	7
Front shock absorbers		
Compressed length:	10.75in	11.4375in
Extended length:	17.5in	18.4375in
Piston diameter:	1.0in	1.0in
Rear springs		
Length:	42in	46in
Width:	1.75in	1.75in
Spring rate:	190lb/in	200lb/in
Load capacity:	800lb	940lb
Number of leaves:	9	9
Rear shock absorbers:		
Compresssed length:	10.75in	11.9375in
Extended length:	17.5in	19.4375in
Piston diameter:	1.0in	1.0in

Willys wasn't reticent about transforming worst case scenarios into examples of the Jeep's go-in-and-get-out-of-anything reputation. "Who says," challenged Willys, "that a 'Jeep' can't pull itself up by its own bootstraps? Here is a Universal 'Jeep' getting out of a tough spot with the help of a winch operated by the front power take-off." (Author's collection)

Examples of these two signs were often displayed by Jeep dealers. By the mid-fifties, Jeep vehicles were being sold worldwide by over 200 distributors and more than 4000 dealers in 116 countries. Willys was also operating manufacturing and assembly plants in 16 foreign countries. (Author's collection)

propeller shaft which locked all four wheels when the CJ-5 was in 4-wheel drive.

At the rear, the CJ-5, like the CJ-3B, had 'Willys' lettering on its tailgate. A '4 Wheel Drive' identification was added to the right side panel.

Willys noted that "new, softer front bucket seats are form fitting with coil springing for a surprisingly comfortable ride. The new covering is attractive, long wearing, and waterproof." The driver's seat adjusted to three positions fore and aft. A double and single front seating arrangement for the driver and two passengers was available at extra cost. With optional rear wheelhouse seat pads seating for four passengers, it was possible to carry a total of seven passengers in a CJ-5. A two-passenger rear seat was also offered. Additional options introduced in 1954 included a 'Passenger Safety Rail' which, said Willys, "provides additional comfort and security," and a cover for the new glove compartment.

Although appearing similar to the CJ-3B's, the CJ-5's full top was of a new design with sidewalls that fastened on the interior and were flush with the perimeter of the Jeep body. A new feature of the top assembly was the provision of stowage straps for the doors above the front seats. There were also fewer bolts to be secured to install the doors. A redesigned, positive latching door handle was easier to operate.

Willys reported that the CJ-5 pressed steel channel frame – with its three intermediate channel cross members and rear channel 'K' cross member – had a new, fully boxed tubular front cross member, "added to further increase the rigidity, carrying strength, and rugged endurance of the Universal 'Jeep' frame." The frame, at 128.4375in in length, was 5.678in longer than that of previous CJ models.

Willys claimed that the use of springs which combined a low deflection rate with a high capacity provided the CJ-5 with "smoother riding, excellent stability, and longer life." As the accompanying table shows, CJ-5 springs and shock absorbers differed from those of the CJ-3B.

Provided as extra equipment for the CJ-5 were 12-leaf front and rear springs with load capacities of 550lb and 1850lb respectively. The dimensions of the rear springs were unchanged; those of the front had a slightly shorter length of 39 inches.

Willys cited six virtues of the CJ-5 which represented its principal sales features: Versatility, Power, Economy, Maneuverability, Ruggedness, and Safety. In regard to its versatility, Willys noted that the CJ-5 "was a passenger car, a truck, farm tractor and a mobile power unit. It can carry seven people with ease over the roughest kind of country in any weather. As a truck the CJ-5 Universal 'Jeep' can carry a payload of 1476 pounds. Extra carrying space – 14sq ft – is available by merely dropping the tailgate to a horizontal position. As a tractor the CJ-5 Universal 'Jeep' has a drubber pull of over 2317 pounds. When equipped with the optional Hydraulic Lift it can draw practically all of the conventional types of farm equipment. As a mobile source of power it can energize generators, welders, winches, and many other powered auxiliary equipment." The CJ-5's combination of 75hp F-head engine, low

By September 1954, when the CJ-5 was introduced, Willys was advertising the F-head Hurricane engine as developing 75hp@4000rpm with a 6.9:1 compression ratio. (Author's collection)

5-HORSEPOWER "HURRICANE"

. . . for greatest economy with normal loads and average service conditions.

4-cylinder, "F-head" type . . . Standard equipment on the Universal 'Jeep' CJ-5 and CJ-3B – optional on all other vehicles in the basic 'Jeep' family.

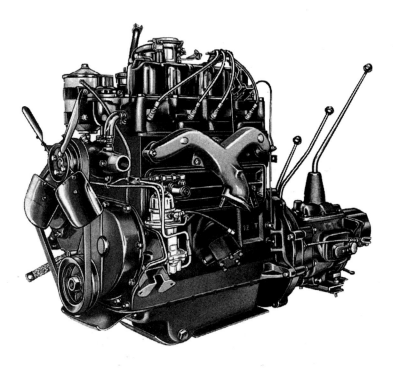

weight, and four-wheel drive (which gave a choice of 12 gear combinations) was capable of transporting payloads up a 60 per cent incline.

Willys promised customers that the CJ-5's blend of "low purchase price, low operating cost and low maintenance cost, together with its multi-purpose and long vehicle life" was more than sufficient to "assure rapid pay-off and economical operation."

If anyone still doubted that the new Jeep wasn't true to its tradition, Willys assured them that the CJ-5's "four-wheel drive means that it will go through any terrain. The four-wheel drive means less slippage in tight spots. The CJ-5 Universal 'Jeep' can turn through passages as narrow as 6 feet and turn in a radius of 1½ times its own length. On the highway the CJ-5 Universal 'Jeep' can travel in two-wheel drive at speeds of up to 70 miles per hour."

In a similar fashion, Willys explained that "the all-steel construction, the extra heavy springs, the airplane-type shock absorbers, and weather resistant upholstery mean that this is a vehicle that can really take punishment." Moreover, Willys asserted that the CJ-5's "low center of gravity prevents side or rear end upsets. The extra large brake linings on all four wheels mean that the CJ-5 Universal 'Jeep' can stop quickly and positively."

Standard CJ-5 equipment is listed in the accompanying table:
Spare wheel
Hood catch (export only)
Front bumper
Single horn
Standard tool kit
Windshield wipers (vacuum operated on driver's side; hand operated on passenger's side)
Rear view mirror (outside mount)
Driver's seat (Deluxe bucket type)
Ventilating windshield (export only)
Single tail, license, and stop light (export only)

The Jeep fire engine, like the World War II Jeeps, carried an axe to the action scene. (Author's collection)

'Jeep' CRASH WAGON

Smothers Fire!
No Water Needed!

FOR AIRPORTS, OIL REFINERIES, OIL FIELDS AND INDUSTRIAL PLANTS OF ALL KINDS

This versatile 4-wheel-drive vehicle is equipped for fighting all types of fires in difficult, hard-to-reach locations where a ready water supply is not always available. Entirely self-sufficient, the 'Jeep' Crash Wagon requires no water supply. It fights fire with chemicals which smother flames quickly.

The 'Jeep' Crash Wagon carries enough equipment to produce over 850 cubic feet of foam and 90 pounds of CO_2 (carbon dioxide gas) — two of the most effective fire-smothering agents known. CO_2 is recommended for electrical fires and foam for oil and gasoline fires. The equipment can be operated by inexperienced personnel and highly-trained fire-fighting crews are unnecessary.

Because of its great maneuverability and selective 2- and 4-wheel drive, the Crash Wagon can travel at fast speeds to reach places where ordinary fire-fighting equipment cannot go. Powered by the highly-efficient *Hurricane* Engine, the 'Jeep' Crash Wagon provides low-cost fire protection.

STANDARD EQUIPMENT
40-Gallon Foam-Type Extinguisher equipped with 50 ft. of 1¼-in. hose and playpipe. 2½-Gallon Foam Hand Extinguisher equipped with 2-ft. of hose and nozzle. 75-Pound CO_2 Extinguisher equipped with 25 ft. of ½-in. hose and nozzle. 15-Pound CO_2 Extinguisher, Hand Type, equipped with 2 ft. of hose and nozzle. Flasher Siren ● Front Passenger Seat ● Radiator Brush Guard ● Draw Bar ● Starting Crank ● Heavy Duty Springs, Rear.

OPTIONAL EQUIPMENT
(At Extra Cost)
Crash Axe ● 4-ft. Crow Bar ● Spot Light ● Recharge for 40-Gallon Foam Extinguisher ● Recharge for 2½-Gallon Foam Extinguisher ● Extra Relief Valve for 2½-Gallon Foam Extinguisher.

Willys claimed the Crash Wagon CJ-5's maneuverability – along with its two and four-wheel drive versatility – enabled it to travel at fast speeds to fires which were inaccessible to ordinary fire-fighting equipment. (Author's collection)

Air cleaner (export only)
Oil filter (export only)
Glove box, door and lock (domestic only)
Access steps (domestic only)

Factory installed, extra cost options for the CJ-5 were:
Radiator guard
Hot water heater and defroster
Belt driven governor
Driver's seat (2/3)
Front passenger seat (1/3)
Front deluxe bucket type passenger seat
Rear passenger seat (wheel housing pads)
Front body top
Complete body top
Belt pulley and pulley drive
Front bumper weight
Tires:
     6.00 x 16 6-ply
     7.00 x 15 4-ply
     7.00 x 15 6-ply

The CJ-5 fire engine was equipped to tow this 200 gallon water tank trailer. (Author's collection)

Dual tail, license, stop lights and directional signals
Air cleaner – oil bath type
Draw bar
Oil filter

Offered as optional equipment at no extra cost was a high pressure radiator cap (hot climate radiator), and the high altitude cylinder head kit

The following items were listed as extra cost accessories:
Dual horns
Gasoline filter
Under hood light
Fog lights
Spare tire lock
Rear reflector
Directional signal lights

This CJ-5 was equipped with an hydraulic lift, allowing a multitude of implements to be easily attached and controlled by the Jeep's driver. The handle controlling the implement was located at the rear of the driver's seat. (Author's collection)

As with previous CJ models, Willys offered the CJ-5 with a large assortment of equipment and specialized components attractive to a wide variety of niche – but highly profitable – markets. One example, intended for airports, oil fields and refineries, and other industrial plants, was the CJ-5 Crash Wagon. Willys described this CJ-5 as "equipped for fighting all types of fires in difficult, hard-to-reach locations where a ready water supply was not always available. To accomplish this task, the Crash Wagon was equipped to fight fires with chemicals, not water.

Crash Wagon equipment included:
– 40gal foam-type extinguisher with 50ft of 1.25in hose
– 2.5gal foam hand extinguisher with 2ft hose and nozzle
– 75lb CO_2 extinguisher with 25ft of 0.5in hose
– 15lb CO_2 hand-type extinguisher with 2ft hose and nozzle

The Crash Wagon was also furnished with a flasher siren, front driver and passenger seats, radiator brush guard, draw bar, starting crank and heavy-duty rear springs.

Optional equipment included a crash axe, 4ft crow bar, spotlight, recharge for 40 gallon foam extinguisher, and an extra relief valve for the 2.5 gallon foam extinguisher. Total fire-fighting capacity consisted of over 850cu ft of foam and 90lb of carbon dioxide. Willys assured buyers that this equipment "can be operated by inexperienced personnel so highly-trained fire-fighting crews are unnecessary."

The CJ-5 could also be equipped as a water pumper,

Passenger seat safety rail
Hydraulic pump and lift
Quick disconnect couplings for hydraulic lift
Starting crank
Pintle hook
Glove box door (export only)
Access steps (right and left, export only)
Ventilating windshield (domestic only)
Hood catch (domestic only)

The following items were mandatory options for the domestic market only:

Both front and rear-mounted winches were available for the CJ-5. This CJ-5 had a Model 151J winch operating off the center PTO. It had three speeds forward and one reverse through the Jeep's regular transmission controls. (Author's collection)

A wide variety of all-steel cabs were offered for the CJ-5. This full cab had safety glass side windows that slid forward for full opening. As seen here, the rear cab panel raised up and was supported by two struts. (Author's collection)

A CJ-5 with a steel half cab. The back panel was removable. (Author's collection)

The Stockland Scoop was available for the hydraulic lift-equipped CJ-5. With a six cubic foot capacity, it was used for a variety of tasks including ditch digging, terracing, leveling and pond building. (Author's collection)

Extended bodies had been a popular Jeep item since the days of the CJ-2A. Most, such as this example for the CJ-5, attached to the body by bolts; cutting or drilling of holes was not required. (Author's collection)

making it suitable for both industrial parks and small rural towns where forested terrains required fire protection. The basic unit carried a centrifugal pumper capable of pumping 500 gallons of water per minute, at a pressure of 120lb, from a source such as a lake. If a free-flowing hydrant was available, this increased to between 550 and 600 gallons a minute. A 200 gallon tank trailer was also offered which provided an immediate water source when the Jeep reached the fire.

When the CJ-5 was introduced, no direct rivals for the British Army, has not yet penetrated the civilian market. However, because it may do so later on, the comparative figures must be given consideration."

Willys acknowledged the Land Rover's sales potential within the British Commonwealth: "For the present, the Land Rover offers some competition in the sterling areas. But the tables still show where the Universal 'Jeep' is the best buy."

Also seen as worthy of consideration as a CJ-5 competitor was the Fiat Campagnola which debuted in

Vehicle	CJ-5	Land Rover	Austin Champ	Fiat
Feature				
GVW	3750lb	3702lb	4840lb	3646lb
Payload	1476lb	1000lb	750lb	1037lb
Wheelbase	81in	86in	84in	94.5in
Clearance	8.125in	7.875in	10in	NA
Length	131.6in	140.75in	140.3in	144in
Width	59.875in	62.562in	61.5in	60.9in
Height	67.13in	76in	71in	71in
Tread	48.44in	50in	48in	49.4in
Specification				
Engine	4 cyl	4 cyl	4 cyl	4 cyl
Type	F-head	F-head	OHV	L-head
Displ (cid) 134.2	121.9	162.2	116.0	
Comp ratio	6.9:1	6.7:1	7.5:1	6.7:1
Horsepower	7 @4000@rpm	52@4000@rpm	78@3750@rpm	53@3700@rpm
Maximum torque	114@2000@ rpm	101@1500@ rpm	140@2000@ rpm	NA
Electrical system	6-volt	12-volt	24-volts	12-volts
Fuel tank (US gal)	10.5	10	20	NA
Maximum draw bar				
Pull	2317lb	1200-2000lb	NA	3300lb
Body	steel	aluminum	steel	steel
Suspension	semi-ellipt	semi-ellipt	torsion bar	semi-ellipt
Axle ratio	5.38:1	4.70:1	NA	4.4:1
Turning radius	20.04ft	18.5ft	35ft	NA

existed in the United States. In spite of this lack of opposition, Willys recognized that the CJ-5 still faced competition from at least two potential adversaries: the British Austin Champ and Land Rover. "The European copies of the Universal 'Jeep'", Willys claimed, "tend to be of the handmade type, and are therefore more expensive. And they do not incorporate, in spite of this high cost, the long life and maintenance-free features of the Universal 'Jeep.'"

Willys noted that: "The Austin Champ, as developed

1951. Jeep dealers were encouraged to learn about these products since "a knowledge of the specifications of competitive vehicles, and comparison with those of the Universal 'Jeep' is highly important in selling."

An example of the material Jeep provided for this purpose illustrates the CJ-5's position relative to these 4WD utility models (see table).

After assuring dealers that "In actual demonstration comparisons the Universal 'Jeep' always proves better than any competitive vehicles," Willys encouraged them to "go through the table and pay particular attention to those points that prove the superiority of the Universal 'Jeep'."

To help dealers become comfortable with this sales technique, Willys offered a few "obvious" examples:
– "The Universal 'Jeep's' maximum brake horsepower is 50 per cent greater than that of the Land Rover."
– "The Universal 'Jeep' weighs 510 pounds less than the Land Rover – the lightest of its competitors. This represents economy all-round: in shipping, importing, and licensing. The light weight, combined with the powerful Hurricane engine, means more power, more payload."
– "The all-steel body of the Universal 'Jeep' has advantages over the aluminum body of the Land Rover because aluminum is difficult to weld in the field, and suffers from metal fatigue very quickly.
– "The Universal 'Jeep' is lower and wider than any of the other vehicles. The result is the low center of gravity that holds the Universal 'Jeep' to the road."
– "The Universal 'Jeep' has greater road clearance than the Land Rover."
– "Generally speaking, the availability of the Universal 'Jeep', its parts, and service facilities, are far superior to those of other lines. Also, the Universal 'Jeep's' price position is generally better."

Dimension	CJ-5	CJ-6
Wheelbase:	81in	101in
Overall length:	135.56in	155.56in
Overall height:	67in	67in
Overall width:	71.75in	71.75in
Front tread:	48.44in	48.44in
Rear tread:	48.44in	48.44in
Front overhang:	22.56in	22.56in
Rear overhang:	32in	32in
Front axle clearance:	8.62in	8.62in
Rear axle clearance:	8in	8in
Bumper to ground:	18.25in	18.25in
Approach angle:	45deg	45deg
Departure angle:	30deg	30deg
Ramp break over angle:	30deg	30deg
Cargo bed length:	39.75in	59.75in
Standard tires:	6.00x16in	6.00x16in
Front axle capacity:	2000lb	2000lb
Rear axle capacity:	2500lb	2500lb
Curb weight:	2274lb	2336lb
Shipping weight:	2163lb	2225lb
Gross vehicle weight:	3750lb	3900lb

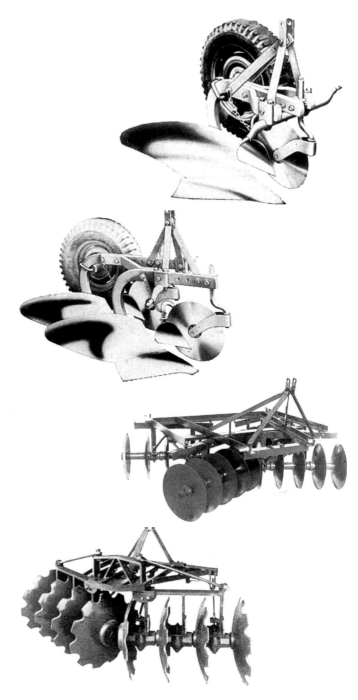

Agricultural equipment for the Universal Jeep was designed with a 3-point linkage for easy attachment to a hydraulic lift. These four examples of general purpose implements available for the CJ-5 are (left to right): single bottom 16in moldboard plow, double bottom 12in moldboard plow, lift-type tandem disc harrow, and a bush and bog harrow. (Author's collection)

In 1959, four years after the CJ-5's debut, a longer wheelbase model, the CJ-6, was introduced. The CJ-6 originated as the military M170 model which had entered production in 1953, and used the same standard equipment springs and shock absorbers as did the CJ-5. It was available in the same six variations, too: Open Body, Convertible Top, Fabric Half Top, Metal Full Cab and Metal Half Cab.

A side-by-side comparison of the CJ-5 and CJ-6 illustrates their similarities and differences (see table on previous page).

After the CJ-6, the next major model development for the Jeep was the introduction of the Tuxedo Park option package in 1961, whose content included two-stage springs, revalved shock absorbers, numerous chrome items – including bumpers, hood hinges, tail lights, and rear view mirrors – fully adjustable padded seats, carpeting, and a column shift.

The following year, Willys identified a CJ-5 with this equipment as the "Tuxedo Park Mark II special CJ-5." On March 5, 1962. a new dress-up option for the Tuxedo Park was introduced. In announcing this item to dealers, Willys

General Part and Service Manager C T Scher explained: "Salt and pepper, Mutt and Jeff, ham and eggs – each go together in traditional fashion. So, too, the new Tuxedo Park Mark II special CJ-5 is complemented by our Parade Blue Convertible Top and Accessory Kit! One is NOT COMPLETE without the other!"

Option components (officially identified as the PB-5 Parade Blue Convertible Top and Accessory Kit), which were also offered for other CJ-5 models, were, said Willys, "specially designed for the Mark II vehicle." They consisted of a convertible top, cover boot, and spare tire cover in the new Parade Blue color. The mildew-inhibiting fabrics were treated with a 'Scotchgard' process which was claimed to provide "long life, color fastness and stain resistance."

Scher worked hard to pump up dealer enthusiasm for this item, many of whom were probably still comfortable with selling the CJ primarily as a utilitarian vehicle. His words, imploring dealers to see beyond those confines, were, in retrospect, visionary. "Once you see the Tuxedo Park Mark II fully 'fitted out' as a unit, sporting the matching Convertible Top and Accessory Kit," he told dealers, "you'll quickly agree that it's a truly marketable package. We're

The CJ-6 cargo area was 50 per cent larger than that of the CJ-5. (Author's collection)

in agriculture   in industry   in government servic

These six views of the CJ-6 illustrate its versatility in a variety of conditions. (Author's collection)

The 1960 Christmas greeting from the "Jeep Folks at the Factory" to the Company's dealers. (Author's collection)

'Jeep' SERVICE AND PARTS

NEWS

DECEMBER 1960

PUBLISHED BY: SERVICE DEPARTMENT, TECHNICAL PUBLICATION SECTION, WILLYS SALES CORPORATION, TOLEDO, OHIO

PLEASE NOTE: GEN'L MGR. ☐ PARTS MGR. ☐ SERVICE MGR. ☐ SHOP FOREMAN ☐   VOL. 9   NO. 11

It gives us great pleasure to extend the Season's Greetings to you, our many friends. We appreciate the cooperation and enthusiasm of all; your success in the past year adds to our joy at this season. Your continuing effort gives hope and promise for a prosperous year to come.

May your Holiday Season be Merry. May the Christmas Spirit abide with you throughout the coming year

From Your 'Jeep' Folks at the Factory

sure you will also agree that the only POSITIVE method of developing a successful sales campaign is by actual DISPLAY and DEMONSTRATION of the Tuxedo Park Mark II with the Parade Blue convertible top, cover boot and spare tire." This kit retailed for $180.19; dealer price was $130.20.

Model	Factory advertised delivered price
CJ-5:	$2211
CJ-5A:	$2306
CJ-6:	$2306
CJ-6A:	$2401

After again being offered as a CJ option in 1963, the Tuxedo Park became a separate CJ model in 1964, identified as the Tuxedo Park Mark IV in either CJ-5A (81in wheelbase), or CJ-6A (101in wheelbase) form. The Tuxedo Park serial number prefix was 8322 (CJ-5A) and 82422 (CJ-6A). Prices, relative to the base prices of the CJ-5 and C J-6 models, were as per the table.

The Tuxedo Park's most obvious features included optional full convertible top, boot and spare tire cover package, exterior and interior bright trim work, a steering column-mounted gear shift lever, and foam-padded

in
public utilities

in
construction

in
personal use

seats upholstered in pleated British calf grain vinyl. After describing the Mark IV as "the newest fashion in 4-wheel drive fun," and asserting that its biggest claim to fame was its "jaunty style", Kaiser Jeep wasn't bashful about calling attention to its numerous chrome-plated exterior components and bright exterior color selection: "no other 4-wheel drive runabout," it claimed, "offers such sporty colors or uses chrome so abundantly."

This CJ-5, with wrecker and plow equipment, is busy clearing snow from a shopping center in the mid-fifties. (Author's collection)

At first glance, it appeared that the Tuxedo Park Mk IV was essentially a CJ-5/6, with chromed and colorful add-ons intended to broaden the Jeep's appeal. But material contained in a 15-page document: *Parts Peculiar To Tuxedo Park Mark IV 'Jeep' Models CJ-5A and CJ-6A*, Kaiser Jeep released in May 1964, indicates otherwise. A sample of its content, which details hundreds of items, illustrates the extent to which the Tuxedo Park differed from other CJ models:

– Chrome fuel cap
– 35amp alternator[1]
– Remote control steering-mounted shift lever ball lever[2]
– Transfer case assembly[3]
– Transfer case shifting decal
– Spicer Model 27AF front axle assembly[4]
– Front and rear brake assembly[5]
– Front and rear spring assembly[6]
– Chrome hood catch, U-bolt, and bracket
– Chrome hood assembly
– Chrome hood-to-windshield catch
– Chrome cowl hood hinges
– Chrome hood hinges
– Chrome windshield bumpers
– Windshield assembly
– Chrome rear bumper arm
– Chrome front and rear bumper bar
– Front license tag bracket
– Chrome footman loop
– Chrome interior and exterior rear view mirrors
– Chrome hand rail assist
– Front floor mats

[1]*The CJ-5 and CJ-6 used a 35amp generator. As options, 40amp and 60amp alternators were available for the Tuxedo Park*
[2]*This gave the Tuxedo Park a relatively uncluttered floor. The Warner Gear T-90, 3-speed transmission had ratios of 3.339, 1.551, and 1.00:1. Reverse ratio was 3.796:1*
[3]*Kaiser Jeep said that the floor-mounted control lever for the Spicer 18 transfer case (with ratios of 2.46 and 1.00:1)*

COMPLETELY
NEW

ALL NEW *STREAMLINED*
MODEL CJ-5 WILLYS 4-WHEEL-DRIVE 'JEEP'

Opposite: Willys used this illustration of the CJ-5 to proclaim it as "... All new Streamlined ..." Not quite the embodiment of a dictionary definition of streamlined, but it's likely that this was of no concern to CJ enthusiasts.

As with earlier CJ models, the CJ-5 was popular with many rural route mail carriers. (Author's collection)

This CJ-5 is busy handling the luggage for passengers of a Boeing Stratocruiser, Pan American Airways Clipper Southern Cross. This plane also flew as Clipper Reindeer and Clipper America. Its first flight was March 11, 1949. It was delivered to Pan American on March 30, 1949. By September 1959 it had flown 31,520.35 hours. It was eventually acquired by the Israeli Air Force and withdrawn from service in September 1972. (Author's collection)

provided "new ease of shifting into and out of four-wheel drive"

[4] *4.27 or 5.38:1 ratios were offered. A Powr-Lok unit was optional*

[5] *The Tuxedo Park was equipped with a new braking system with double-action servo brakes with 10in drums and 174sq in of effective lining area. The CJ-5 continued with 9in drums with an effective lining area of 102.65sq in*

[6] *The Tuxedo Park used two-stage front springs with six leaves and five-leaf rear springs*

Kaiser Jeep reported that the Tuxedo Park was available in a choice of adjustable bucket or ⅔rd width driver's seats as well as front passenger seats in either bucket style or ⅓rd width standard height. The British calf grain vinyl cover was offered in Sylvan Green, Nordic Blue, Black or President Red.

Since Willys often accommodated individual customer tastes, It's likely that some models left the factory with special order color schemes. In most cases, however,

the basis for the Tuxedo Park's color selection had these parameters: all interior surfaces were painted to match the exterior color. The seat and convertible top colors either matched or harmonized with the exterior color, depending on color selection. The top boot and spare tire cover (constructed of the same material as the convertible top) matched the color of the top.

Four body colors were offered: President Red, Sierra Blue, Parkway Green, and White Cap. Sources disagree over the number of colors offered for the Tuxedo Park Top. A Tuxedo Park sales brochure lists six colors: Black, White Cap, Nordic Blue, Park Blue, President Red, and Sylvan Green. However, a press release mailed to journalists on October 7, 1964 listed only White, Sylvan Green, Nordic Blue, and President Red. The spare tire cover and top boots matched the convertible top colors.

The Tuxedo Park's standard equipment included dual vacuum windshield wipers, seat belts, directional signals, 7.35x15 black wall tires with highway service tread (other sizes and types, including white sidewalls were optional), and adjustable driver's seat.

In addition to features already noted, optional equipment for the Tuxedo Park included a chrome outside passenger mirror, 9.25in clutch, floor mats, fresh air heater and defroster, high altitude cylinder head, locking gas cap, and wheelhouse cushion pads. Far rarer than the Tuxedo Park Jeeps were the CJ-5 models powered by the Perkins diesel engine.

Bruce Phillips, then a pilot for American Airlines,

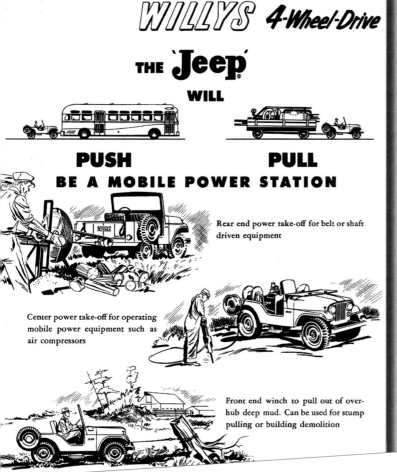

WILLYS *4-Wheel-Drive*

THE 'Jeep' WILL

PUSH   PULL

BE A MOBILE POWER STATION

Rear end power take-off for belt or shaft driven equipment

Center power take-off for operating mobile power equipment such as air compressors

Front end winch to pull out of over-hub deep mud. Can be used for stump pulling or building demolition

This promotional artwork illustrated the ease with which the CJ-5 handled a wide variety of tasks. (Author's collection)

acquired his diesel CJ-5 in 1965. "Hardly anybody in the country knew anything about there being a diesel Jeep available from the factory at that time," he told the author. "I was in the market for a new Jeep when I was flying around the country and having layovers in different cities. I visited the local Jeep dealerships whenever I could, and in one of them I found a small brochure that had one paragraph in it mentioning a diesel engine being available. So I said right there, 'that's what I want.'"

When Bruce Phillips returned home to Buffalo, New York, he stopped by several nearby Jeep dealers. "I would go into them and say that I was interested in learning about what kind of deal they could give me on a diesel Jeep. They would say 'What are you talking about? There is no such thing as a diesel Jeep.' So I would show them my little folder and they would say, 'Oh we don't know anything about that. We haven't heard anything about that.' They would try to sell me one they had on the lot.

"I eventually found a dealer in North Tonawanda, New York, who said he'd get one for us. He knew about the

FOR EXTRA-RUGGED JOBS...
YOU NEED THE EXTRA-RUGGED CJ-6!

Bruce Phillips' 1965 diesel-powered CJ-5 as seen when new in the Adirondack Mountains of New York State. Bruce purchased his first Jeep, a CJ-2A, in 1948 and has accumulated over fifty years of experience with Jeeps on the Adirondack's highways, and byways, and in its backwoods. (Courtesy Bruce Phillips)

Kaiser Jeep suggested that "for extra-rugged jobs ... you need the extra-rugged CJ-6!" Exactly what type of 'extra-rugged' job is being done here is not clear ... (Author's collection)

As this illustration from a 1963 CJ-6 sales brochure shows, the CJ-6 had the capacity to carry a seven-member work crew without difficulty. (Author's collection)

Jeep® UNIVERSAL
MODEL CJ-6
4-wheel drive
G.V.W. 3900 lbs.

diesel because he had sold a couple of them for use in the salt mines at East Aurora, New York. He'd converted a couple other regular gas Jeeps to Wakashaw diesel engines.

"The engine's retail price was $850, but the salesman was kind of tickled to sell one, so he gave it to me for $650. The total price was $3800.

"He said that the factory didn't send for an engine from Perkins until they got an order for a diesel Jeep, so it would probably take about eight weeks to get it. But in about six weeks he called and said 'It's here.' Apparently there had been an engine in Toledo at the time and they didn't have to order one. The Perkins fit right in there. The engine mounts were a little bit different. But the engine just barely made it into the compartment so that the back end of the engine only had about a half inch between it and the firewall.

"I used it for years and years. It got kind of rusty and I had to repair the body a few times. But we had a great time with it."

Bruce recalls only two problems he experienced with the diesel during the time he drove it some 80,000 miles. One was that it smoked a lot. "People

who followed me complained about their eyes burning. We never could do anything about adjusting that fuel to stop the smoke. It always smoked a little. "At one point it started overheating. I took the cylinder head off and discovered there was a sand hole from the casting located right behind one of the intake valves, that was letting the water run right into the engine. I found a new head for it at a Perkins facility in Boston and I put that on and never had any more trouble with it.

"It gave me twice the gas mileage

Two 1964 Tuxedo Park Mark IV CJ-5s with White Cap bodies and President Red tops and interiors. (Author's collection)

The Tuxedo Park's standard wheel cover is seen here in combination with optional white sidewall tires. (Author's collection)

The Tuxedo Park's standard foam padded seats were covered with pleated British calf grain vinyl. (Author's collection)

and the fuel only cost half as much as gasoline at that point, so I had a big saving. It was fun to take it into a gas station and pull up to the diesel pump and the attendant would say 'the gas pump's over there. You don't put diesel in a Jeep.' I'd say, 'Well, it has been running OK on it.'

"It was a great experience to have that Jeep. They didn't make very many of them and it was fun to have one of the few. I enjoyed it. I wish I still had it today."

After acquiring the diesel CJ-5, Bruce equipped it with one of the most popular aftermarket items offered for CJ-Jeeps, a Warn 'All Range Overdrive' unit which had been introduced in 1961. As he explains, the motivation for this was the CJ-5's limited top speed: "The CJ-5 had the 5.38:1 differential ratio and when I brought it home from the shop the first time I noticed that the best I could do was 50mph with the engine wind right on out". Responding to an ad in *Popular Science*, in which Warn promised that the unit was "easy to install in less than two hours," Bruce ordered the Warn overdrive and proceeded to install it himself. "The last gear on the shaft in the transmission runs a gear over into the transfer case." he explains. "All you do is take the cap off the back end of the transmission, pull that gear off and stick the overdrive in, bolt it on and it's in business"

Hooking up the handle was also not difficult. "You just mount that handle up through the floor, right beside the other four-wheel drive handles;" he says, "it's alongside the main shift lever, so you can use both handles together."

On the road, the Warn overdrive was both functional and easy to use. "It is synchromesh so it doesn't clash when you shift it or anything," says Bruce. "It has a planetary gear setup inside of it with two speeds. It's direct drive and 15 per cent overdrive and when you have to shift gears you can get a half a step in gear change instead of the whole step; in high gear/overdrive, it gives you a good 15 per cent overdrive. I could go 65mph on the thruway after I installed that. It made a lot of difference in fuel mileage and time in traveling, I got around 35mpg on diesel fuel before I installed the unit and the overdrive increased it quite a bit.

"Of course the engine was turning a lot less. It was quieter on the highway; the engine speed was way down when you were cruising. It was a well-designed unit that did a great job. It really made the Jeep perfect for trailer loads and things like that because you could just get a half step shift when you got to a hill and keep right on going without dropping way down into a lower gear. It was a great addition to the Jeep."

With the transfer case and standard 3-speed transmission, the Warn overdrive-equipped CJ-5 had twelve speeds forward and four in reverse. "With that overdrive, remembers Bruce, "I could start out and shift all the way out of town before I got in high gear. You could shift it at anytime; just push in the clutch and shift the overdrive.

"My CJ-5 has the Powr-Lok differentials front and rear. They offered that setup only for a short time because it made the Jeep steer hard, but it would go places that the regular ones wouldn't go."

On August 24, 1965, Kaiser Jeep introduced a new Dauntless V-6 as an option for the CJ-5 and CJ-6. With 155hp, this engine more than doubled the Universal Jeep's power.

Kaiser Jeep wasn't shy about predicting the impact this output would have upon the CJ-5's performance. "The

The Tuxedo Park was equipped with double-action servo brakes with 10in drums. (Author's collection)

Variable rate springs in the Tuxedo Park Mark IV were intended to provide a softer, smoother, more comfortable ride regardless of load. (Author's collection)

power boost provides substantially greater smoothness and efficiency in the four-wheel drive traction which enables 'Jeep' Universals to climb precipitous hills and operate over the most difficult types of terrain, including snow, mud and sand.

"It gives the rugged Universal series a greater power-per-pound of curb weight than competitive vehicles and increases its versatility for recreational and general utility service."

Also adding to the V-6's appeal was its compact size, which allowed it to fit into the CJ's engine compartment with plenty of space left over.

The Dauntless V-6 originated as an aluminum V-8 for the 1961 Buick Special. It was also offered as an option for the Oldsmobile F-85. At that time it was credited with 185hp@4800rpm. High production costs – together with corrosion and reliability problems – led to a V-6 engine that, whilst based on this aluminum V-8, was of cast iron construction. Due to its V-8 origin, the Dauntless was a 90° V-6 with a thin wall block design, and a lighter overall engine weight as compared to several smaller V-8 engines. In addition, it had hydraulic valve lifters, aluminum alloy pistons, stamped rocker arms, wedge-shaped combustion chambers, four main bearings, and steel-backed aluminum connecting rod bearings.

See accompanying table (right) for additional specifications of the Dauntless V-6.

Displacement:	225cu in
Bore x stroke:	3.75 x 3.40in
Compression ratio:	9.0:1
Maximum horsepower:	160hp@4200rpm
Maximum torque:	235lb/ft of torque @ 2400rpm
Recommended fuel:	Regular
Cooling system:	9qt; 10qt with heater
Carburetor:	Dual barrel downdraft; 1.4375in barrel sizes
Intake valves:	1.375in head diameter; 0.401in lift
Exhaust valves:	1.625in head diameter; 0.401in lift

Motor Trend, reporting on the test of a V-6 model in its May 1966 issue, reminded readers that "stuffing the V-6 into a Jeep was an invigorator known to the off-road fraternity long before the factory in Toledo got around to officially engineering its installation." The magazine also mentioned that the exhaust pipe on early V-6 models had been routed to run below the transfer case skid plate, leaving it exposed to damage when the Jeep was taken

The model's steering column-mounted shift lever linked it with the MA models of 1941 and early CJ-2A Jeeps. Kaiser-Willys said it provided "finger-tip control and more floor space for legs." (Author's collection)

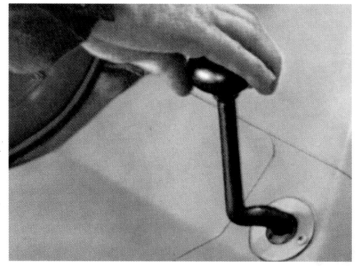

This floor-mounted lever shifted the Tuxedo Park Mark IV in and out of 4-wheel drive. (Author's collection)

off-road. This was soon corrected on new examples and a retro-kit made available to owners of the original models.

Both 4-cylinder and V-6 Jeeps were available with an optional heavy-duty, four-speed transmission. The specifications of these transmissions are shown in the accompanying table.

Engine:	Hurricane	Dauntless
Transmission:	Warner T98A	Warner T18
Input torque capacity (ft/lb):	240	340
Gear ratios:		
First	6.398	4.020
Second	3.092	3.092
Third	1.686	1.686
Fourth	1.0:1	1.0:1
Reverse	7.820	7.439

To accommodate the weight differences between the V-6 and Hurricane engines, the specification of the standard front and rear springs installed on the CJ Jeep depended on which engine was used (see table, right).

In 1966, the Tuxedo Park – like the CJ-5 and CJ-6 – was offered with the 160hp Dauntless V-6. This engine option was accompanied by a change in the Tuxedo Park's suspension, which now had variable rate leaf springs at the rear and conventional leaf springs up front. Together with the appeal of an engine with more than double the power of the previous Tuxedo Park, the latest model was also available with a new and wider selection of body, convertible tops and seat colors. The latest body

Front springs	CJ/Hurricane 4	CJ/Dauntless V-6
Number of leaves:	5	10
Spring rate (lb/in):	188	176
Length x width (in):	39.63 x 1.75	39.63 x 1.75
Total thickness (in):	1.242	1.940
Capacity at pad (lb):	875	865
Capacity at ground (lb):	1035	1025
Rear springs		
Number of leaves:	5	10
Spring rate (lb/in):	155-230	155-230
Length x width (in):	46.00 x 1.75	46.00 x 1.75
Total thickness (in):	1.593	1.593
Capacity at pad (lb):	1240	1240
Capacity at ground (lb):	1370	1405

colors included Indian Ceramic, Empire Blue, Beechwood, Glacier White, and President Red. Three seat colors were offered: Charcoal (available with all body colors), Marlin Blue (available with Empire Blue and Glacier White), and

1966 CJ Jeep major option prices

Option	Price
Front passenger seat:	$51.00
Rear seat:	$78.25
Heater:	$84.00
AM radio:	$61.00
White sidewall tires:	$12.70
Full soft top:	$165.00
Steel cab:	$475.00
External mount fuel cans (each):	$6.50
External mount carrying racks (each):	$3.00
Power winch:	$360.00
Rear limited-slip differential:	$45.15
Warn lock-out front hubs:	$67.50
Cutlass lock-out front hubs:	$55.00
Heavy-duty clutch:	$7.71

This 1965 Tuxedo Park Mark IV is equipped with the ²/₃rd driver, ¹/₃rd passenger seat combination. (Author's collection)

A fully-occupied 1966 Tuxedo Park Mark IV powered by the new 155hp Dauntless V-6 engine. (Author's collection)

**Black Top
White Cap Body**

**White Cap Top
White Cap Body**

**White
Sierra**

**Black Top
President Red Body**

**White Cap Top
President Red Body**

**Presid
Preside**

Prospective Tuxedo Park Mark IV owners were told that "half the fun of buying a Tuxedo Park is picking your own color combination." These ten exterior colors choices were available. The spare tire cover and top boots matched the colors of the convertible top. (Author's collection)

A view of a 1966 Tuxedo Park Mark IV equipped with the optional front bucket seats and 2/3rd-1/3rd rear bench seat. (Author's collection)

**Nordic Blue Top
Sierra Blue Body**

**Parade Blue Top
Sierra Blue Body**

**White Cap Top
Parkway Green Body**

**Sylvan Green Top
Parkway Green Body**

Top
Body

d Top
Body

President Red (available with President Red and Glacier White). The convertible tops and seats were offered in Marlin Blue, Charcoal, Glacier White and President Red, offering a range of 21 different color combinations. The Tuxedo Park was offered with new bucket seats also, and, like the other CJ-5 models, had a new, high impact safety windshield.

Tuxedo Park models with the V-6 engine had the same general specification as their CJ-5 and CJ-6 siblings. 1967 was the final year of Tuxedo Park manufacture. During its production life a total of 7394 Mark IV models had been built.

With Kaiser Jeep introducing its new Jeepster and Commando models in 1967, availability of the V-6 engine remained the CJ's major appeal in 1967/68. By mid-1968 over 75 per cent of Jeeps (including the Jeepster and Commando models) were being ordered with the V-6.

The V-6's popularity led to negotiations between General Motors and Kaiser Jeep resulting in Kaiser Jeep's acquisition of the unit's manufacturing equipment from Buick, which was installed in a new, 100,000 sq ft building in Toledo. By mid-1968 this facility was operational, producing engines at the rate of 30 a day. Buick had planned to drop this engine after the 1967 model year, and was happy to sell its tooling to Kaiser after production of its 1967 models ended. Kaiser's investment, both in the new plant and the equipment, exceeded six million

dollars, just a fraction of the costs Kaiser would have incurred in designing and producing an entirely new engine. Moreover, the purchase allowed Kaiser Jeep to begin production at least two years sooner than if it had decided to manufacture an entirely new engine.

The 1968 advertised delivered prices (ADP) of the CJ models and their options were as per the following table.

Model/vehicle code number	ADP[1] Open body	ADP Half top
CJ-5/8305	$2630.37	$2682.94
CJ-6 8405	$2723.96	$2778.46
DJ-5[2] 8505	$2110.65	$2152.83

[1]Advertised delivered price effective as of May 15, 1968
[2]The DJ-6 was not listed in the revised price list of May 15, 1968

Option	Code no	ADP
Dauntless V-6 engine:	312	$210.95
Seats:		
Front passenger seat (⅓rd type):	20N	$65.34

Option	Code no	ADP
Front passenger seat (bucket):	20Y	$68.81
Rear seat:	54	$67.08
Driver seat (⅔rd type):	131	$24.21
Tires:		
8.45 x 15 (4-ply) suburbanite:	805	$48.51
Rear locking differentials, 4-cylinder models:		
4.27:1 ratio:	4.27 L/A	$46.75
5.38:1 ratio:	5.38 L/A	$46.75
Rear locking differentials, 4-cylinder models:		
3.73:1 ratio:	3.73 L/A	$46.75
4.88:1 ratio:	4.88 L/A	$46.75
High altitude cylinder head (4-cylinder only):	24	No charge
Heavy-duty springs and shocks (CJ-5):	60	$29.26
Heavy-duty springs and shocks (CJ-6):	60	$24.63
4-speed transmission (4-cyl only):	174	$174.76

Dealer installed accessory equipment		
Item	Part number	Price
Cigar lighter:	916589	$3.14
Locking gas cap:	931662	$2.40
Chaff screen kit:	818688	$11.25
Magnetic drain Plug (4-cyl only):	915863	$1.60
Draw bar:	947378	$33.75
Helper air spring kit (front):	924457	$39.90
Helper air spring kit (rear):	924458	$39.90
Pintle hook:	923091	$42.99
Passenger safety rail:	961594	$5.67
Passenger safety railkit:	94509	$2.10
Left outside rearview mirror (tripod type):	970671	$8.00
Spare wheel lock:	934292	$3.40
Wheelhouse cushion pads	689819	$10.50
Windshield washer:	9428793	$7.50

The chrome windshield latches, steering column-mounted gear shift lever, and foam-padded seats of the Tuxedo Park were upholstered in pleated British calf grain vinyl. (Courtesy Joe Caprio)

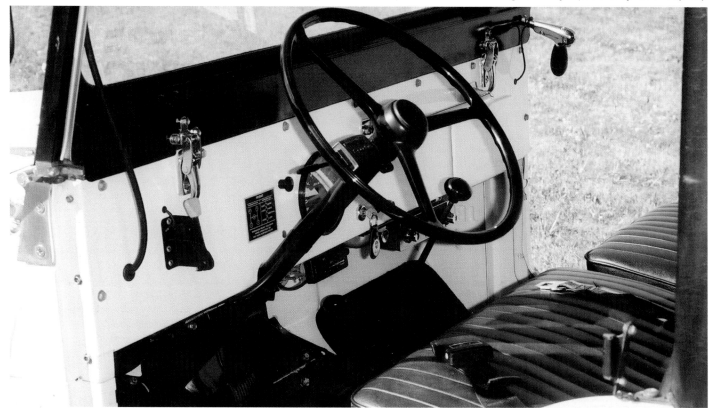

*Joe Caprio's Tuxedo Park combined
a White Cap body with a Black top.
(Courtesy Joe Caprio)*

Kaiser Jeep depicted the V-6 engine as the major feature of the 1969 CJ Jeeps. "Universal models in the world famous 'Jeep' vehicle line," it reported, "offer a high performance V-6 as the top horsepower option in the series.

"The 'Dauntless' V-6 engine, which the company manufactures in a new plant in Toledo, more than doubles the normal power of 'Jeep' Universals ... It is the first 6-cylinder power plant ever made available in the Universal series.

"The remarkable margin of power afforded by the V-6 effects substantially greater smoothness and efficiency through the power train. This in turn improves the characteristic four-wheel drive traction enabling 'Jeep' Universals to move dependably over the most trying and difficult terrain."

Kaiser-Willys graphically defined the impact the V-6 had upon the CJ's off-road performance: "Added horsepower boosts the power-per-pound of curb weight far beyond that of competitive vehicles, a decisive factor in running through mud, snow or sand, and over rocks, ruts and steep hills. These unassailable performance advantages form the 'plus' needed for maximum versatility in recreational as well as general utility service."

One of the most unique packages offered for the CJ-5, the 'Jeep' Camper' option, debuted in 1969. While this unit would fit on any existing CJ-5 manufactured since 1955, Kaiser Jeep told prospective buyers that "it is strongly recommended that you utilize only Jeep Universal models equipped with the Dauntless V-6 engine and 4.88:1 axle." For those interested in purchasing a new

CJ-5, it was possible to order the camper unit separately or in combination with the CJ-5 as a complete unit.

Calling it the "greatest idea in trailblazing rigs since the horse and buggy," Kaiser Jeep said "there's really nothing like the new Jeep Camper ... you're not limited to the highways ... get off the road, pick out your site and set up camp ... On location, the camper is easily detached ... and that means in a few short minutes you've got a vacation home that doesn't have to be moved until you say the word. Your Jeep Universal is free for more adventure."

The cost of the complete Camper with the following standard equipment (effective January 2, 1970), was $2198.00:

Above & top right: Included in the Tuxedo Park's side trim was a V-6 logo as well as Tuxedo Park Mark IV identification on the hood. (Courtesy Joe Caprio)

Camper features:
– Dual lighting system (12v and 115v)
– Sleeping and dining area for four adult campers
– Toilet with built-in water supply and holding tank
– 20 gallon pressure water system
– Approved oven/stove with thermostat and stove hood
– Inlaid vinyl linoleum
– 100 pound ice box
– Galvanized storage compartment for two

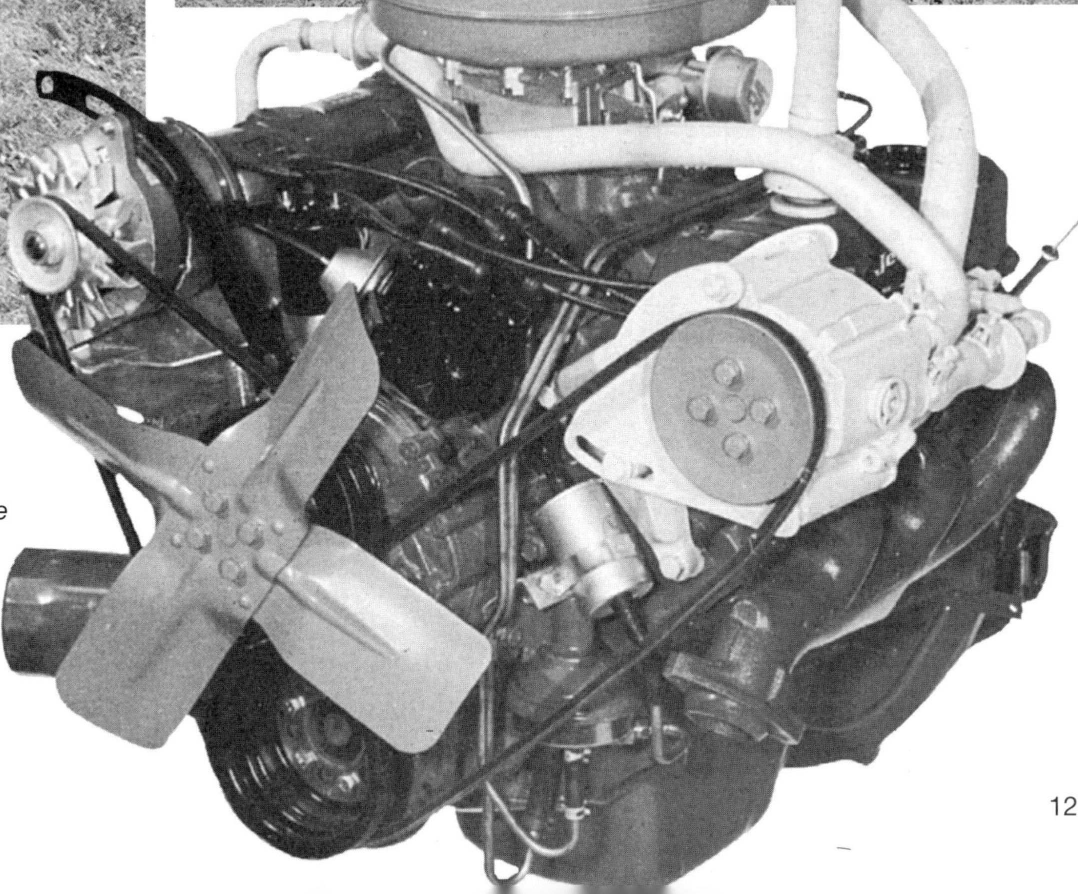

The Dauntless V-6
engine was a compact,
short stroke V-6 that
operated on regular grade
gasoline. (Author's
collection)

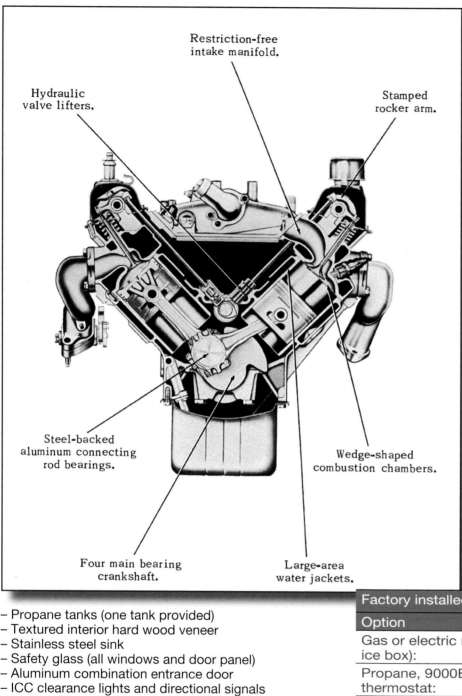

Restriction-free
intake manifold.

Hydraulic
valve lifters.

Stamped
rocker arm.

Steel-backed
aluminum connecting
rod bearings.

Wedge-shaped
combustion chambers.

Four main bearing
crankshaft.

Large-area
water jackets.

A head-on view of the Dauntless V-6 engine identifying a number of its design features. (Author's collection)

Right: The Warn overdrive unit for the CJ Jeeps was compact, weighing only 22 pounds. (Author's collection)

– Goodyear 8.55 x 15 BSW power cushion tires
– Camper Mounting Kit (front and intermediate attaching parts boxed and shipped with each Camper)

Kaiser Jeep offered the Camper in four basic forms:

Description	Reference code
Standard Camper plus roof vent and gas light:	JC-1
Standard Camper plus furnace, roof vent, Monomatic toilet, gas light:	JC-2
Standard Camper plus refrigerator, furnace, roof vent, Monomatic toilet and gas light:	JC-3
Standard Camper plus roof vent, gas light and furnace:	JC-4

– Propane tanks (one tank provided)
– Textured interior hard wood veneer
– Stainless steel sink
– Safety glass (all windows and door panel)
– Aluminum combination entrance door
– ICC clearance lights and directional signals
– Four unloading jacks
– Seven wire electrical main entrance connector
– Adequate reinforcement at all mounting points
– One standard roof vent
– Wiring for optional Monomatic toilet installation
– Rear axle brakes with Brake Control Kit
– Shock absorbers
– Square tubular bumper

Factory installed optional equipment	
Option	Price
Gas or electric refrigerator (in lieu of ice box):	$235.00
Propane, 9000BTU furnace with thermostat:	$99.50
Roof vent (in overcab extension):	$19.30
Monomatic toilet (substitute for standard Sani-Matic; only at time of manufacture):	$149.00
Gaslight:	$24.00
A mandatory option was the draw bar (option code 53) and electric wire	

WARN "All Range" OVERDRIVE

FOR WILLYS 'JEEP' AND I-H SCOUT 4-WHEEL DRIVES

more 'GO' in every gear

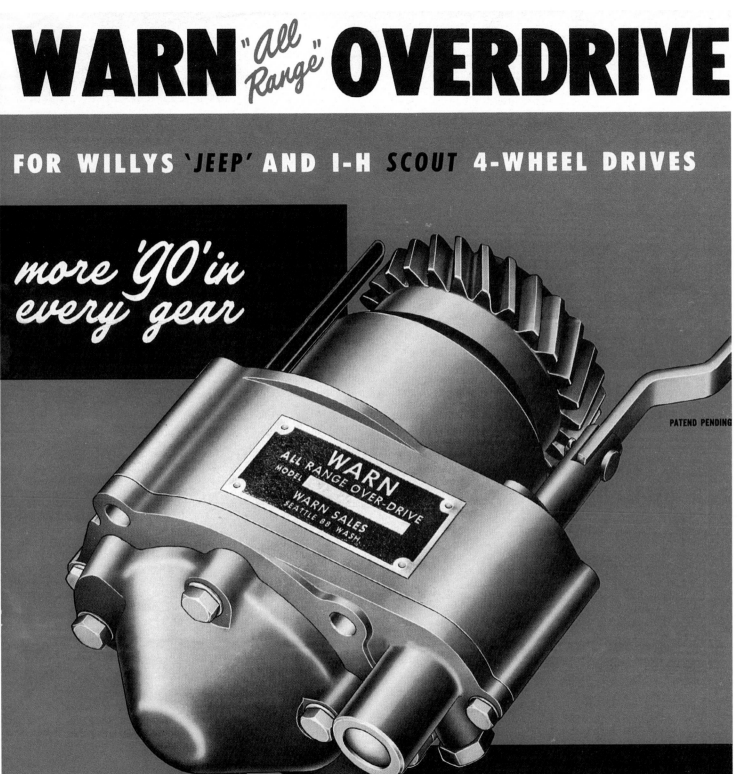

PATEND PENDING

WARN
ALL RANGE OVER-DRIVE
MODEL
WARN SALES
SEATTLE 88 WASH.

3/4 ACTUAL SIZE · WEIGHS ONLY 22 LBS.

MODEL 20
LOW GEAR RATIO
Fits most 4-wheel drives

MODEL 30
HIGH GEAR RATIO
For use with large engines

SYNCHROMESH TRANSMISSION

SHIFT ON-THE-GO...AT ANY SPEED...
UP OR DOWN...IN ANY GEAR...IN
ANY RANGE...FORWARD OR REVERSE
...IN 2-WHEEL OR 4-WHEEL DRIVE!

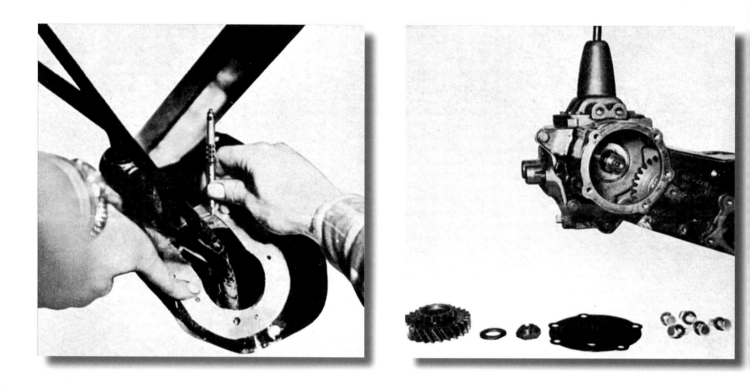

These four views show the ease with
which the Warn overdrive unit could
be installed in under two hours.
(Author's collection)

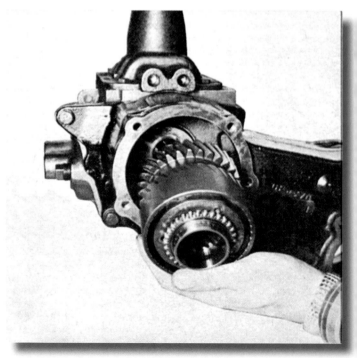

The 1969 Camper option for the CJ-5. Kaiser Jeep called it "an exclusive camper unit that capitalizes on Jeep 4-wheel drive for the ultimate in off-road advantages in finding and reaching remote campsites." (Author's collection)

The CJ-5 was equipped with a Dauntless V-6 engine and 4:88:1 rear axle to handle the weight of the camper coach. (Author's collection)

Exterior colors offered for the 1969 CJ-5 and CJ-6 models included Gold Beige, Bronze Mist, Prairie Gold, Glacier White, Empire Blue, President Red, and Spruce Tip Green.

In 1969 and 1970, Kaiser Jeep introduced two limited production CJ-5 models, reflecting market trends which were shifting the 4WD market away from its traditional utility vehicle core toward customers who recognised the Jeep's aptitude as a recreational/sports vehicle. The first consisted of a small group of special CJ-5s that Kaiser Jeep identified as the 462, or the 'Four-6-Two.' Features included a roll bar, front bucket seats, rear seat, a heavy-duty oil pan and heavy-duty oil pan skid plate, electric ammeter and oil gauges, engine coolant temperature gauge, swing-out spare tire carrier, red-striped H70 x 15 Polyglas tires, and full wheel covers. Required options included V-6 engine, heavy-duty frame, heavy-duty springs, locking rear differential, padded sun visors, and padded instrument panel.

The 462 was followed in 1970 by the CJ-5 Renegade I. In promoting the Renegade, Kaiser Jeep demonstrated an awareness that the Jeep market was on the verge of a dramatic transformation. "Way-out action," said Kaiser Jeep, "is what is happening with the way-out vehicle ... The 'Jeep' Renegade I built by Kaiser Jeep Corporation." The Renegade I was available in two colors: Renegade Purple or Lime Green. The content of what Kaiser Jeep described as the Renegade I's "special 'super' accessory package" included the following:

– 'Racing-type' roll bar
– Rear swing-away spare tire carrier
– Heavy-duty oil pan skid plate
– Electric oil and ammeter gauges
– Black Renegade hood stripes
– Kelsey Hayes 15 x 8in steel wheels
– G70 x 15 4-ply 'Polyglas' white-striped tires
– Front bucket seats
– Rear seat
– Draw bar
– Heavy-duty frame and suspension
– Locking rear differential
– Dual sun visors
– Safety rail
– Padded instrument panel
– 225cu in V-6

For 1970 the mass-produced CJ Jeeps were available in nine exterior and and three interior colors in the combinations shown in the table.

Interior colors	Marlin Blue	Charcoal	Rawhide
Exterior colors:			
President Red:	NA	X	NA
Champagne White:	X	X	X
Empire Blue Metallic:	X	NA	NA
Sprucetip Green Metallic:	NA	X	X
Burnished Bronze Metallic:	NA	X	X
Prairie Gold:	NA	X	X
Avocado Mist Metallic:	NA	X	X
Spring Green:	NA	X	X
Vintage Gold. Metallic:	NA	X	X

The camper coach provided sleeping accommodation for four adults, a stainless steel sink, storage cabinets and a dining area. (Author's collection)

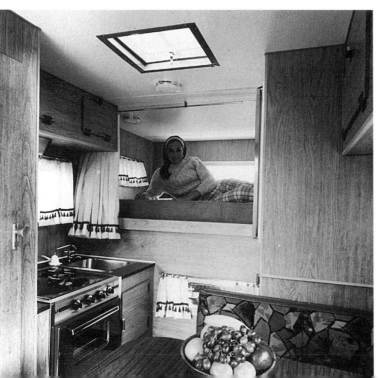

Prices for 1970 model Universal Jeeps, and their options, were, as of January 2, 1970:

Vehicle code number	ADP[1]	ADP[2]
8305 (CJ-5 /Hurricane F4 motor):	$2868.23	$2929.90
8405 (CJ-6/Hurricane F4 motor):	$2962.32	$3026.07
8505 (DJ-6/Hurricane F4 motor):	$2345.15	$2395.59

[1]Advertised delivered price with open body, no top
[2]Advertised delivered price with half top

Prices of the CJ-5 (vehicle code 8305A) and the CJ-6 (vehicle code 8405A) with the Dauntless V-6 engine were $210.95 higher than the corresponding model with the Hurricane 4-cylinder engine.

Option prices for the 1970 CJ Jeep were:

Option	Code number	ADP
Engine:		
Dauntless V-6:	312	$215.30
Seats:		
⅓rd front passenger seat:	20N	$66.69
Bucket front passenger seat:	20Y	$75.80
Rear seat:	54	$89.58
⅔rd driver seat:	131	$24.71
Tires:		
8.55 x 15 (4 ply) Suburbanite:	805	$56.24
H78 x 15 Polyglas Suburbanite:	821	$83.05
H78 x15 Polyglas power cushion WSW:	823	$115.49
Additional equipment:		
Locking rear differential (4-cyl):		
4.27:1	4.27L/A	$49.43
5.38	5.38L/A	$49.43
Locking rear differential (6-cyl):		
3.73:1	3.73L/A	$49.33
4.88	4.88L/A	$49.33
High altitude cylinder head (4-cyl only):	24	No charge
Draw bar:	53	$28.25

Option	Code number	ADP
Heavy-duty springs and shocks (4-cyl):	60	$29.86
Heavy-duty springs and shocks (6-cyl):	60Y	$35.92
Heavy-duty rear springs (6-cyl):	60M	$20.53
4-speed transmission (4-cyl only):	174	$178.36
Heavy-duty 70amp battery:	187	$7.34
55amp alternator:	359	$28.15

Dealer installed accessory equipment

Item/part no	Suggested list price	Approx
Cigar lighter/916589:	$3.68	0.2 hr
Locking gas cap/931662:	$3.15	None
Chaff screen kit/981007:	$15.14	0.2 hr
Draw bar/947378:	$39.54	–
Magnetic drain plug*/915863	$1.63	None
Front helper air spring kit/924457:	$48.51	1 hr
Rear helper air spring kit/924458:	$36.90	1 hr
Pintle hook/923091:	$50.35	1 hr
Passenger safety rail/961594:	$6.66	0.2 hr
Passenger safety rail kit/94509:	$2.94	0.5 hr
Spare tire lock/934292:	$3.98	0.1 hr
Wheelhouse cushion pads/689819:	$13.74	None

*Hurricane engine only

The CJ-5 easily detached from the camper unit once a base camp was chosen. (Author's collection)

The Camper unit was also available to current owners of the CJ-5. Kaiser Jeep assured them that the camping unit could be easily installed without alteration to their vehicle. (Author's collection)

The Camper option, the Dauntless V-6, and the 462 and Renegade I models were among the last major CJ developments made by Kaiser before Kaiser Jeep was consolidated with American Motors, effective from October 1, 1969.

The 1969 model was the last CJ-5 produced by Kaiser Jeep Corporation. Kaiser Jeep sent it off in style, explaining that "deep foam bucket seats, a full set of safety features and a wide selection of trim fabrics and colors go with the basic model." The exterior color selection for 1969 included Gold Beige, Bronze Mist, Prairie Gold, Glacier White, Empire Blue, President Red and Spruce Tip Green. Note the location of the windshield wipers at the bottom of the windshield. (Author's collection)

7

"FOR FUN & FAMILY ... FOR ADVENTURE & DURABILITY" – THE AMC CJ-5 & CJ-6 JEEPS

The acquisition of Kaiser Jeep Corporation by American Motors Corporation (AMC), was formally completed on February 5, 1970, the day after stockholders approved the move at the annual meeting with a shares vote total of 10,689,78. Those opposed numbered 297,142. The value added to the company by the total purchase price of approximately $70 million meant that American Motors became a billion dollar corporation. The combined fiscal 1968 sales of American Motors (which had begun on May 1, 1954 when Nash-Kelvinator acquired the Hudson Motor Car Company), and Kaiser Jeep totaled $1.2 billion, making AMC the 75th largest industrial corporation in the US.

AMC's Board Chairman Roy D Chapin Jr noted in his report to shareholders that "by acquiring Kaiser Jeep, we gain entry into the commercial and recreational vehicle market" which had more than tripled in the last 10 years, with sales of 125,000 units a year. In that context Chapin added that "Jeep brings us an established organization, distribution facilities, manufacturing facilities and a brand name which is known in virtually every corner of the world."

Time Magazine (October 31, 1969) began its report on AMC's acquisition by reminding its readers of the origin of the Jeep's international reputation. "Like Spam, Betty Grable and the big band sound," it noted, "the Jeep is a memorable symbol of World War II."

Along with AMC President William Lundberg, Chapin went to great length in AMC's 1970 annual report to assure shareholders that the acquisition of Jeep was one of the company's most important actions. At the same time he identified several factors that had prevented Jeep from becoming all that it could be. "Jeep can, and will be a major profit contributor to American Motors," he asserted. "There are a number of reasons why Jeep has considerable potential. Its commercial vehicle lines are well engineered and well known.

"What has been lacking to a degree is the kind of complete program our combined companies are now in a position to carry out – research to gain specific market information, then product development and aggressive merchandising and sales programs based on realistic assessments of what buyers of four-wheel drive vehicles require."

During the 1970 model year, Jeep retail sales had totaled 30,000 units, or about 20 per cent of the four-wheel drive market. This was down from the share Jeep had in the 1960s when fewer competitors existed. However, explained AMC, "it provides a sizable base from which to re-establish Jeep as the sales leader." By acquiring Jeep AMA depicted itself as becoming "an important factor in the four-wheel drive market which has grown by almost 500 per cent in the past decade to approach 140,000 units annually. This growth is expected to continue, or even accelerate, during the 1970s."

A 1970 CJ-5 in company with a Jeepster Commando Pickup. (Author's collection)

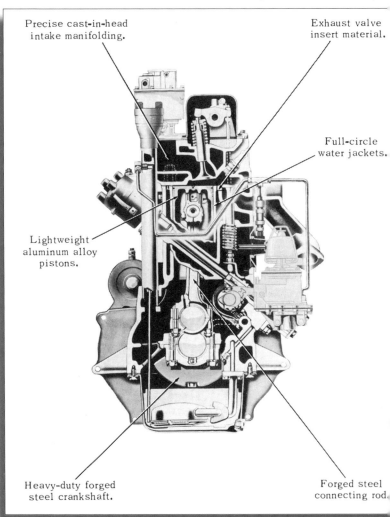

sophisticated developments in safety and off-road performance made possible only by 4-wheel drive."

As displayed at the New York show, the XJ001's hand-laid fiberglass body had a pearlized lime finish. A molded hood scoop was functional and the one-piece molded foam seats had metal backs with integral headrests finished with black calf grained vinyl. The padded dash and console were also covered with this material. A roll-bar was built into the windshield, and the rocker panels and front bumper utilized a simple bolt-on system allowing for ease of replacement. The fuel tank was located in the rear with a capacity expected to be in the 20 gallon range. The XJ001's wide-mouth filler opening was, said AMC: "an

Detailing of the Hurricane's primary features: this illustration was provided to Jeep dealers in 1970. (Author's collection)

Precise cast-in-head intake manifolding.

Exhaust valve insert material.

Full-circle water jackets.

Lightweight aluminum alloy pistons.

Heavy-duty forged steel crankshaft.

Forged steel connecting rod.

For the first two quarters of 1970 Jeep operated at a loss as wholesale vehicle sales were held back by existing dealer inventories But with October 1970 Jeep wholesale commercial vehicle sales up 31 per cent over the previous year's level, Jeep Corporation was operating at a profit as the year came to an end.

Initially, AMC didn't make any major changes in the CJ design, but, eager to stamp its imprint on the Jeep's future, it selected the 1970 New York International Automobile Show (April 4-12, 1970) for the first public showing of the XJ001, described as the latest and most advanced "4-wheel drive 'idea' car created by Jeep Corporation."

Work on the XJ001 had begun two years earlier, with final development work handled by AMC's design facilities in Detroit under the direction of James E Anger, and by the development and research division in Toledo, managed by Ivan N Schatzka, Chief Development Engineer. Based on the CJ-5 and thus having an 81in wheelbase, XJ001 overall length was 144 inches; width was 72 inches and height, measured at the windshield top, was 57 inches. Describing it as a "two-place research vehicle," AMC said the XJ001 "embodies racy, European-flavored sports car styling with

important feature, especially to racing buffs interested in running such a vehicle in the fast-growing, off-road racing activities around the country. Additional 'racing items' found on the XJ001 included 'racing-type' hood latches and steering wheel, wide-wheels, low-profile tires, and full Stewart-Warner instrumentation.

The XJ011's tread width was an "extra-wide" 54 inches. Ground clearance was 8.75 inches.

The XJ001 was designed to use a variety of engines and drive train components. Noting that "there are allowances for many variations in power plants that will make desirable installations," AMC said the "most likely candidate" was its 360cu in V-8 with a 2bbl carburetor. At one point the XJ001 was demonstrated with a Dauntless V-6 engine. As shown in New York, the XJ001 was fitted with a 4-speed manual transmission controlled by a console-mounted shifter. The news that "there are also provisions for automatic transmission and Hurst shift linkage options," preceded introduction of the Hurst-Jeepster in 1971.

The three seat colors offered for the 1970 CJ-5andCJ-6. (Author's collection)

The XJ001 was an "Idea Jeep" built by Jeep Corporation shortly after American Motors acquired Jeep from Kaiser in 1970. Its reinforced plastic body was mounted on a slightly modified CJ-5, 81in wheelbase chassis with a widened tread. It was equipped with wide aluminum wheels, H60 x 15 Goodyear Polyglas GT tires, a spoked 'racing-type' steering wheel, competition-oriented instrumentation, hood latches and rally stripes. In the early 1970s it was destroyed in a fire when the van in which it was being transported overturned and caught fire. (Author's collection)

After noting that the XJ001 had been designed to allow for the use of a "large variety of power plants", Jeep Corporation hinted at future plans for production model CJ Jeeps by noting that "the engine most likely to be used will be a 360cid, 2-barrel V-8." Driver and passenger sides of the XJ-001 were slightly different in appearance. (Author's collection)

The XJ001 was equipped with Stewart-Warner instrumentation, and a 'racing-type' steering wheel. (Author's collection)

A view of the XJ001 in the Jeep design studio. American Motors' caption for this photo explained that "Design proposals for future commercial and recreational vehicles are developed in a new Jeep styling studio in Detroit." (Author's collection)

Future AMC president Gerald Meyers, then AMC's Vice President of Product Development, emphasized that the role of the XJ was to "function only in testing design and engineering ideas and will not be placed in production in its present configuration." But by noting that it "was created as an experimental test platform for innovations that can be applied in the rapidly-expanding off-road recreational vehicle field," he drew attention to what was to be one of the XJ001's enduring influences on Jeep design history; its four-wheel drive system.

AMC provided just enough information about this unit at the New York show to add substance to Meyers' comment, describing it as "a center-differentiated, full-time four-wheel drive system ... now well along in development for 'Jeep' vehicles. It will give the XJ001 the advantage of traction at all four wheels automatically as driving conditions demand. This new transfer case has been named Quadritrac by the company. it is chain-driven and offers a low range for moving through extremely rough terrain or weather hazards."

In its Nine Months Report to stockholders dated August 1970, AMC noted that "Long-range, we are planning development of Jeep products to meet needs of recreational markets. Short-term, we are improving the present line of sports-utility, station wagon and light truck vehicles in the Jeep commercial line. Some changes will come next year."

As 1971 began, AMC shareholders were given an upbeat assessment of the future of the 4WD market: "The commercial four-wheel drive market," they were told in the First Quarter Report, "presents exciting possibilities because it is still a very young market and a very diverse one. Real growth did not begin until the past decade, when annual sales skyrocketed 500 per cent to the 150,000 unit level. With uses for four-wheel drive vehicles varying from business to agriculture to family transportation to sports and recreation, the market seems certain to grow to substantial proportions in the 1970s."

Indicative of AMC's recognition that the Jeep's sales potential had barely been tapped was its promotion of the publicity accorded the Renegade II. Displaying an early example at the company's annual meeting in February 1971 just after its introduction, AMC described the Renegade II as "a limited edition model with special performance accessories."

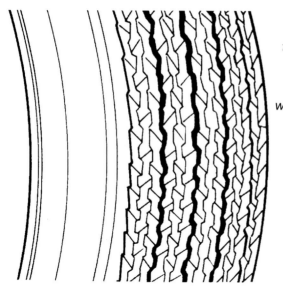

This power cushion tubeless tire in blackwall 7.35 15, 4-ply form was standard for 1970 CJ-5 and CJ-6 Jeeps with the Dauntless V-6 engine. It was considered "especially suitable for highway use." (Author's collection)

Those items included a roll bar, front bucket seats, safety rail, rear seat, heavy-duty oil pan skid plate, electric ammeter and oil gauge, engine coolant temperature gauge, rear spare tire carrier, white-striped H70 x 15 Polyglas tires, Charcoal striping, hood side and center, 15 x 8in aluminum alloy wheels, large driver's side exterior mirror, V-6 engine, heavy-duty frame and springs, locking rear differential, and padded sun visors and instrument panel.

This 8.55 x 15, 4-ply Suburbanite tire in either black or white sidewall form was optional for the 1970 CJ-5 and CJ-6. Kaiser Jeep explained that its "thousands of sharp edges combined with deep cleats provide better pull-away grip, surer climb on slippery hills, and safer stops on slick surfaces." (Author's collection)

The Renegade II was available in Baja Yellow, Mint Green, Plum Metallic, Riverside Orange, and Sierra Blue. Production totaled approximately 600 units.

While the Renegade was destined to become a key element of the CJ model line and the Jeep's expanding image, the Camper option was an early casualty of the ownership change as it was not listed in the *1971 Data Book* issued by American Motors.

Although AMC didn't make any substantial changes to the CJ's design until 1972, it wasted no time in aggressively promoting the CJ-5/6 (as well as the other models in the Jeep range). One full line 1971 sales brochure was headlined "Introducing the one that goes where others can't." In regard to each Jeep model, AMC declared "It has Guts (to get you through)." Referring to the Universal, AMC declared: "Jeep guts have made it a legend in its own time." In addition to reminding readers about traditional CJ virtues: "this is the one that goes where others can't. Conquers hills, rocks, muck, slush, sand – even rips out tree stumps .." AMC also publicized the CJ's success in off-road racing and endurance events such as the Baja 500, the Mint 400, and the Riverside Grand Prix.

The table shows 1971 interior/exterior colors, and available combinations.

1971 prices for CJ models and their options (effective January 4, 1971) are given in the following table.

Interior trim			
	Buckskin	Marlin Blue	Charcoal
Exterior color			
Sprucetip Green Metallic:	X	NA	X
President Red:	X	NA	X
Avocado Mist Metallic:	X	NA	X
Champagne White:	X	X	X
Spring Green:	X	NA	X
Vintage Gold Metallic:	X	NA	X
Island Blue Metallic:	NA	X	NA
Candlelight Yellow:	X	NA	X

Jeep Corporation's performance, as measured by domestic wholesale sales of all models, made steady improvement under AMC. In the first six months of 1971 sales increased 26 per cent to 17,878 units, compared with 14,196 in the corresponding period in 1970.

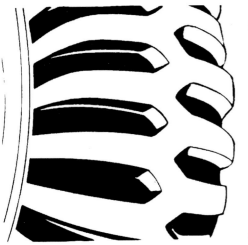

The familiar 6.00 x 16, 4-ply black sidewall, All Service tube-type tire was standard for the 1970, Hurricane 4-engined CJ-5 and CJ-6 Jeeps. "As its name implies," said Kaiser-Jeep, "this is a general purpose tire for vehicles that must operate without interruption on the road or off in any kind of weather. Non-directional tread design provides adequate non-slip traction for forward and reverse driving." (Author's collection)

Model code/model	MSDP*
83050/CJ-5:	$2886.00
84050/CJ-6:	$2979.00

Manufacturer's suggested delivered price

Option	Code number	
Meyer Metal full cab:	62N	$399.00
225 V-6 engine:	312	$100.00
4-speed manual trans (4-cyl only):	174	$174.65
Optional axle ratios:		
5.38 (4-cyl only):	–	$12.65
4.88 (V-6 only):	–	$12.65
Trac-Lok rear diff:	–	$61.35
4.27 (4-cyl only):	–	$61.35
5.38 (4-cyl Only):	–	$61.35
3.73 (V-6 only):	–	$61.35
4.88 (V-6 only):	–	$61.35
Cigar lighter:	13A	$6.50
Dual sun visors:	14	$13.95
Padded instrument panel:	267	$37.95
70amp battery:	187	$11.70
55amp alternator:	359	$27.60

Option	Code number	ADP*
Heavy-duty cooling system (4-cyl):		
6 blade fan:	52N	$9.75
Heavy-duty cooling system (6-cyl):		
(radiator & 6 blade fan):	52	$23.35
Heavy-duty frame:	356	$19.50
Front & rear springs & shocks (military wrap):		
4-cyl	60	$38.85
6-cyl	60Y	$38.85
12-leaf rear springs:		
(6-cyl only)	60M	$20.15
Tires:		
8.55 x 15 4-ply BSW, Suburbanite:	805	$55.15
8.55 x 15 4-ply WSW, Suburbanite:	856	$87.50
H78 x 15 BSW Polyglas Suburbanite:	821	$81.05
H78 x 15 WSW Polyglas power cushion:	822	$113.40
Draw bar:	53	$27.65
Fuel tank skid plate:	103	$19.95
Spare tire tailgate mount:	133	$9.95
Nitrox Emission (6-cyl) and fuel vaporization system**:	24W 262	$37.00

***Mandatory for California. Price listed is for 24W and 262*

Warn Semi-automatic hubs:	296	$64.75
Front passenger bucket seat:	20Y	$74.30
Full bench (⅔ -⅓) front seat:	131	$89.45
Rear seat with dual seat belts:	54	$92.10

Advertised delivered price

The 1972 CJ Jeeps, reflecting the influence of AMC's marketing strategy, were introduced to the press at Catalina Island, California. In his presentation, Marvin W Stuckey, Vice President for Jeep Product Development, offered a glimpse of AMC's future plans: "We plan to continue to move fast and aggressively. We are developing some very interesting plans for capturing a larger share of the four-wheel drive market." As far as the latest models were concerned, Stuckey explained that "what we have achieved for 1972 is the first phase of a longer-range plan to capitalize on this potential." Driving this point home, he told his audience that "a principal reason the four-wheel drive market is exciting is that it is a relatively young and diverse market. In only the past decade, sales skyrocketed by more than 500 per cent."

AMC's strategy to position the Jeep at this market's focal point included enhancing its reputation for reliability and durability, improving driver and passenger comfort, and placing greater emphasis on contemporary styling

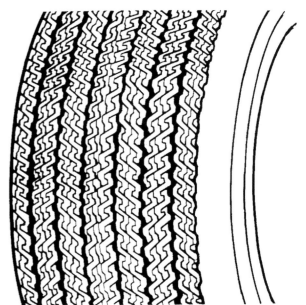

Also optional for the 1970 CJ-5 and CJ-7 models was this G-70-15 Polyglas white sidewall tire. (Author's collection)

A 1970 CJ-5. American Motors' acquisition of Kaiser Jeep in 1970 nearly coincided with the 30th anniversary of arrival of the first Bantam model at Fort Holabird on September 23, 1940. (Author's collection)

and features. Symbolizing this new era of Jeep history was abandonment of the Jeep Universal series designation in favor of Jeep CJ-5/CJ-6 identification.

Accompanying this change were numerous others for 1972. AMC's 232 cubic inch, in-line six became the CJ's

This photo of the CJ-5 Renegade, powered by the V-6 Dauntless engine, was included in one of the first Jeep press packs prepared by American Motors after it acquired Jeep. It was postmarked September 22, 1970. (Author's collection)

It is likely that this is the same Renegade as that in the previous photograph. Its chrome front bumper is evident in this view. (Author's collection)

standard engine, with 258cid 6-cylinder and 304cid V-8 engines optional. No longer available were the 134cid four and 225cid V-6 engines.

The three AMC engines had the specifications shown in the table overleaf.

All three engines operated on Regular, Low-Lead or No-Lead gasoline. These larger, heavier and more powerful AMC engines came with many new, high capacity components in the CJ drive train and suspension. New, increased capacity standard and optional front springs had the ratings shown in the following tables.

An employee identification badge from American Motors' ownership of Jeep. (Courtesy Marshall Rimland collection)

Type:	232 Six	258 Six	304 V-8
Bore:	3.75in	3.75in	3.75in
Stroke:	3.50in	3.90in	3.44in
Displacement (cu in)/cc	232/3802	258/4299	304/4983
Comp ratio:	8.0:1	8.0:1	8.4:1
Main bearings:	7	7	5
Net horsepower:	100@3600rpm	110@3500rpm	150@4200rpm
Net torque (lb/ft):	185@1800rpm	195@2000rom	245@2500rpm
Carburetor:	1bbl	1bbl	2-bbl
Intake valves			
Head dia (in):	1.787	1.787	1.787
Lift (in):	0.372	0.372-in.	0.425
Exhaust valves			
Head dia (in):	1.406.	1.406	1.406
Lift (in):	0.372	0.372	0.425
Capacities			
Radiator:	10.5qt*	10.5qt*	14qt

*9.5qt without heater for 6-cylinder engines

The cover of American Motors' 1970 annual report positioned the CJ-5 – along with other Jeep vehicles and a military 6x6 – in close proximity to the AMC passenger car models for 1971. (Author's collection)

Standard front springs	1971[a]		1972	
Model:	4-cyl	V-6	CJ-5	CJ-6
Number of leaves:	5	10	7	9
Rate (lb/in):	188	176	190	210
Length (in):	39.63	39.63	39.75	39.75
Width (in):	1.75	1.75	1.75	1.75
Total thickness (in):	1.242	1.940	1.575	1.926
Capacity at pad (lb):	875	865	855	1040
Capacity at ground (lb):	1035	1025	1015	1200
Standard rear springs Model:	4-cyl	V-6	CJ-5	CJ-6
Number of leaves:	5	6	5	5
Rate (lb/in):	155-230	155-230	155-235	155-235
Length (in):	46.00	46.00	46.00	46.00
Width (in):	1.75	1.75	1.75	1.75
Total thickness (in):	1.593	1.593	1.593	1.593
Capacity at pad (lb):	1240	1240	1240	1240
Capacity at ground (lb):	1370	1405	1405	1405

[a]Spring rates for the CJ-5 and CJ-6 were identical in 1971

Optional front springs	1971	1972
Model	4-cyl/V-6	CJ-5/CJ-6
Number of leaves:	12	10
Rate (lb/in):	236	270
Length (in):	39.50	39.75
Width (in):	1.75	1.75
Total thickness (in):	1.242	2.250
Capacity at pad (lb):	1240	1300
Capacity at ground (lb):	1400	1460
Optional rear springs	1971[b]	1972
Model	4-cyl/V-6	CJ-5/CJ-6
Number of leaves:	12	13
Rate (lb/in):	410	225
Length (in):	46.00	46.00
Width (in):	1.75	1.75
Total thickness (in):	3.573	2.887
Capacity at pad (lb):	1850	1260
Capacity at ground (lb):	2015	1425

[b]If the CJ-5/6 was ordered with the optional 12-leaf front springs, rear springs with these specifications were mandatory

The GVW ratings of the CJ-5/CJ-6 – with standard and optional springs – were as follows:

Model:	GVW (standard springs)	GVW (optional springs)
CJ-5:	3750lb	4500lb
CJ-6:	3900lb	4750lb

CJ-5 Jeeps at the end of the assembly line at the Toledo, Ohio plant. (Author's collection)

The 6-cylinder engines were linked to a new Warner T14A 3-speed manual transmission with an input torque capacity of 230ft/lb, and ratios of 3.1, 1.6132 and 1.0:1. The reverse ratio was 3.1:1. The 304 V-8 had a standard Warner T15A 3-speed manual, rated at 325ft/lb, with ratios of 2.997, 1.832 and 1.0:1. Reverse ratio was 2.997. The CJ-5's optional 4-speed manual for both 6-cylinder engines was a 340ft/lb rated Warner T-18 with ratios of 4.02, 2.41, 1.41 and 1.0:1. Reverse ratio was 4.73:1. All forward gears

American Motors described the 1971 CJ-5 Universal as "the one about which legends have been made – a direct descendant of the vehicle that probably did more crucial jobs for more people under more trying conditions than any other in automotive history – the Jeep model of World War II." (Author's collection)

A trio of colorful 1971 CJ-5 Renegade II models. As seen here they were available in three colors: Baja Yellow, Riverside Orange/Big Bad Orange and Mint Green. (Courtesy DaimlerChrysler Media Services)

were fully synchronized on 3-speed transmissions; the 4-speed had synchromesh on its top three forward gears.

These developments resulted in a new arrangement of power train combinations shown in the accompanying table.

A 10.5in diameter clutch with a torque capacity of 290ft/lb was used with all engines. Replacing the 10in x 2.0in brakes of 1971 were increased capacity 11in x 2.0in units with a total effective lining of 180.8sq in. CJs with the 304 V-8 were available with new optional power brakes. For easier access, the brake master cylinder was relocated from the frame to the engine compartment.

A new Dana 30 open knuckle, fully-floating front axle

Engine	Transmission	Axle ratios	
		Standard	Optional
232 3-speed:		3.73	4.27
4-speed:		3.73	4.27
258 3-speed:		3.73	4.27
4-speed:		3.73	4.27
304 3-speed:		3.73	4.27

replaced the Dana 27 unit used previously. Aside from having increased capacity (up to 2300lb from 2000lb), its open end, ball joint wheel ends were easier to service, and minimized any tendency of wheel shimmy. This change also reduced the CJ's curb-to-curb turning diameter:

Model	1971	1972
CJ-5	38.6ft	32.9ft
CJ-6	42.3ft	37.6ft

An increased capacity (up to 3000lb from 2500lb), semi-floating, flanged shaft Dana 44 rear axle was also utilized. A Dana 20 transfer case without a park brake (this transfer case had been used previously for the J-series and Jeepster models) replaced the park brake-equipped Dana 18 model used in 1971. Aside from being quieter, it had a 2.03:1 low range, instead of the older model's 2.46:1. The transfer case was operated by a new, longer shift lever that reduced shifting effort.

Replacing the older cam and lever steering system was a Saginaw recirculating ball setup. AMC said it reduced steering effort and provided improved recovery. With fewer steering joints, it was also easier to service, and reduced the possibility of steering 'play' developing. For the first time a Saginaw

power steering system was optional for all engines. After asserting that "Jeep handling has never changed too much," *Off-Road Vehicles* (Jan/Feb 1972) reported that "the addition of power steering is certainly the most marked improvement so far!"

These developments were accompanied by numerous other changes, including longer 84in and 104in wheelbases for the CJ-5 and CJ-6, resulting in an extended front end (hood and fenders) that added 3.3 inches to the Jeep's overall length. The CJ's major dimensions for 1972 were as per the table on page 145.

Standard and optional seating choices for the CJ remained unchanged. A driver full-foam seat was standard. Optional choices consisted of a passenger full-foam bucket seat, a 2/3rd-1/3rd split front bench seat, and a rear bench seat. Replacing the frame mount type clutch and brake pedals were suspended units. This change eliminated water and dust leaks associated with the prior setup's floor holes A foot-operated park brake replaced the older hand lever: AMC said this allowed for easier actuation. The standard heater/defroster had increased capacity. A new cigarette lighter and ashtray – as well as new oil and ammeter gauges – were optional. AMC retained the CJ's standard movable tailgate and right-side mounted spare tire for 1972, but offered as an option a new solid, fixed

The 1971 CJ-5 was available with a variation of the hood striping used on the Renegade II. (Author's collection)

Dimension	CJ-5	CJ-6
Wheelbase:	84in	104in
Overall length:	138.9in	156.9in
Overall height:	69.5in	68.3in
Front tread*:	51.5in	51.5in
Rear tread*:	50.0in	50.0in
Front overhang:	22.9in	22.9in
Rear overhang:	32.0in	32.0in
Approach angle:	45°	45°
Departure angle:	30°	30°
Ramp breakover angle:	29°	29°
Front axle clearance:	8.6in	8.6in
Rear axle clearance:	8.0in	8.0in
Platform to ground:	23.3in	23.3in
Bumper to ground:	18.2in	18.2in

*AMC reported that the CJ's wider front and rear tread improved lateral stability. The front tread was increased by 3 inches; the rear by 1.5 inches. Off-Road Vehicle magazine (Jan/Feb 1972) essentially agreed, noting that it made the CJ-5 "much more comfortable and more stable to handle."

Body color code number	Color
432	Champagne White
494	Light Skyway Blue*
492	Medium Jetset Blue Metallic*
491	Julep Green Metallic*
431	Avocado Mist Metallic
493	Yucca Tan Metallic*
490	Butterscotch Yellow*
495	Canary Yellow*
226	President Red

*New colors for 1972

432	Raven Black
135	Omaha Orange
81	Transport Yellow
394	Marlin Blue Metallic
221	Federal Gray
504	Forest Green

tailgate with a rear-mounted spare tire. AMC claimed this provided a "better appearance and more convenient spare location."

New Buff or Black Wellington all-vinyl seats were available with nine exterior colors (see following table).

Six fleet colors (available only if three or more vehicles were ordered) were also offered in 1972 (table above right).

In the midst of these changes, AMC still found time to promote the 1972 Renegade. "This limited production vehicle leaves little doubt about its true purpose," it reported. "The sport Jeep Renegade is built for the man who wants all the excitement

Jeep
'72 new Jeep guts get you closer to the action.

When the crackle of a driftwood fire, laughter, and the crashing of waves are the only sounds for miles around, chances are you'll find a Jeep original nearby.

This is the one that goes where most other vehicles in the world can't go.

It's built to take you where the crowd can't follow. It's built with Jeep guts. And this year Jeep guts are stronger than ever.

he can get out of 4-wheel drive. That's why the specially priced Renegade equipment package includes a hefty 304 cubic inch V-8. A Track-lok differential is included, too. And that's not all. Cast-aluminum 7 inch wheels (American racing alloy), bucket seats, fuel tank skid plate, roll bar, custom paint job, and many other features which are available only as separately priced options on ordinary 4-wheel drive vehicles are all part of the Renegade package. This one has what it takes to do just about everything for fun. If you're in the market for this kind of excitement, better see your Jeep dealer soon. Scheduled Renegade production is limited."

At the end of 1972, AMC had 1550 Jeep dealers

The roll bar on this 1971 CJ-5 was a dealer installed option. (Author's collection)

American Motors set the tone for this evocative view of a 1972 CJ-5 by assuring Jeep enthusiasts that "when the crackle of a driftwood fire, laughter, and the crashing of waves are the only sounds for miles around, chances are you'll find a Jeep original nearby." This CJ-5 had a Canary Yellow exterior. The V-8 emblem positioned below the body side 'Jeep' lettering identifies it as powered by the optional 304 V-8. (Author's collection)

who were steadily improving their sales performance. For example, in the quarter ending December 31, 1972, Jeep vehicle sales had risen 44 per cent over the 1972 level to an all-time quarterly record of 17,216 units.

At AMC's February 1973 annual meeting, the corporate response to a shareholder question concerning Jeep advertising illustrated the stature of the Jeep's public image: "Jeep vehicles are not specifically identified with American Motors in advertising because the Jeep name

This pair of 1972 CJ-5 Jeeps were powered by the two alternatives to the standard 232cid six. The Presidential Red model has the 258cid 6-cylinder; the Canary Red CJ-5 is fitted with the 304 V-8. (Author's collection)

Jeep

The 1972 CJ-5's standard movable tailgate and side-mounted spare tire. (Author's collection)

The CJ-5 was available with this optional fixed tailgate and rear-mounted spare. (Author's collection)

These oil and ammeter gauges were new options for 1972. (Author's collection)

Model code/model	MSDP
83050/CJ-5:	$2955.00
84050/CJ-6:	$3045.00
Option	*Price*
Free-wheeling hubs:	$98
Power steering:	$148
Power brakes:	$46
Limited slip rear differential:	$62
Oil and ammeter gauges:	$17
Heavy-duty frame:	$20
Heavy-duty springs & shock absorbers:	$39
Front passenger bucket seat:	$74
Split front bench seat:	$89
Rear bench seat:	$92
55amp alternator:	$38
70amp battery:	$12
Cigarette lighter:	$7
Draw bar:	$28
Padded instrument panel:	$38

is particularly strong in four-wheel drive markets and the company wants to emphasize this strength."

In the midst of the Jeep's sale momentum, AMC President Roy Chapin made a comment that surely must have piqued the interest of many long-time Jeep enthusiasts. "We believe," he said, "rotary engines will play an important future role in the auto industry ... in February the company signed agreements with Curtiss-Wright Corporation which give American Motors a non-exclusive license covering the manufacture and sale by American Motors of rotary combustion engines for passenger cars and Jeep vehicles produced in North America."

Prices of 1972 Jeeps and selected options were as shown in the accompanying table (left).

With AMC focusing most of its effort for 1973 on the new Quadra-Trac full-time 4WD system option for the Jeep Wagoneer and several Jeep truck models, changes to CJ models were relatively minor. Replacing the five digit sales reference number was a two digit system:

Model	Old	New
CJ-5	83050	83
CJ-6	84050	84

The instrument panel was modified to accommodate 'soft-feel' control knobs with international code symbols. Green lighting was used for both cluster and the optional oil and ammeter gauges, which were relocated to each side of the instrument cluster for easier reading. The

1972 CJ-5 equipped with a front winch at work. During AMC's 1972 fiscal year, Jeep sales totaled a record 46,000 units, up 25 per cent on the previous year. (Author's collection)

gauge needles changed from white to fire orange. New bright trim rings were added to the gauges and cluster.

Other changes included relocation of the parking brake handle to the lower left corner of the instrument panel; lighted heater controls with black and bright knobs for 'air,' 'def,' and 'Temp,' a separate toggle switch for the fan, and new standard electric windshield wipers (in place of the old hand pump/vacuum system) with integrated washer and two-speed wiper control operation. A new connector at the wiper motor switch allowed for easier removal of the fold-down/detachable windshield.

No changes were made in engine/transmission availability, but the exhaust valve seats in the six-cylinder engines were now induction hardened for improved service life. All engines operated on regular, low lead or non-leaded gasoline of 91 octane or higher. A mechanical clutch linkage replaced the cable setup, and more durable, extended life joints were incorporated into the front axle and propeller shaft. Added to the CJ-5/CJ-6 standard equipment list was a fuel tank skid plate, previously listed as a dealer installed option. A roll bar – also formerly available only as a dealer installed option – was now a factory option. The use of new paint highlighted the 'JEEP' lettering on the CJ's cowl side.

AMC also instituted the following new or improved factory inspection facilities and equipment for better quality control at the CJ's Toledo assembly plant:
– Checking equipment for air conditioning and heaters
– Additional air conditioning system inspection on the final assembly line
– Upgraded brake testing and checking equipment
– Additional fuel system testing and inspection
– Wheel balance and tire fill equipment
– Front end alignment equipment
– Body and frame checking equipment
– Final assembly electrical inspection

This 1972 CJ-5 has optional custom chrome wheel covers, a fabric full top and an Avocado Mist Metallic exterior. (Author's collection)

– Speedometer and axle ratio check equipment
– Added inspection equipment for purchased parts

Nine exterior colors (five of which were new) were offered for 1973 (see table, top right).

1973 CJ model prices, along with selected options, were as per the table on page 149.

Sales of the latest CJ-5 Renegade (which AMC said was "bound for glory,") began in January 1973. Standard equipment included the 304 V-8, roll bar, American racing forged aluminum wheels, H78 x15 white sidewall tires, wheel well extensions, transmission skid plate (in addition to the standard CJ-5 fuel tank skid plate), oil and ammeter gauges, dual mirrors and sun visors, rear mounted spare, and a blackout hood with side-positioned 'Renegade' racing stripe. Included in the

Left to right: The standard driver seat for the 1972 CJ models and the optional split front seat. (Author's collection

Body color code no	Color
32	Champagne White
92	Medium Jetset Blue Metallic
31	Avocado Mist Metallic
90	Butterscotch Yellow
14	Fawn Beige*
12	Fairway Green Metallic*
17	Cooper Tan Metallic*
13	Daisy Yellow*
15	Trans-Am Red*

New for 1973. The six fleet colors from 1972 were continued. All exterior colors were available with Wellington vinyl seats in either Buff r Black

recorded in the entire 1972 fiscal year.

One of the rarest CJ-5 Jeeps of the early 1970 era, the 'Super Jeep,' was marketed from May through July 1973 (and briefly again in 1976). AMC advised Jeep dealers that the Super Jeep was a "mod and colorful showroom traffic builder." The caption of one Super Jeep advertisement would surely have aroused public interest: "Not a bird. Not a plane. But a new thrill under the sun – 4-wheel drive fun-mobiling. At first glance, the same familiar profile, but underneath that super stripe stands a baby brute with the guts to go where others fear to

Renegade's selection of "bright, sporty body colors" were Renegade Plum and Renegade Yellow. Mandatory Renegade options included a rear Trak-Lok differential and a heavy-duty cooling system.

Jeep sales momentum continued into 1973. In the first six months of AMC's 1973 fiscal year, ending on March 31, 1973, retail sales of all models reached 33,166 units, 49 per cent higher than the previous yearl. Three months later, in August 1973, AMC had more good news to report to stockholders: Jeep retail sales in the nine months of the fiscal year 1973 were 49,619, exceededing the volume of 46,000 units

Model code/model	MSDP
CJ-5:	$3086.00
CJ-6:	3176.00
Option	Price
Rear Trac-Lok diff (3.73:1):	$59.40
H78 x 15 Polyglas Suburban tires:	$81.10
4-speed manual trans:	$107.30
Cigar lighter:	$8.65
Front passenger bucket seat:	$72.10
Dual sun visors:	$13.55
Heavy-duty cooling:	$25.60
Draw bar:	$26.80
Rear bucket seats:	$72.10
Power steering:	$143.25
Passenger safety bar:	$6.85
Padded instrument panel:	$31.90
Semi-automatic hubs:	$59.80
Heavy-duty frame:	$18.90
Heavy-duty front and rear springs and shocks:	$37.60
Heavy-duty 70amp battery:	$11.30
Heavy-duty cooling:	$25.60
51amp alternator:	$26.75
258cid 6-cyl engine:	$53.85
Oil and amp gauges:	$16.65
Roll bar:	$54.65
Draw bar:	$26.80

A Butterscotch Gold 1973 CJ-5 in the service facility of a new AMC/Jeep dealership in West Allis, Wisconsin. The Jeep dealer organization was strengthened under AMC's control. Although the total remained at about 1500, over 400 new Jeep dealers had been added since 1970. Nearly 450 were selling both AMC and Jeep vehicles. (Author's collection)

A 1973 CJ-5 with a Jetset Blue Metallic finish was powered by the optional 304cu in, 150hp V-8. Its roll bar, previously available only as a dealer installed item, was now a factory option. (Author's collection)

This off-roader most likely appreciated the addition of a fuel tank skid plate as standard equipment for his 1973 CJ-5. (Author's collection)

Cluster and optional oil and ammeter gauges in the CJ-5 had new green lighting for 1973; gauge needle color changed from White to Fire Orange. Both gauges and cluster received new, bright ring moldings. Other changes included lighted heater

controls with black and bright knobs, and a separate toggle switch for the fan. (Author's collection)

For 1973 CJ instrument panel modifications included using 'soft-feel' control knobs and moving the parking brake release to the lower left corner of the instrument pane. The bucket seats seen here were optional, as were the relocated oil and ammeter gauges. New 2-speed electric windshield wipers with integrated washers were standard.
(Author's collection)

tread. 'Super Jeep' is all guts from the brawny suspension to the heavy-duty axle – an open-end design that can turn in just 32.9ft. And while you're checking out the special color treatment on the front and rear seats, the roll bar's saying 'go!' and the 258 six answers 'r-r-r-ight!' Oversize L78 x 15 Polyglas whitewall tires are included, along with those black rubber hp extensions on the fenders, plus chrome front bumper and a safety rail for your more easily flustered passengers. She's available in all kinds of color combinations and lots of extra goodies. So don't just sit there, hit the trail in a gen-u-ine Super Jeep."

Additional features of the Super Jeep included full-length body stripes,

The 1973 Renegade went on sale in January 1973. Powered by the 304cu in V-8, it was, said AMC, "bound for glory ... the Jeep with even more muscle and flair." This example was finished in Renegade Plum. (Author's collection)

Body color	Striping colors
Jetset Blue	Red and Blue
Champagne White	Red and Blue
Butterscotch Gold	Orange and White
Daisy Yellow	Orange and White
Copper Tan	Orange and White
Fairway Green	Orange and White

In this depiction of Jeep body styles in 1973, AMC regarded the Renegade as a separate model. (Author's collection)

white-trimmed instrument panel and sun visors, 8in steel wheels, and a chrome front bumper.

The Super Jeep was available in the body/striping color combinations shown in the table.

All 1974 CJs had a new brake system with proportioning valves, new drums, linings and master cylinders. They were also fitted with stronger body-to-chassis mounts, a higher output heater, and new optional bumpers that met the Federal 5mph standard. Induction hardened exhaust valve seats were specified for the 304 V-8 engine. All engines were modified to meet evaporative and exhaust emission standards for utility vehicles, which came into effect for 1974.

Body Styles:

CJ5   CJ6   Renegade

Full top   Half-cab

All CJ models had new frames for 1975 with increased gauge side rails, as well as an improved exhaust system. Their ignition systems now included an electrical wiring harness for faster, more reliable starts in all kinds of weather. The use of a new dash disconnect plug allowed easier diagnosis and servicing of the electrical system. Replacing the ammeter on the CJ dash was a voltmeter, indicating battery condition and the alternator's status.

For the first time the CJ was offered with a factory installed AM radio. Mounted below the instrument panel, it was packaged in a weatherproof case and connected to a fixed length whip-type antenna. Additional new options included a column-mounted tachometer, HR-78 x 15 radial tires, a 'Cold Climate Package' consisting of an engine block heater, a 70amp battery and a 62amp alternator. A new, more durable Whitco top, featuring improved visibility and larger door openings, was also a factory option. As in previous years, it could also be installed by the dealer.

The fuel economy and throttle response of the six cylinder engines were improved by the use of a modified intake manifold, allowing them to operate on a leaner air/fuel mixture. All CJ engines required no-lead gas. Drivers were alerted to this development by warning labels ('UNLEADED FUEL ONLY') located on the instrument cluster and the fuel filler area. The 304 V-8 was fitted with a catalytic converter. Both the CJ-5 and CJ-6 had improved insulation to reduce heat intrusion from the engine compartment into the cab.

The 1975 Renegade's new hood tape had thin red surround lines with white 'RENEGADE' lettering and a main color contrasting with the body color. Its interior contained new Levi's vinyl front bucket seats and matching rear seat, instrument panel pad, and padded sun visors. Dealer installed carpeting was available for the Renegade. The Renegade could also be ordered with the Whitco top in either Blue or Tan. The Levi's seats were optional for the base CJ-5, which had standard CJ Wellington vinyl interior in either Light Beige or Black.

AMC introduced the 'Levis' trim in 1973 as an interior option for Gremlin and Hornet hatchback models. It quickly became the most popular special interior treatment in AMC history. Putting this popularity in a perspective that owners of Levi's jeans quickly embraced, AMC explained that "more than 65,000 pairs of blue jeans pants could be made from the 'Levi's' material used by American Motors for interior trim in Gremlin and Hornet hatchbacks since 1973."

The Levi option for the CJ-5 was available in what AMC described as "the classic blue denim look" or an all-new orange/and blue combination. "Because of the more rugged trail use accorded CJ-5s," AMC explained, "the Jeep's 'Levi's' cloth will be vinyl instead of spun rayon as in the passenger car adaptation."

Included in the Renegade's standard equipment was the 304 V-8, roll bar, forged aluminum wheels with H78 x 15

A 1974 CJ-5 Renegade in Renegade Yellow. At the start of the 1974 model year, Jeep had 17 per cent of the domestic 4-wheel drive market. Since 1970, the average Jeep dealer's annual sales rate has increased from 19 to 46. (Author's collection)

A 1975 CJ-5 Renegade in Mellow Yellow equipped with optional front winch and auxiliary lighting. (Author's collection)

Suburbanite XG Polyglas tires, heavy-duty cooling, Whitco top, wheel lip extensions, passenger safety rail, ash tray, cigar lighter, spare tire lock, and rear-mounted spare tire. A red and white Levi's logo was positioned above the

Jeep lettering on the Renegade's front cowl. The base CJ Jeeps had appropriate CJ-5 or CJ-6 identification below the Jeep lettering.

Available for the Renegade only were two new colors: Renegade Blue and Renegade Orange. The exterior colors offered for the base CJ models for 1975 consisted of these ten colors: Alpine White, Raven Black, Fawn Beige, Mellow Yellow, Red, Copper Metallic, Green Apple, Reef Apple Metallic, Pewter Gray Metallic, and Medium Blue Metallic. With the exception of Green Apple Metallic and Reef Green Metallic, the Renegade was also available in these colors.

Prices of the CJ models and those of the popular options were as per the accompanyng table.

Although the CJ-5 was continued with major improvements – many of which were shared with the new CJ-7 – for 1976 the much more sophisticated CJ-7 was the final rendition of the original CJ design concept.

Model	FADP
CJ-5:	$4099.00
CJ-6:	$4195.00
Option	*Price*
Hardtop:	$399.00
Rear passenger seat:	$89.00
Padded dash:	$39.00
70amp battery:	$18.00
Outside passenger mirror:	$7.50
Free-wheeling front hubs:	$85.40
Rear Trac-Lok diff:	$69.40
H78 x 15 tires:	$84.75
304 V-8:	$125.65
Heavy-duty springs & shocks:	$39.60
AM radio:	$69.00
Lighter & ashtray:	$9.95
Rear seat:	$89.35
Passenger safety rail:	$7.95
Padded instrument panel:	$34.90
Rear spare tire mount:	$9.60

A 1975 CJ-5 Renegade in Renegade Orange. Many elements of the Renegade package – such as forged aluminum styled wheels, 304cu in V-8, and roll bar – were available as individual options for standard CJ-5 and CJ-6 models. (Author's collection)

Renegade/Renegade Orange

These two views illustrate the distinctions between the 1975 Renegade interior and the standard CJ-5 version. The Renegade's Levi's vinyl seats were offered in blue or tan. The standard Wellington vinyl seats were available in black or buff. (Author's collection)

This 1975 Renegade's color, Renegade Blue, was – along with Renegade Orange – exclusive to the Renegade. (Author's collection)

On August 7, 1975 a new age of Jeep history began when American Motors announced that "a new CJ-7 model with optional one-piece removable hard top, automatic transmission and Quadra-Trac drive joins the Jeep line of four-wheel drive vehicles for 1976 ... For the first time in a CJ model, the Jeep enthusiast can enjoy the on-road and back-trail flexibility and performance of Turbo Hydra-Matic transmission and Quadra-Trac full-time four-wheel drive."

AMC had earlier introduced Quadra-Trac in 1973 as an option for the Jeep Wagoneer models with the 360 cu in V-8 and automatic transmission. At that time AMC indirectly referred to the XJ001 by adding that "Jeep was the first US manufacturer to announce full-time four-wheel drive, a development which has been under way for a number of years."

The new 1976 CJ-7 Jeeps on the Toledo, Ohio assembly line. (Author's collection)

Comparing the basic specifications of the CJ-5 and CJ-7 in the accompanying table illustrates their differences.

AMC's statement that the CJ-7 "retains the traditional ruggedness, durability and character of the CJ family," was reminiscent of Kaiser-Willys' assurances to the Jeep community in 1955 that the new CJ-5 didn't compromise established Jeep virtues.

Changing the CJ in any way required both deliberation and caution. "You have to be careful," said Tom Walsh, AMC's Vice President of Product Engineering, in an interview with Ken Kelley of *Pickup, Van and 4WD* magazine, "not to do away with the many things which have made Jeep vehicles so successful. Yet, you have to remember that no matter how successful any product is, you can't stand still. Automotive history includes more than one product that enjoyed outstanding success for a time, but fell from favor because the manufacturer tried to stand still for too long."

Model	CJ-5	CJ-7[a]
Wheelbase:	83.5in	93.5in
Overall length:	138.4in	147.9in
Front/rear overhang:	23.5in/31.4in	23.5in/30.9in
Overall width[b]:	68.6in	68.6in
Overall body width:	59.9in	59.9in
Overall height:		
Open body:	67.6in	67.6in
Soft top:	71.4in	71.3in
Hardtop:	71.3in	70.5in
Cargo floor height:	25.2in	25.1in
Step height:	27.0in	26.1in
Front/rear tread:	51.5in	51.5in
Rear tread:	50.0in	50.0in
Minimum ground clearance:	6.9in	6.9in
Mininum turning diameter:	33.5ft	35.9ft
Leg room:	37.9in	39.1in
Head room:		
Soft top:	39.8in	40.6in
Hardtop:	40.8in	39.9in
Hip room:	55.4in	53.8in
Shoulder room:	55.4in	53.8in
Gross vehicle weight:		
Standard open body or soft top:	3750lb	3750lb
Standard with hardtops:	4150lb	4150lb
Optional[c] with open or soft top:	4150lb	4150lb
Curb weight (open body):	2680lb	2720lb

[a]With the introduction of the CJ-7, the CJ-6 model was no longer offered in US and Canadian markets, though was still available for export sale until 1981. Total production was 50,172
[b]With side-mounted spare
[c]Four-leaf front and rear springs were standard. The optional extra duty suspension included seven-leaf, two-stage front and rear springs, heavy-duty shock absorbers and a front frame tie bar

In the CJ-7's case, early sales indicated that AMC had made the right moves at the right time. Early in 1976 it added 300 workers to the Toledo labor force and increased CJ output to a record daily high of 450 units, approximately 40 per cent of which were CJ-7 models.

The full 1976 Jeep vehicle line. From front to back: CJ-7, Cherokee Chief, Wagoneer, Jeep truck, and CJ-5. (Author's collection)

Just over half of the CJ-7 Jeeps produced were equipped with the Quadra-Trac system, which, with either the 258-six or 304 V-8 engine, automatically provided differentiated power at all times (both forward and reverse) to front and rear axles. Unlike the CJ-7's standard Dana 20 4WD setup, there were no mechanical shift levers beneath or inside the driver compartment. The basic unit consisted of a single range system with a 1:1 ratio silent chain drive transfer case, including a modified type of limited-slip differential with a cone clutch arrangement. This provided controlled bias front to rear, permitting speed variations between the two driving axles for optimum performance. For example, when the CJ-7 was negotiating a turn, all four wheels were pulling in the direction of the turn, providing the maximum tractive force for safe handling. The biasing unit worked continuously, delivering torque to front and rear propeller shafts for the best balance of power to the wheels for all types of driving conditions.

A vacuum-controlled 'lockout' device included in Quadra-Trac protected the biasing unit under extreme conditions such as propeller shaft failure, or in an off-road

The new CJ-7 for 1976. This example has the optional one-piece removable hardtop and roll bar. (Author's collection via American Motors)

A 1976 CJ-7 Renegade in Sunshine Yellow. Both its Levi's vinyl interior and 15 x 7in forged aluminum styled wheels were standard with the Renegade package. (Author's collection)

A 1976 CJ-7 Renegade in Renegade Orange. The rear swing-away spare tire carrier was included in the Renegade package. (Author's collection)

Availability of an automatic transmission and Quadra-Trac for the CJ-7 was an historic first in the history of the CJ Jeep. (Author's collection)

situation where the Jeep was high centered. In such situations, this component deactivated the differential and biasing unit, resulting in a conventional four-wheel drive mode. When a control knob, located in the glove box, was turned fully counterclockwise, the lockout was engaged and a light, indicating four-wheel drive lockout, appeared on the instrument panel.

In addition to the single range Quadra-Trac, an optional self-contained, low range reduction unit – consisting of a planetary gear set giving a 2.57:1 reduction – could be mounted directly to the transfer case at the end of the transmission main shaft. Rather than use a floor-mounted lever, AMC provided a instrument panel-mounted push/pull control to the right of the steering column to operate the clutching mechanism. To engage low range, transmission was placed in neutral at a speed of below 5 miles per hour. When the vehicle came to a stop, the handle was pulled out firmly, To disengage, the transmission was placed in neutral and the lever was pushed in (again, firmly). The lockout feature could be used in both low and high range positions.

The CJ-7's extra cost one-piece polycarbonate, injection molded removable top (a soft top was also optional) was available in either white or black. It was installed along with steel side doors (with a 33.8in opening), roll-down windows, vinyl door trim panels, and a steel lift

gate. The standard CJ-7 tailgate was flush-mounted with double wall, dual latch construction. A rear-mounted, swing-away spare tire carrier was optional.

All 1976 CJ models had larger tail lights with integral backup lights, a new folding windshield, and a new, "more attractive" instrument panel and pad with relocated controls and switches. The radio and speaker were now located in the instrument panel. New floor and dash panels provided increased leg room. The defroster outlets were redesigned for improved air distribution. A new four-bar design for the passenger-side seat (in place of the older fold-and-tumble seat) allowed the entire seat to move forward for easier entry to the rear.

The CJ-7 Jeeps, as well as the CJ-5 models, also had a new frame and suspension, new energy absorbing steering columns with anti-theft ignition and new steering wheels, and standard three-speed transmission.

The bending strength and torsional rigidity of the new frame were greater than those of the older unit, and a key feature was a full box section construction from the front to the fuel tank cross member, and increased depth side rails. Integral with the frame were stronger cross members and a combination cross member skid plate for the engine, transmission and transfer case extending the full width of the vehicle. A standard fuel tank skid plate was also included. The frame's splayed side rail design widened from front to rear, providing a wider suspension foundation. The result, wider-spaced and longer multi-leaf springs, in conjunction with new shock absorbers, improved the Jeep's lateral stability. New body hold-down mounts contributed to a reduction in vibration and noise.

Use of an electric assist choke on six-cylinder engines improved fuel economy and performance. An exhaust gas recirculation system and new fuel return line (also used on the 304 V8) improved hot engine starting.

The new standard three-speed, fully synchronized transmission with heavier gears, shafts and synchronizers was capable of handling higher engine torque loads as well as giving easier, smoother operation. Its ratios – along with those of the optional four-speed manual and the three-speed Hydra-Matic automatic transmission used with Quadra-Trac – were as shown in the table.

Transmission	3-speed manual	4-speed manual	H-M
First gear:	3.00	6.32	2.48
Second gear:	1.83	3.00	1.41
Third gear:	1.0	1.69	1.00
Fourth gear:	–	1.0	–

Both the CJ-5 and CJ-7 had new frames for 1976 with splayed side rails, stronger cross members and a built-in engine/transmission skid plate. (Author's collection)

New options included a tachometer and rally clock, full-foam ⅔rd-⅓rd seat, indoor/outdoor-type carpeting, sports or leather-wrapped steering wheel, and a front stabilizer bar. A new Convenience Group (courtesy lights,

CJ interiors for 1976. Above: The standard CJ-5, the Renegade, and (below) the ⅔rd-⅓rd bench seat option. CJ-5 seats were finished in a Wellington vinyl in black or buff. The back seat was optional for all CJ models. The Renegade's Levi's vinyl bucket seats were offered in blue or tan. The ⅔rd-⅓rd seat was offered in either black or buff Wellington vinyl. (Author's collection)

passenger-side mirror, passenger assist handle, cigar lighter, ashtray and 8in day/night mirror), and a new Decor Group (rocker panel protection molding, instrument panel pad and overlay, and a sports steering wheel) were also offered.

Both the Renegade and 'Levi's' options were continued for the CJ-5 and available for the CJ-7. Added to the Renegade package were courtesy lights (mounted under the dash), an 8in day/night mirror, sports steering wheel, instrument panel overlay, and bright rocker panel protection between the front and rear wheel wells. Two hood tape combinations were available for the Renegade: blue with orange and white accents, or gold with brown and white accents. 'Levi's' seat trim in blue or tan with matching instrument panel pad and sun visors was included. The 'Levi's' trim was also offered as a separate option on models without the Renegade package.

AMC seemed to be taking a risk by entering the new CJ-7 in the highly visible and well publicized Press-On-Regardless (POR) Rally of November 7-9, 1975, but driver Gene Henderson and navigator Ken Pogue had won back-to-back national championships in the Sports Car Club of America's Professional Rallye Series in 1973 and 1974 with a Jeep Cherokee, and in 1972 they had won the POR with a Jeep Wagoneer. Henderson's rallying friends and competitors laughed when he headed a team of two Wagoneers in the 1200-plus mile POR, then North America's only World Championship rally. Previously, this

northern Michigan event had been dominated by small sports cars. Taking his cue from the naysayers, Henderson publicly named the two Jeeps 'Moby Dick I' and 'Moby Dick II.' The cynics were silenced when Henderson and Pogue won the POR and the second Wagoneer, teamed by Erhard Dahm and Jim Callon, finished third.

Henderson retired from competition at the end of the 1974 season but the challenge of preparing and competing with the CJ-7 proved too appealing to resist. Asked to explain his change of plans, he explained "It's taking an unlikely vehicle and making it a winner. You shouldn't be able to beat sports cars with a Wagoneer, but we did then again with the Jeep Cherokee."

Preparing the CJ-7 for its POR debut involved about 400 skilled man hours and the use of dozens of standard and heavy-duty parts. "The CJ-7 Jeep is a new car for us," explained Henderson, "and we are using the proven AMC 360 cubic inch V-8 to give it the performance required for this tough rally ... It possesses a large amount of flexibility. When running a rally of 1000 to 1500 miles you can't have an engine in a high state of tune, because it won't stay that way. The flexibility is needed because we run from 2000rpm up to 6500rpm."

The engine was clearanced, blue-printed and carefully balanced. It was equipped with needle bearings,

This 1976 CJ-7 has the redesigned soft top with both improved vision and larger door openings. If ordered with the standard interior, it was available in black or white. For Jeeps with the Levi's interior color choices were tan or blue. (Author's collection)

a Crane camshaft, shot-peened connecting rods, a Holley carburetor, and an Edelbrock high rise manifold.

The CJ-7's Quadra-Trac full-time 4WD system was expected to handle the tasks of pulling the Jeep out of the mud and maintain traction on the ice and snow-covered sections of the rally. But Henderson's previous experience guaranteed that he would not leave well enough alone. "We have beefed up the CJ-7's suspension," he noted, "so that these 4000 pound vehicles can stand flying three and four feet off the ground, bounce in and out of frozen ruts at 100 miles an hour, straddle boulders and bounce off trees, as they do in the POR." With those conditions in mind, the CJ-7's standard fuel tank skid plate was augmented by a special skid plate that extended the Jeep's full width to provide protection for the engine and transfer case.

Suspension changes included the use of eight heavy-duty Monroe shock absorbers; two at each wheel. Bendix metallic disc brakes were installed at all wheels. The brake system used a silicone brake fluid with a higher boiling point that Henderson, in 1972, had helped Dow chemists

develop. Henderson graphically described the effect previous rallies had upon the brakes: "The brakes got so hot they annealed to the return springs, and the springs stretched out like baling wire."

For use in the POR, the CJ-7's Turbo Hydra-Matic transmission was modified to provide quicker downshifts and higher rpm upshifts. Additional alteration included installation of a 32gal Aero-Tec fuel cell, Stewart-Warner dual fuel pumps, full Stewart-Warner instrumentation, a heavy-duty roll bar, CBIE driving lights and Goodyear L78 x 15 Suburban six-ply tires with safety inner liners. An intercom system was built into the driver's and navigator's safety helmets.

Although Henderson had never prepared – or even driven – a CJ-7 before preparation for the POR began, he was confident it could be a winner of what AMC described as "America's oldest, richest, longest and meanest car rally."

Although, ultimately, the CJ-7 wasn't the winner, as it went out in the rally's early stages with a sheared distributor drive, Henderson and Poque ended the season on a high note with a second place finish in the final event of the 1975 Pro-Rally Series, the December 6-7 El Diablo Rally. The CJ-7 won the same number of stages (seven) as the winning Volvo 142, but was 1.8 minutes behind the Swedish car at the finish.

The production model CJ-7 and CJ-5 were available in twelve body colors for 1976: Sand Tan, Dark Cocoa Metallic, Sunshine Yellow, Firecracker Red, Brilliant Blue, Nautical Blue, Medium Blue Metallic, Reef Green Metallic, Pewter Gray Metallic, Renegade Orange, Classic Black and Alpine White. The first six listed were new for 1976.

In direct contrast with what American Motors described as an "unexpected, substantial decline" in sales of its Gremlin and Hornet passenger cars was the increasing popularity of the Jeep line. In the first three months of 1976 domestic Jeep retail sales were a record 20,581 units, up from 12,187 in 1975. In its 1976 annual report, AMC told shareholders that: "Jeep continues as a real success

The Gene Henderson-prepared CJ-7 being tested prior to the 1975 Press-On-Regardless Rally.
(Author's collection)

The Jeep CJ-7 crew for the 1975 Press-On-Regardless Rally. Left: Gene Henderson, driver; right: Ken Pogue, navigator. (Author's collection)

An artist's colorful depiction of Henderson and Pogue in the midst of the 1975 POR. (Author's collection)

story. Retail sales in the US and Canada were a record 95,718 units in 1976, up from 67,771 in 1975. In the past six years, production has increased 10 times, from 175 units a day to 600."

These developments affected the composition of AMC's dealer network. As of September 30, 1976, there were 1713 AMC dealers in the US, compared with 1797 the year before. "On the Jeep," AMC reported, "dealers had an excellent year, and the number of dealerships increased from 1531 to 1608 during 1976. More importantly, the number selling both AMC and Jeep products climbed from 910 to 1049."

In announcing the 1977 Jeep on September 1, 1976, AMC noted that: "in each of the seven model years since acquisition of Jeep Corporation, the American Motors subsidiary has made significant improvements and refinements in its Jeep vehicles that have strengthened and broadened their appeal."

Both the CJ-5 and CJ-7 had stronger frames with full, rather than the partial box section side rails of 1976. The fuel tank was now enclosed in a protective material, and the rear body panels were strengthened.

Front disc brakes, with 11.75in rotors, in either manual or vacuum assist form replaced power drum brakes as options for all CJs. Remaining as standard were 11 x 2in

drums, front and rear. New wide wheels and tires were also optional. To accommodate these developments, the front axle and wheel spindles were upgraded. For the first time the CJ Jeeps were available with factory air conditioning as well as a center console. To make room for the air conditioning air ducts, the ashtray was moved to the upper portion of the dash. All models could be fitted with indoor/outdoor carpeting. Also introduced in 1977 was a "soft feel" molded rubber sports steering wheel, available either as a separate option or as part of the Decor Group. A six-way tilt steering wheel was a new option for CJ-7s equipped with both manual and automatic transmission.

The Renegade package, with several changes, remained available for both CJ models. For 1977 new 9.00 x 15 Tracker A/T raised white letter tires replaced the H78x15 whitewalls used previously. Replacing the forged aluminum wheels of earlier years were 8in wide, white painted, styled steel wheels with a red pinstripe. A new hood tape striping in either gold or blue was included. The CJ-7 Renegade continued to include a rear swing-away spare tire carrier. All CJ-7s were again available with the optional one-piece removable top, installation of which was accomplished in less than two minutes. All CJ models had optional soft tops in black or white, and with Levi's trim, in Levi's blue or tan.

The ratios of the CJ's optional 4-speed manual transmission (available only with the Dana 20 manual 4-wheel drive system and the 258cid 6-cylinder engine) were changed to make them common with other Jeep vehicles (see table).

AMC reported that this change "will give the CJ increased pulling power and engine braking – especially desirable for mountain driving or rough off-road terrain."

As a result of the various technical changes made for 1977, the curb weight of the CJ-7 slightly reduced from 2720lb to 2701lb.

For 1977 twelve body colors were offered, including five new ones: Autumn Red Metallic, Loden Green Metallic, Midnight Blue Metallic, Mocha Brown Metallic and Tawny Orange. Other existing colors included Alpine White, Brilliant Blue, Classic Black, Firecracker Red, Pewter Gray Metallic, Sand Tan and Sunshine Yellow.

The CJ-7's availability with Quadra-Trac and Hydra-matic, growing popularity of the Renegade package (25 per cent of all CJ-5 and CJ-7 models produced in 1977 were Renegades), plus increased output at Toledo, enabled the Jeep Corporation to repeatedly set new production and sales records in 1977. Total Jeep vehicle sales in the US and Canada were a record 153,000 units. At year's end, Jeep vehicle sales had risen over year-ago periods for 37 consecutive months.

The CJ model's popularity had received an added shot of adrenalin with the introduction of the Golden Eagle package in early 1977. AMC described this option, available for CJ-5 and CJ-7 models with soft tops, as: "a

Gear	1976 trans	1977 trans
First:	4.02	6.32
Second:	2.41	3.00
Third:	1.41	1.69
Fourth:	1.00	1.00
Reverse:	4.73	7.44

A 1977 CJ-7 Renegade. (Courtesy DaimlerChrysler Media Services)

The Golden Eagle package for the CJ-5 was introduced in early 1977. (Author's collection)

new dimension in the Jeep line ... an exciting yet distinctive vehicle." Jeep distributors were told by C N Busch, Jeep's Director of Marketing Services, that "You will recognize this as a 'golden' opportunity to create more enthusiasm for Jeep vehicles. The 'Golden Eagle' should be used to capture potential customer's interest and stimulate all Jeep sales."

The Golden Eagle content consisted of these items:
– Thrush Brown exterior color
– Gold, black and white eagle hood decal
– Golden Eagle name on hood side (black lettering edged in gold)
– Gold, black and white pinstriping on body side and front fender
– Limited edition decal on grille panel
– Gold stripe on grille panel
– 15in x 8in styled wheels (painted gold with black accent stripe)

Included in the Golden Eagle package were these regular production options:
– 9-15 Tracker RWL tires
– Rear-mounted spare tire
– Levi's tan vinyl soft top
– Levi's tan interior
– Levi's tan instrument panel pad
– Roll bar
– Wheel lip extensions
– Spare tire lock
– Convenience Group
– Decor Group (black anodized rocker molding)
– Tachometer and clock
– Brown carpeting

Options in conflict with Base Golden Eagle package*:
– Exterior colors
– Interior trims
– Hardtop options
– Optional tires
– Wheel covers
– Side mounted spare
*Except for the items listed, the Golden Eagle could be ordered with all regular production options

The Golden Eagle program originated as a limited edition basis with a one-time production run scheduled for January 1977. But by early April 1977, Toledo Plant Manager David J McFeggan Jr had announced that the first order for 2000 Golden Eagles had been filled and production was under way of another 2000 units. The Jeep's popularity in foreign markets was

equally impressive with unit sales increasing 44 per cent over 1976. Total international Jeep volume grew from 26,500 units in 1976 to 30,300 units in 1977.

The Jeep's worldwide popularity was easily explained by AMC: "Jeep is successful because the company has adopted a range of choices for customers – not just vehicle forms, but a growing list of comfort, convenience and appearance options. Jeep buyers increasingly want style and individuality to go with toughness and durability. Their vehicles are used for recreation and work, and as multi-purpose family transportation."

To enable Jeep to take full advantage of the increasing popularity of four-wheel drive vehicles around the world, AMC's International Operations concentrated its efforts in four areas: expansion of existing markets, cultivation of new ones, development of new models for specific needs, and participation in joint venture manufacturing operations. These objectives led to an agreement to build Jeep vehicles in Egypt in 1977 at a plant which was to have the capacity to produce 10,000 to 12,000 vehicles annually when completed in 1981.

Other countries, specifically identified by AMC, where the Jeep was particularly popular were Venezuela and Iran. In the former, AMC reported that the Wagoneer and

An artist's rendering of the Jeepster II, a concept design shown to AMC shareholders in early 1978 and later displayed at many auto shows around the US. It had a 100 inch wheelbase, a built-in roll bar, and fiberglass detachable doors. It reputedly could be powered by either 4-cylinder turbo-charged gasoline or diesel engines. (Author's collection)

CJ models commanded a significant share of the market and that "a major expansion of output of the assembly plant at Tejerias is under way to better match production capacity with increasing demand. The Venezuelan market is growing, reflecting the country's large petroleum income and a growing middle class." In Iran, sales had increased to the point where Jeep vehicles commanded nearly 75 per cent of the four-wheel drive market.

The 1977 CJ Jeeps and their options were priced as per the accompanying table.

AMC President Gerald Meyers' February 1978 remarks that "It may not be obvious, but if you take the time to look you can see they're different than they were before and better. This shows what can be done with product even if there's not a lot of money to throw around for retooling." were backed up by many revisions to and new features for the 1978 CJ Jeep.

All CJs had a completely redesigned heater and ventilation system with improved heat distribution (especially to the rear), higher defroster temperature, increased air flow rate and improved outside fresh air ventilation. A new ambient air intake system lowered engine temperature and improved engine efficiency.

Standard equipment that was previously optional included manual front disc brakes, ashtray and cigar lighter, passenger assist handle, passenger-side exterior mirror, and H78 Suburbanite XG fiberglass-belted tires. A new under hood light became part of the Convenience

Model	FADP*
CJ-5 (open body):	$4399
CJ-7 (open body):	$4499
*Factory advertised delivered price	
Option	Price
258 engine:	$73
304 engine:	$140
4-speed manual transmission:	$144
Turbo-Hydra-matic/Quadra-Trac (high range):	$345
Turbo-Hydra-matic/Quadra-Trac (high and low range):	$482
Power steering:	$166
Power disc brakes:	$73
Manual disc brakes:	$53
Air conditioning:	$499
AM radio:	$73
Renegade package:	$799
Extra duty suspension package:	$63
Front stabilizer bar:	$27
Convenience Group:	$41
High altitude package:	$50
Soft top:	$239
Levi's soft top:	$275
Hardtop with doors (CJ-7)	$525
Trac-Lok rear differential:	$77
Free-wheeling hubs:	$95
Heavy-duty cooling system:	$34
Heavy-duty battery:	$31
Heavy-duty alternator:	$40
Tilt steering wheel:	$68
Center console:	$49
Swing-away spare tire:	$52
Tachometer and rally clock:	$73
Roll bar:	$66
Body side step:	$19
Removable carpet (front and rear):	$69
Wheel covers:	$37
Vinyl bucket seats with Levi's trim:	$69
Vinyl bench seat:	$33
Rear seat:	$100

A 1978 CJ-5 in Sunshine Yellow. (Author's collection)

A 1978 CJ-7 Golden Eagle. The Golden Eagle package was now offered in a choice of seven colors. (Author's collection)

Group. Flax replaced Buff as the color for seats and door panels.

Fourteen body colors were offered, including these three new ones: Sun Orange, Golden Ginger Metallic and Captain Blue Metallic. Existing colors included Alpine White, Loden Green Metallic, Mocha Brown Metallic, Autumn Red Metallic, Oak leaf Brown, Brilliant Blue, Classic Black, Firecracker Red, Pewter Gray Metallic, San Tan and Sunshine Yellow. The $1249 Golden Eagle package was offered in a wider choice of colors (Oak Leaf Brown, Golden Ginger Metallic, Mocha Brown Metallic, Loden Green Metallic, Sand Tan, Alpine White and Classic Black).

With domestic wholesale sales of all Jeeps models in the three months

During 1978 AMC converted its Brampton, Ontario plant from passenger car to Jeep production, adding – it explained – "important capacity to supplement output at the main Jeep plant in Toledo, Ohio." At a 1979 Geneva Auto Show press conference, AMC President Paul Tippett, Jr said this would increase Jeep capacity by about 50,000 units. During 1979 gasoline shortages forced AMC to severely cut Jeep production at Toledo and Brampton. (Author's collection)

Below: A 1979 CJ-7 equipped with the Renegade Package in Russet Metallic. (Author's collection)

Ohio Governor James A Rhodes was invited to drive the 150,000th Jeep vehicle built in 1978, a Firecracker Red CJ-7 Renegade, from the Toledo assembly line. His passenger was AMC President Gerald Meyers. (Author's collection)

ending December 31, 1977 a record 31,328 units (up from 26,689 the year before), AMC increased 1978 Jeep production from 630 to 660 units per day beginning mid-February. AMC also scheduled Saturday overtime at the Toledo plant for a seven week period through March 18, 1978.

Worldwide, the news about Jeep sales was also very positive. "Jeep has set records for two years in a row," said AMC President Meyers in February 1978. "We sold 150,000 Jeep vehicles throughout the world in 1977, and will probably go to 170,000

A 1979 CJ-5 equipped with the Golden Eagle Package in Alpaca Brown Metallic and tan denim vinyl soft top. Its 8 inch painted spoke wheels were standard. (Author's collection)

in the current year. We are going to build on our Jeep success with product again the hero. We'll be shouting about Jeep vehicles – and selling them."

American Motor's awareness of the potential of the international market led to the introduction in 1978 of 4-cylinder diesel powered CJ models for Europe, Latin America and Asia. Selected as the power plant for these Jeeps was the 2.7 liter, 4-cylinder Perkins engine that, as noted in Chapter Six, had been installed in a few CJ-5 Jeeps in the mid-sixties. This engine's specification was as per the table.

Displacement:	2.71 liters (164.9cu in)
Bore x stroke:	92 mm x 101mm (3.62in x 4.0in)
Horsepower:	70@3600rpm
Torque:	115lb/ft@2050rpm
Compression ratio:	20:1
Oil capacity with cooler:	11.4 liters
Cooling system capacity:	11.4 liters

Describing the combination of the CJ's legendary toughness and the Perkins engine's reputation for longevity as "A marriage made in hell," Jeep explained that "When we built the new Jeep CJ Diesel, we wanted a power plant as tough and dependable as the Jeep CJ chassis. We found it: a 2.7 liter 4-cylinder diesel from Perkins, the world's largest manufacturer of diesel engines. This engine incorporates the most advanced engineering features and represents state-of-the-art design in lightweight diesels."

The Perkins engine's credentials included many impressive achievements. Its durability had been demonstrated by numerous 1000-hour tests, including one run at full speed under full load without a failure of any kind. It was designed to complete 240,000km (approximately 150,000 miles) before a major overhaul was required. Its pistons were oil-cooled and had controlled expansion skirts to maintain correct piston position under

a wide range of loads and engine speeds. Armored top piston ring grooves were specified, as was an induction hardened, five main bearing crankshaft. Aside from routine oil and filter changes, the only other recommended maintenance for the diesel engine consisted of valve clearance adjustments every 15,000km and injector adjustment every 90,000km.

The results of tests conducted under a wide range of conditions indicated that the fuel consumption of a diesel-engined CJ was between forty and fifty per cent less than the same CJ equipped with a gasoline engine. The outcome of durability tests conducted in the American southwest were equally impressive. "In the desert outside Yuma, Arizona," reported AMC, "daytime temperatures often reach 48 degrees C (118 degrees F). The air is filled

This Saxon Yellow 1979 CJ-7 has the optional injection molded hardtop. (Author's collection)

A view of the dash of a 1979 CJ-7 equipped with Turbo-Hydramatic and Quadra-Trac. (Author's collection)

with abrasive dust so fine that it hangs in the air for hours. Here, we tested the new Jeep CJ Diesel. Up winding roads, down sheer canyons, through deep sand, along boulder-strewn river beds. Then on to the test track for hours at sustained speeds from 120 to 136kph. Up and down thirty per cent grades to strain the drive train and through acceleration/deceleration courses to test the transmission and clutch. When we were done, we were satisfied that the new Jeep CJ Diesel was a 4-wheel drive vehicle worthy of the Jeep name."

The Perkins CJ was marketed to a wide variety of potential customers. AMC's Jeep Corporation, which handled international Jeep sales, reported that "The new Jeep CJ Diesels are winning a new place in construction, mining, lumbering, agriculture, and in personal usage round the world."

Perkins was the world's largest manufacturer of diesel engines and in addition to Jeep dealers in 130 countries, the CJ Diesels were also backed by over 2000 Perkins diesel dealers and distributors worldwide.

The Diesel CJ was available in CJ-5, CJ-6 and CJ-7 forms. All three shared the specifications shown in the table on page 172.

Along with the other Jeep models, both the CJ-5 and CJ-7 had improved fuel economy ratings for 1979. A weight reduction of approximately 80lb was achieved in both models, which were required to meet a 1979 federal standard of 15.8mpg. All Jeeps were also equipped with a single catalytic converter to satisfy federal emissions standards.

The Renegade package now included a new stripe design with varying widths in three graduated shades of either blue or orange with gold borders. The Golden Eagle package was continued for 1979.

A new convertible vinyl soft top with cotton polyester fabric backing

was offered for both the CJ-5 and CJ-7. This incorporated significant design improvements including better fit, greater strength and increased leak resistance. Blue, black, white, and tan colors were offered.

The 258-cid 6-cylinder with a 2bbl carburetor was the CJ's standard engine, though in 1978 it had been standard only for vehicles sold in California. The 2bbl 304cid V-8 remained optional. A four-speed manual transmission with an upgraded shift tower and a new shift pattern was optional for CJ-5s with the 6-cylinder engine and for CJ-7s with the 304 V-8.

A moon roof was optional for the 1979 CJ-7 hardtop. (Author's collection)

A 1979 CJ-7 Levi's edition owned by Rick and Melanie West. (Courtesy Bob Christy)

Transmission:	Model T-1250, 3-speed synchronized
Ratios:	
First:	2.990
Second:	1.750
Third:	1.00
Reverse:	3.170
Optional:	

'3 plus 1' transmission (three synchronized road gears plus one extra duty low)	
Ratios:	
Low:	6.32
First:	3.09
Second:	1.59
Third:	1.00
Reverse:	7.44
Clutch:	Single dry plate, diaphragm spring type
Diameter:	27.9cm (11in)
Transfer case:	Dual range (2.03 and 1.0:1)
Axle ratios:	4.09:1, front & rear

Prices of the 1978 CJ Jeeps and those of selected options were as follows:

Model	FADP*
CJ-5 (open body):	$5095
CJ-7 (open body):	$5195

Factory advertised delivered price

Option	Price
Golden Eagle package:	$1249
Renegade package:	$799
Hardtop:	$610
Tachometer and clock:	$77
Rear bench seat:	$106
258 engine (standard in California):	$77
304 engine:	$186
4-speed manual trans. (258 engine):	$153
Turbo Hydra-matic/Quadra-Trac:	$366
Turbo Hydra-matic/Quadra-Trac (high and low range):	$511
Free-wheeling hubs:	$101
Limited slip rear differential:	$82
Power steering:	$176
Power brakes:	$73
Extra duty suspension:	$85
Front stabilizer bar:	$29

Fourteen body colors, including twelve that were new, were offered for the 1979 CJ models (see table).

Color	All models & Renegade package	Golden Eagle package
	Availability	
Olympic White*	X	X
Morocco Buff*	X	X
Wedgewood Blue*	X	NA
Cumberland Green Metallic*	X	X
Sable Brown Metallic*	X	X
Russet Metallic*	X	X
Arrowhead Silver Metallic*	X	NA
Alpaca Brown Metallic*	X	X
Saxon Yellow*	X	NA
Firecracker Red	X	NA
Classic Black	X	X
Ensign Blue*	X	NA
Mandarin Orange*	X	NA

***New for 1979**

The 1979 Silver Anniversary CJ-5 in its attractive Quick Silver finish, chrome 15 x 8in wheels, and special silver-toned Renegade stripes. (Author's collection)

The 1979 Silver Anniversary CJ-5 had this commemorative crest positioned on its instrument panel. (Author's collection)

Jeep (UK) Limited marketed a wide range of rhd Jeep products, including the CJ-6 and CJ-7 models. The 1979 CJ7 Renegade was equipped with automatic transmission, the 4.2 liter 6-cylinder engine and Quadra-Trac. With a soft top, it retailed for £7079.95; with hardtop for £7818.85. (Author's collection)

On December 1, 1978 five CJ-7 Jeeps began the "Expedicion De Las Americas", a venture starting at Punta Arenas Chile, the southernmost tip of South America, and ending some 20,000 miles later at Prudhoe Bay in northernmost Alaska in April. The most difficult part of this ambitious and risky endeavour (since failure was entirely possible) involved crossing a 250 mile section of Central American jungle and swamp known as the Darien Gap. In 1978 this stretch of land was the last obstacle preventing the Pan-American highway from linking North and South America.

The only previous successful crossing of the Darien Gap had been accomplished in 1972 by a British Army unit of two hundred men and two Land Rovers. It had taken them over three months to complete the passage.

The leader of the CJ-7 expedition was 52 year old Mark Smith, who portrayed himself as a 'Jack of all trades.' He had previously worked as a logger, airport manager, real estate broker, and building contractor. To Jeep enthusiasts, Smith was far better known as part of a group of residents of Georgetown, California who launched the first Jeepers' Jamboree across the Sierra Nevada Mountains over the Rubicon Trail in 1953.

The staff of the 1978 expedition consisted of sixty people, with seventeen members crossing the Gap in the five CJ-7s. A Jeep Cherokee was also involved, but was shipped around the Gap; a J-20 Jeep truck was used on portions of the trip. Due to the unavailability of unleaded gasoline in South America, the expedition obtained permission to have the vehicles converted to use regular gas. All of the CJ-7 Jeeps were equipped with Johnson roll bars, luggage racks, brush guards, 8000lb Ramsey winches, Warn locking hubs, CB radios, and oversized Wrangler R/T tires mounted on Cragar wheels. They had 6-cylinder, 258cid engines and 4-speed manual transmissions. The expedition also had an array of specialized equipment including a set of customized aluminum 'ladders' for spanning ditches, climbing almost vertical banks, and improving traction in the mud and mire of the swamps.

When the Jeeps entered the Darien Gap, construction had begun on a highway that would end its isolation. Undoubtedly, this aided the Jeep expedition in completing the crossing in 30 days, some 14 days less than had been planned, since it was able to make use of about 70 miles of partially-cleared right-of-way for the new highway. Nonetheless, it was still an impressive achievement, involving the crossing of nearly eighty miles of swamp and one hundred miles of jungle, through which narrow paths had to be cut for the Jeeps by indigenous people using machetes. "One day," recalled Smith, "we moved only 50 feet in nine hours. Other days we covered as many as 10 or 11 miles."

Smith had plenty of praise for his crew who performed their tasks in 100 degree heat and 95 per cent humidity. "Never a harsh word was spoken," he recollected, "even though conditions were almost unbearable at times." In spite of an abundant insect population, there were no illnesses during the journey through the Gap. "We started a '100 Club' when we entered the Gap," Smith said. "To qualify for membership, you had to be able to count at least 100 bites on your body. Everybody was a member by the third or fourth day." Shortly after the five red Jeeps emerged from the jungle, Smith had 'Darien Conquistador' painted in very large letters on their hoods.

The 1979 model year began with new AMC President Paul Tippett Jr predicting that Jeep production would double in three years. AMC had already switched over its Brampton, Ontario facility to Jeep production, and was planning to spend over $30 million to convert part of its Kenosha, Wisconsin plant to Jeep production also. Speaking at the 1979 Geneva Auto Show in February 1979, Tippett explained that: "We have a project going that will add 50 per cent to the output of our main Jeep plant in Toledo by 1981.

"Put it together and our output of Jeep vehicles will have increased from about 170,000 units a year in 1978 to more than 350,000 – and in just three years.

"All of this," explained Tippett, "is big change, but it's a bold response to what's happening. The four-wheel drive market in the US and Canada will go over a million units in 1978. It was 200,000 a few years ago. And this is just the beginning. Basic lifestyle changes are behind this phenomenon, so it isn't going to stop ... The Jeep product

Jeep UK identified the standard CJ-7 as the 'Basic Model.' Retail price of the soft top was £5535.97. The hardtop version listed for £6323.85. The CJ-6, available as a soft top, was priced at £5576.69.
(Author's collection)

The 1979 CJ-7 Golden Eagle for the UK market had the same power and drive train as the Renegade. The distributor noted that it had "a customized trim that can make the interior like a luxury saloon." Its exterior "makes it strikingly different from any other 4-wheel drive vehicle – even another Jeep." Golden Eagle CJ-7 prices were identical to those of its Renegade comtemporaries. (Author's collection)

line is the best known in the world, and we think we're the best in the world and we're going to keep it that way."

This momentum continued into early 1979. Included in AMC's announcement of the results of its second fiscal quarter, ending on March 31, was news that Jeep sales had risen more than 40 per cent over a year earlier. This upward sales trend was reversed in mid-1979 when events in the Middle East and subsequent governmental reactions led to the destabilization of gasoline supply in the US.

On December 1, 1978 an expedition of five CJ-7 Jeeps, began the Expedition De Las Americas, a two continent, two hemisphere trek of 20,000 miles, from Punta Arenas at the southernmost tip of South America to Prudhoe Bay in northernmost Alaska. The leader of the adventure was 53 year old Mark Smith, a self-styled jack-of-all-trades and creator of the Jeepers Jamboree. (Author's collection)

The crews of the CJ-7 Jeeps made good use of the Ramsey winches in their 30-day passage through the Darien Gap. Mark Smith said the group never would have conquered the Gap without winches that made it possible to navigate stretches such as the river seen here. (Author's collection)

Almost lost from view is one of the five CJ-7 Jeeps used to cross the Darien Gap. (Author's collection)

Just another day of work in the Darien Gap for two members of Mark Smith's Expedition De Las Americas. American Motors' claim that the CJ-7 was "undaunted by Darien!" failed to give the crew a fair share of the credit for the Jeep's success. (Author's collection)

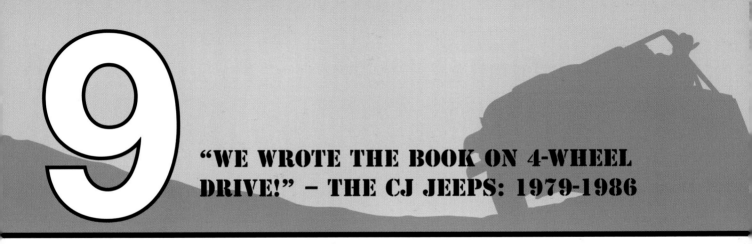

9

"WE WROTE THE BOOK ON 4-WHEEL DRIVE!" – THE CJ JEEPS: 1979-1986

Long queues at gas stations and rapid increases in the price of gasoline had a sudden and negative impact on AMC's ambitions for the Jeep.

In late May 1979, AMC announced it had "temporarily delayed" partial conversion to Jeep production of the Kenosha plant. Earlier, AMC had announced that Jeep sales had fallen fifteen per cent in April, halting months of consecutive sales increases. More bad news came in the form of AMC scheduling three one-week closures and personnel layoffs at the Toledo plant to keep Jeep inventories under control. The first layoff involved 3700 of the plant's 6100 hourly employees.

By early May, as Jeep sales declined further still from their April level, *The Wall Street Journal* of May 6, 1979 quoted one AMC/Jeep salesman as saying that "there's just no showroom traffic for anything that doesn't get 30 miles per gallon." His dealership attempted to move Jeeps off its lot by selling them to other dealers at cost. In late June AMC announced further cutbacks.

For the 1979 calendar year Jeep vehicle sales were 140,431, compared to 161, 912 in 1978. Yet sales of CJ models, when measured against its competitors, enabled it to remain at the top of the small utility vehicle class, as the accompanying table shows.

In the midst of this sales downturn, in May 1979 a limited edition Silver Anniversary CJ-5 was introduced in recognition of the CJ-5's 25th birthday. The package included the following features:

A 1980 CJ-7 Renegade in Cardinal Red with Orange/Gold hood and body stripes and optional roll bar. A soft-feel sports steering wheel was added to the Renegade package for 1980. (Author's collection)

Vehicle	1979 calendar year sales
Jeep CJ	74,878
Ford Bronco	69,724
Chevy Blazer/GMC Jimmy	62,185
International Scout/Traveler	24,269
Dodge Ramcharger	18,863

– Quicksilver Metallic paint
– Chrome 15 x 8in spoked style wheels
– Black vinyl soft top
– Renegade stripes in special silver tones
– Seat trim (buckets and rear) in black vinyl with silver thread contrast switching and silver buttons

This 1980 CJ-7 is equipped with the new-for-1980 Laredo option. Seen in this view are the package's standard 15 x 8in steel chrome plated wheels, 9R-15 Goodyear Wrangler tires, and chrome front bumpers. Contrasting with its Classic Black finish is special Silver striping. This CJ-7 also has dealer installed driving lights. (Author's collection)

– Unique 25th Anniversary panel crest

Regular options applied to the package included L78 x 15 Tracker PG tires (9 x 15 Tracker AT tires were optional), wheelip extensions, black anodized rocker panel moldings, roll bar, spare tire lock, Convenience Group, Decor Group, tachometer and clock, full gray carpeting, and a center console.

Silver Anniversary CJ-5s were also available with all CJ options that did not conflict with the package's content.

A 1980 CJ-5 with the Laredo package in Dark Brown Metallic and Gold striping. The high-back front bucket seats and rear seat were standard Laredo features. The high-back seats were also available in Renegade and Golden Eagle models. The roll bar was an option. (Author's collection)

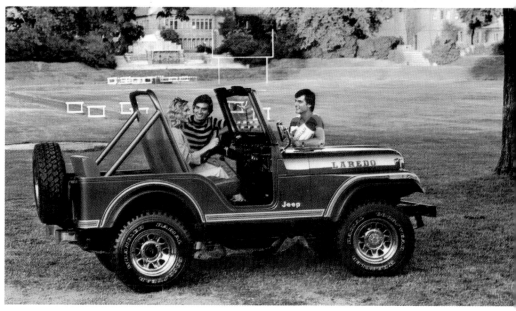

A 1980 CJ-5 Renegade in Saxon Yellow equipped with a dealer installed Sun Bonnet top. The hood and body stripes are Blue/Gold. (Author's collection)

AMC provided its dealers with a history lesson and plenty of promotional suggestions to make the most of the occasion. Dealers were told that George Marshall had made his famous appraisal of the Jeep as "America's greatest contribution to modern war" only after "the 1941 Willys MA had distinguished itself in the sands of Africa, mountains of Italy, in South Pacific jungles and remote outposts where US servicemen and their allies were stationed." AMC's copywriters may have been overly generously in their depiction of the MA's wartime activities at the expense of the far more numerous MB, but most dealers got the idea!

Turning to the postwar success of the CJ-models, AMC explained that "production of a peacetime Jeep for the civilian market began as soon as war ended in 1945. Military equipment was discarded in favor of snow plows, post hole diggers, trenchers, etc. And thousands of 'Universal' CJ-2A Jeeps were sold to farmers and other businessmen. A more refined vehicle – the CJ-3A Jeep – was successfully introduced in 1950."

AMC defined the introduction of the CJ-5 in 1954 as a pivotal moment in Jeep history: "The transition from the familiar olive drab utility vehicle of the war years to a colorful sports utility vehicle was complete. Previously impossible tasks in remote off-road areas were performed with ease with the help of the incomparable CJ-5. And its ruggedness, reliability and unparalleled 4-wheel drive performance have made it the standard in sports utility vehicles the world over."

To make the most of the limited supply of Silver Anniversary models, AMC suggested that dealers order other Jeeps in Arrowhead Silver Metallic to tie in with the Silver Anniversary campaign that could include a special "Silver Preview" evening for local media representatives.

Also proposed was the sponsorship of an "Antique Jeep Rally" with prizes for the oldest CJ-5 in the best condition. Another idea suggested by AMC was to offer a Silver Anniversary CJ-5 to local dignitaries as a courtesy car.

For its part, AMC – ensuring that Jeep enthusiasts learned of the Silver Anniversary model – circulated an ad featuring a large illustration of the new CJ-5, reading "25 and goin' strong! That's our rugged CJ-5. And to celebrate we've created a limited edition that'll knock you out! Just listen to these one-of-a-kind features: slick Quicksilver Metallic finish; racy silver-toned Renegade accent striping; black soft top, black vinyl buckets and bold silver accents. And if that isn't enough, a dashboard plaque commemorating the occasion. So, what're you waiting for? An anniversary like this only comes around once every 25 years! The Silver Anniversary CJ-5 at your Jeep dealer now!"

Prices of the 1979 CJ Jeeps and selected options were as shown in the accompanying table.

For the 1980 model year both CJ-5 and CJ-7 were

Model	FADP
CJ-5 (open body):	$5488
CJ-7 (open body):	$5732
Option	Price
Goodyear Tracker A-T 9 x15 tires:	$50.00
Renegade package:	$849.00
Golden Eagle package:	$1158.00
Free-running front hubs:	$107.00
4-speed transmission:	$161.00
Draw bar:	$37.00
Power steering:	$188.00
Power front disc brakes:	$70.00
Tilt steering wheel:	$76.00
AM radio:	$91.00
Heavy-duty cooling:	$41.00
Steering damper:	$12.00
Front stabilizer bar:	$31.00
Front and rear carpeting:	$77.00
Soft top:	$307.00
Hardtop (CJ-7):	$656.00

This Laredo is equipped with a new CJ-7 option for 1980: steel doors with roll-up windows in combination with a soft top. All CJ-7 Jeeps for 1980 had a standard swing-away spare tire mount.

Jeep

Beginning with the 1980 model year, Pontiac supplied this 2.5 liter, 4-cylinder engine to AMC for use in the CJ-5 and CJ-7. (Author's collection)

179

available with a 2.5 liter, 4-cylinder 'Hurricane' supplied by the Pontiac division of General Motors Corporation. Agreement to go with this unit had been announced by AMC in mid-January 1978, and the following month AMC Chairman Roy Chapin and AMC President Gerald Meyers presented the idea's rationale to stockholders. "The decision to purchase the 4-cylinder 2.5 liter engine from General Motors is," they said, "a lower investment solution in a time of major capital demand. Another important consideration is the need for a substantial volume of smaller engines for both future car and Jeep vehicle programs in response to new fuel mileage requirements."

Meyers made no apologies to shareholders about this decision, describing it as "a clear indication of how your new team can move quickly. We needed a stronger and more efficient 4-cylinder power plant for cars and Jeep vehicles of the 80s, and we're not reluctant to get that engine from General Motors. It meant speed and huge cash savings."

The specification of the Hurricane engine, which joined the 258 6-cylinder and 304 V-8 in the CJ engine line, is as per the table.

This thin wall design engine, which AMC noted was the "first 4-cylinder power plant offered in a Jeep vehicle manufactured for commercial sale in the US or Canada in nearly a decade," was

Displacement:	151cid (2.5L)
Bore x stroke:	4 x 3in
Carburetion:	1 x 2bbl
Comp ratio:	8.2:1
Horsepower:	82@4000rpm
Torque (lb/ft):	125@2600rpm

An artist's rendering of the new Toledo paint facility which was operational in 1981, showing various Jeep models including CJs being painted. The facility had a capacity of 1000 bodies a day – 50 per cent more than the operation it replaced. (Author's collection)

used in combination with a new SR-4 Borg-Warner, all-synchromesh, 4-speed manual transmission, which replaced the 3-speed manual used in 1979 as the CJ's standard gearbox. It had ratios of 4.07, 2.39, 1.49 and 1.0:1. Among its key features was the use of aluminum for the case, top cover and adapter housing.

A second new all-synchromesh, 4-speed manual, a Temac Model T-176, was used for CJs with either the 258 6-cylinder or 304 V-8. Its ratios were 3.52, 2.27, 1.46 and 1.0:1. The previously optional 4-speed manual with a 6.32:1 non-synchromesh first gear was no longer offered. Concluding the transmission revisions for 1980 was replacement of the 3-speed Turbo-Hydra-matic, previously used in the CJ-7, with a lighter weight Chrysler TorqueFlite unit.

A Model Dana 300 part-time four-wheel drive system, an upgraded version of an earlier model, was used with all transmission/engine combinations offered for the 1980 CJ-5 and CJ-7. Compared to the 2.03:1 low range of the preceding Dana 20 unit its low range had a 2.62:1 ratio. AMC explained that "the basic concept of the new transfer case was to minimize losses in efficiency during highway driving, reduce the weight of the four-wheel drive assembly and provide a low range transfer case ratio compatible with lower numerical axles needed for peak highway fuel economy."

The axle ratios for the 1980 CJ Jeep were as per the table.

Engine	Standard	Optional
4-cyl:	3.54:1	4.09:1
6-cyl:	3.07:1	3.54:1
V-8:	3.07:1	3.54:1

The full-time Quadra-Trac system with automatic transmission was not available with 1980 CJ models. Manual free-wheeling hubs, previously optional, became standard. Together with the combination of free-wheeling hubs and new transfer case contributing to the CJ Jeep's significantly improved fuel efficiency was the use of a new lighter weight, high efficiency battery, and a self-adjusting, low-friction hydraulic clutch on CJs with the 4-cylinder engine/4-speed transmission.

AMC's assertion that "the lightweight, highly efficient 4-cylinder, 2.5 liter engine will enable 1980 CJ models to achieve significant increases" was supported by an EPA estimated 21mpg and 25mpg highway rating for the 4-cylinder CJ-5.

A new Laredo option for the CJ-5 and CJ-7 in either soft or hardtop version and priced at $1950, was the top level CJ trim package. It consisted of 15 x 8in styled steel chrome plated wheels with a center hub cover, new Goodyear Wrangler 9R on-or-off road radial tires, chrome front and rear bumperettes, swing-away spare tire carrier with chrome latch and stop, chrome mirror heads and arms, black rocker moldings, hood insulation, body striping in either silver or blue tones, indoor/outdoor carpeting, leather-wrapped steering wheel and passenger assist bar, chrome grille panel with pinstriped instrument panel, covered console with special trim pad, special door trim panels, and a Laredo nameplate on the instrument panel.

CJ-7s with the Laredo option had hardtops with tinted glass in the side quarter windows. Offered for the first time on a Jeep, and standard on the Laredo, were high-back bucket seats in black and silver or beige and brown; the Laredo had matching rear seats. These bucket seats were also included in Renegade and Golden Eagle packages which were priced at $899 and $1450 respectively. With only one color, Classic Black, carried over from 1979, CJ customers enjoyed a virtually all-new palette of colors in 1980 (see table page 184).

In the midst of what AMC characterized as an

A 1981 CJ-5 Renegade. (Author's collection)

The CJ-5 Jeeps had new one-sided galvanized rear body panels for 1981. The Renegade had a revised striping scheme. (Author's collection)

The 1981 Laredo package listed for $2049. (Author's collection)

182

A 1981 CJ-5 Laredo in Classic Black with optional styled chrome wheels. Body striping and Laredo lettering were color-coordinated with the exterior color; in this case Silver and Gray. (Also available in Nutmeg and Brown.) (Author's collection)

A base 1981 CJ-7 in Copper Brown Metallic. The standard roll bar could be equipped with optional padding and saddle bags. Its white 15 x 8in styled steel wheels and black wheellip extensions were optional. (Author's collection)

"industry-wide recession," sales of all Jeep models declined. Nonetheless their share of the domestic four-wheel drive market increased during calendar year 1980 to 19.1 per cent from 18.2 per cent in 1979. AMC asserted that "much of the increase could be attributed to strong sales of Jeep CJ models as consumers turned to more fuel-efficient vehicles."

Prices of 1980 CJ Jeeps and selected options are listed in the accompanying table (below right).

Calendar 1980 year sales of CJ Jeeps totaled 47,304 units.

In terms of quality 1981 models benefited from the completion of a $30 million paint facility at the Toledo plant. Speaking to shareholders at the April 29, 1981 annual meeting, AMC Chairman Gerald C Meyers called it "the newest and best automotive paint system in the world ... Earlier this month," he added, "because of my personal commitment to quality improvement, I went to Toledo to be on hand for the start-up of the new paint facility. And I came away very proud of what I saw, confident that our Toledo plant is well prepared to turn out the kind of paint finish that the mighty Jeep brand suggests."

The painting process which, AMC claimed, "incorporates the world's most advanced automotive painting technology," began with an initial stage at which a protective primer was applied to the bodies. After receiving a negative electrical charge the bodies moved through a dip tank filled with rust-resistant primer which had a positive charge. Since the primer was attracted to

Color	Base	Renegade	Golden Eagle	Laredo
Olympic White:	X	X	X	X
Cameo Tan:	X	X	X	X
Medium Teal Blue:	X	X	NA	NA
Dark Green Metallic:	X	X	X	NA
Dark Brown Metallic:	X	X	X	X
Russet Metallic:	X	X	X	NA
Bordeaux Metallic:	X	X	X	X
Smoke Gray Metallic:	X	X	NA	NA
Alpaca Brown Metallic:	X	X	X	NA
Saxon Yellow:	X	X	X	X
Cardinal Red:	X	X	NA	NA
Classic Black:	x	X	X	X
Navy Blue:	X	X	NA	X
Caramel	X	X	X	NA

Model	FADP
CJ-5 (open body):	$6195
CJ-7 (open body):	$6445

Option	Price
Renegade package:	$1075.00
Golden Eagle package:	$1450.00
Laredo package:	$1950.00
Tachometer and rally clock:	$84.00
Limited slip rear differential:	$90.00
Power front disc brakes:	$73.00
Power steering:	$194.00
Tilt steering wheel:	$79.00
Front anti-roll bar:	$41.00
Steering damper:	$21.00
Extra duty suspension:	$93.00
258 engine:	$129.00
304 engine:	$383.00

An Oriental Red 1981 CJ-5 Renegade. Revised Renegade graphics for 1981 were available in gradations of yellow, blue or, as seen here, red, depending on base exterior color. (Author's collection)

A 1981 CJ-7 Renegade in Moonlight Blue with blue exterior graphics and optional molded hardtop.

The dash panel of a 1981 CJ Renegade. with soft-feel sports steering wheel in nutmeg. Options include clock and tachometer, and an AM/FM radio.

the bodies by reverse polarity, all sheet metal was covered, providing added rust protection. After the bodies passed through a cleansing rinse, a second coat of special primer was sprayed on prior to the application of three coats of finish enamel.

One-sided galvanized steel was used for the top front fender panels on 1981 CJ-5 and CJ-7 models, the rear corner panels and inner and outer door panels of the CJ-7, and the rear body panels of the CJ-5. Product Group AMC Vice President Dale E Dawkins explained to Jeep buyers the relevance of the expanded use of galvanized steel: "Our expanded galvanized program is believed to be the most extensive in the industry," he stated. "The consumer benefits of galvanizing become very apparent when steel is subjected to American Society of Test Materials (ASTM) engineering tests. When a sample of unprotected cold-rolled steel 30 thousandths of an inch thick is exposed to a five per cent salt solution using the ASTMB117 salt spray test, the steel will show 'daylight' or become perforated after only 2500 hours. One-side galvanized steel the same thickness will show no indication of perforation or structural loss after the same time period in this closed cabinet test."

While Jeeps were not exposed to the 'closed cabinet' in everyday use, they were constantly subjected to corrosive agents. In the northern tier of the United States in the early 1980s, some ten million tons of salt were used annually to melt ice and snow on highways and streets; in fact, more salt was spread each year on highways than was used for food, farming and industry combined! In coastal areas, Jeeps were exposed year round to salt spray. Air pollution was also a source of corrosion, especially in areas where levels of sulfur dioxide and chloride were high.

Also improving Jeep quality was the utilization of a $3.5 million Final Inspection Acceptance (FIA) facility at the Toledo plant. Each Jeep was driven over a short road test to the FIA line after being approved at the final inspection station on the assembly line. In addition to the road test,

the Jeeps were retested for water leaks, and received over 150 additional checks before being released for shipment to dealers. The FIA line had large plate glass windows facing a busy Toledo street: North Cove Boulevard. The attention of passing motorists was attracted by a large sign reading 'Jeep Quality – Come See for Yourself.'

The result of a long-term AMC engineering project, an extensively redesigned version of the CJ's optional 258 6-cylinder engine was introduced for 1981. Whereas the earlier version weighed 535 pounds, the new version weighed in at just 445 pounds. This significant reduction was achieved by revising many primary components and, wherever possible, replacing steel parts with those constructed of lighter materials, mainly aluminum. Additional program objectives were to improve engine reliability, reduce maintenance costs, and lessen noise levels throughout its operating range.

The revised engine block weighed thirty pounds less than its 1980 counterpart, achieved by decreasing thickness of the wall, the web and many flanges. Straightening and reshaping the rocker cover flange eliminated a great deal of unnecessary cast iron. Replacing a stamped steel rocker arm cover with one fabricated of glass-filled nylon gave a net two pound weight reduction. Both the oil and water pumps now used aluminum housings instead of cast iron. The exhaust manifold was simplified by being separated from the intake manifold and doing away with the heat valve. The new intake manifold was constructed of aluminum instead of cast iron and incorporated an electrically heated warm-up device and a water-heated circuit to replace the exhaust heat valve.

Changes to the camshaft profile reduced valve overlap without compromising maximum horsepower output. The new overlap allowed a lower idle speed for reduced fuel

The 1981 Laredo interior. Seen here is the Laredo's standard black, leather-wrapped steering wheel. Not visible is its leather-wrapped passenger assist handle, available in either black or Nutmeg. The high-back front bucket seats and rear bench seat are trimmed in a Cara grain vinyl of Nutmeg with a Honey accent strap. Also offered was a black seat and gray strap color combination.

consumption whilst also increasing low speed torque output. The California version of this engine (the 304 V-8 was not available in California for the CJs) had a new front accessory drive system which used a single belt routed through and around all engine pulleys.

An additional fuel economy measure was the incorporation of a locking torque converter in the Chrysler TorqueFlite transmission used with the 6-cylinder engine. This also reduced engine wear and lowered transmission temperatures by decreasing friction that resulted from slippage in a conventional torque converter. In the revised transmission, a clutch engaged automatically when the output shaft reached approximately 1100rpm. With the

This 1982 Jeep CJ-7 Limited has a Mist Silver Metallic finish. Two other exterior colors were offered for the Limited: Slate Blue Metallic and Olympic White. (Author's collection)

engine speed and that of the output shaft now equal, power was transferred more efficiently from the engine to the drive train.

The CJ Jeeps had EPA estimated mileage ratings* for 1981 as shown in the table.

Engine	Highway	Overall
4-cyl:	27mpg	22mpg
6-cyl:	24mpg	27mpg

As did most other manufacturers, Jeep cautioned customers not to become overly excited about these mpg numbers, advising them to "use these figures for comparison. Your results may differ due to driving speed, weather conditions and trip length. Actual highway mileage will be less."

A useful option not available in 1980 was a wide ratio automatic transmission for 4-cylinder CJ-7s. CJs with the

The 1982 CJ-7 Limited interior featured special door trim and high-back bucket seats, seen here in Slate Blue Western Weave cloth. A rear bench seat was also included. (Author's collection)

6-cylinder engine now had a 2.73:1 instead of 3.07:1 axle ratio. A 3.73:1 was optional. First gear ratio of the manual transmission was 4.07:1 rather than 3.5:1 as in 1980. CJs with the V-8 engine had a first gear ratio of 3.82:1 in place of the 3.52:1 ratio used in 1980. Their standard axle, regardless of transmission, was 2.73:1, which replaced the 3.07:1 of 1980. The optional ratio was 3.31:1.

Minor design changes for 1981 included a longer optional sidestep, new body graphics for the Renegade package, and addition of a vent window in the optional soft top/metal door of the CJ-7.

The 1981 color selection consisted

A 1982 CJ-7 Laredo in Classic Black with Silver and Gray hood lettering and body striping. (Author's collection)

of Cameo Tan, Vintage Red Metallic, Classic Black, Autumn Gold, Moonlight Blue, Steel Gray Metallic, Dark Brown Metallic, Deep Maroon Metallic, Olympic White, Copper Brown Metallic, Oriental Red, Montana Blue, Sherwood Green Metallic and Chestnut Brown Metallic.

List price of the CJ-5 rose $1045 to $7240 for 1981. The CJ-7's base price increased by the same amount to $7490. Most Jeep options were also more expensive. The Renegade package retailed for $1316; the Laredo package for $2049. Prices for other options are listed in the accompanying table.

Only 30,564 CJs were sold in calendar year 1981, a drop of 16,740 units from 1980, which might have been even greater if AMC hadn't reduced Jeep prices by ten per cent in April. Although 1981 model year sales of all Jeep models declined to 63,275 from 77,852 in 1980, Jeep's market share moved up to 21.2 per cent.

Option	Price
258 engine:	$129.00
Power steering:	$194.00
Power front disc brakes:	$73.00
Tilt steering wheel:	$83.00
Body side steps:	$22.00
Halogen head lamps:	$45.00
Fog lamps:	$79.00

International sales of Jeep vehicles increased in nearly every major market. In Venezuela, where AMC had a 45 per cent equity position in Jeep de Venezuela, a joint venture partnership which was the largest assembler of Jeep vehicles outside the US, nearly half of the four-wheel vehicles sold were Jeeps.

AMC significantly expanded its operations in Africa during 1981 by creating Jeep Africa in Nairobi, Kenya, a joint venture partnership in which AMC had a 51 per cent equity. Far Eastern operations set sales records with an 82 per cent increase in volume over 1980. Sales of CJ-7 Jeeps manufactured in Indonesia nearly doubled with around 16 per cent of the local four-wheel drive market.

Several changes were made to the CJ Jeep's front and rear tread measurements for 1982 (see table on the following page).

Together with the use of new Arriva tires, these

This 1982 CJ-7 Renegade has its hood lettering and body graphics in gradations of yellow. Body color is Copper Brown Metallic. "Renegade," said Jeep, "is the boldest and most familiar of all CJ appearance packages." (Author's collection)

	1981 CJ-5	1981 CJ-7	1982 CJ-5	1982 CJ-7
Front tread:	51.5in	51.5in	52.4in	55.8in
Rear tread:	50.5in	50.5in	50.5in	55.1in

The 1982 CJ-7 in its base form was refreshingly reminiscent of early postwar models. (Author's collection)

A posed picture of the 1982 CJ-7 Jamboree Commemorative Edition. (Author's collection)

revisions resulted in better roadability. All CJ models were offered with several new options, including a 5-speed manual transmission, a wide ratio automatic transmission, and a 20 gallon fuel tank.

A new Jeep CJ option package, the Limited, debuted in 1982. Beyond the basic CJ equipment, the $2895 Limited option included power steering, power front disc brakes, AM/FM radio with two speakers, a monochromatic paint theme with color-keyed hardtop and wheellip extensions, special dual color body side striping, special grille panel strips, exterior 'Limited' nameplates, chrome front bumpers and rear bumperettes, body side steps, black painted windshield and window frames, special dual exterior mirrors, 15 x 7in steel spoke wheels with bright trim rings, Decor and Convenience Groups, high-back front bucket seats with rear bench seat in Slate Blue or Nutmeg western weave (Nutmeg leather seats were optional), special sound/heat insulated carpeted floor, trim panels for the wheel housing, tailgate, inner body and cowl sides, carpet protective front floor mats, low gloss finish for the sports console, steering column and bezel and air conditioning housing, color-keyed padded roll bar, special door trim and headlining, door activated dome and courtesy lights, leather-wrapped steering wheel and passenger assist handle, and rear quarter belt line trim molding. The Limited was also offered with an "improved ride package" which had softer front and rear springs and shock absorbers.

Exterior colors offered for 1982 included Olympic White, Mist Silver Metallic, Classic Black, Sherwood Green Metallic, Jamaica Beige, Cooper Brown Metallic, Slate Blue Metallic, Deep Night Blue, Oriental Red, Sun Yellow, Vintage Red Metallic and Chestnut Brown Metallic. The Limited CJ-7 was available in five exterior/interior color combinations: Mist Silver Metallic, Slate Blue Metallic and Olympic White exteriors with a Slate Blue interior or Copper Brown Metallic or Olympic White exteriors with Nutmeg cloth or optional leather interior.

Jeep described an even more unique 1982 CJ as a "bossy, gleaming, dressed-up and decked-out 4WD dream machine." Officially it was the Commemorative Edition CJ-7 Jamboree, a very special CJ-7 produced to mark the 30th Anniversary of the world-famous Jeepers Jamboree. Jeep considered this off-road event "as legendary as Jeep CJ itself" and gave anyone wanting to own a new a CJ-7 Jamboree fair warning that they would be hard to come by. "You had better take a long, hard,

A 1982 CJ-7 Jamboree with factory approved, dealer installed special equipment including Ramsey electrical winch, off-road driving lights mounted on an over windshield bar, and grille and brush guards. (Author's collection)

The 1982 CJ-7 Jamboree's rear chrome bumperettes and black vinyl spare tire cover with its Jamboree logo. (Author's collection)

loving look at Jamboree now," they were told, "for it will be a 4x4 rarely sighted in Jeep Country. Only 2500 Jeep CJ-7 Jamboree models will be offered for limited sales, making it an instant off-road classic."

Each Jamboree had a numbered instrument panel plaque indicating its chronological placement in the total build. In addition, each owner received a signed certificate of authenticity.

Along with the dash plaque, the Jamboree interior was distinguished by the following items:
– High-back black vinyl bucket seats and rear bench seat with special gold accents
– Center console
– Black floor and wheelhouse carpeting
– Black padded roll bar and saddle bags
– 'Jamboree' hood lettering
– Black vinyl spare tire cover with 'Jamboree' logo
– Choice of either special Topaz Gold Metallic or Olympic White paint
– Chrome styled wheels
– Chrome front bumper
– Chrome rear bumperettes
– Black vinyl soft top
– Decor Group

Required options not included in the Jamboree Packet were:
– 258cid engine
– 5-speed manual transmission
– Power steering
– Power disc brakes
– Wrangler radial tires
– 20 gallon fuel tank
– Tachometer and rally clock
– Halogen fog lamps
– Tilt steering wheel
– Heavy-duty battery
– Heavy-duty alternator
– Heavy-duty cooling
– Heavy-duty suspension

Jeep also issued this list of "Factory Approved Dealer Installed Special Equipment" for the Jamboree:
– Ramsey electric winch and mounting kit
– AM/FM stereo CB radio with antenna
– Off-road driving lamps and over windshield light mounting bar
– Fire extinguisher
– Grille guard
– Brush guard

When he introduced the new CJ-7 to the media, Jeep Corporation's Director of Marketing, D Greb, said: "we're pleased to present a Commemorative Edition Jeep CJ-7 Jamboree model in honor of the 30th anniversary of an

The Jamboree's standard high-back front bucket seats in Black vinyl with Gold accents. (Author's collection)

event that has become synonymous with four wheeling ... the Jeepers Jamboree. It's an excellent package with special trim and equipment designed to appeal to serious off-roaders. It will be available for limited sale only. We're sure it's going to live up to its illustrious name."

After evaluating the Jamboree CJ-7, Mike Anson, publisher of Petersons' *4-Wheel & Off-Road* magazine, considered it "a very impressive machine. The special gold color is super. And Jamboree is dressed the way off-roaders like their vehicles. More significantly, with the Jamboree model, Jeep Corporation demonstrates its continued strong support of off-road activities, epitomized in the famous Jeepers Jamboree."

1982 CJ Jeep and selected options prices were as per the table on page 193.

Calendar year sales of CJ models totaled 29,718 units.

For 1983, the 4.2 liter 6-cylinder that was standard for the CJ-5 had a higher, 9.2:1 compression ratio, up from 8.6:1 in 1982. A new MCU-Super D electronics and pulse-air injection system improved both fuel efficiency and throttle response. The 4.2 liter engine was available for the CJ-7 which had the 2.5 liter 4-cylinder as standard. Both the CJ-5 and CJ-7 were offered with the same appearance/equipment packages as in 1982. CJ sales increased to 36,308 units for 1983.

Ten exterior colors were available for 1983 CJ

Model	Price
CJ-5	$7515
CJ-7	$7765

Option	Price
258 cubic inch engine	$145.00
5-speed manual transmission	$199.00
3.31:1 axle ratio	$33.00
Extra duty suspension	$103.00
Power steering	$229.00
Power front disc brakes	$99.00
Air conditioning	$681.00
Front and rear carpeting	$108.00
AM radio	$99.00
Tilt steering wheel	$99.00
Heavy-duty battery	$45.00
Spare tire lock	$8.00
Halogen head lights	$51.00
Halogen fog lights	$90.00
Cold Climate Group	$115.00
20gal fuel tank	$49.00
Roll bar accessory package	$113.00
Laredo package	$2149.00
Limited package	$2895.00

Details of the Jamboree's chrome styled wheels. (Author's collection)

Jeeps: Olympic White, Mist Silver Metallic, Classic Black, Jamaican Beige, Copper Brown Metallic, Sherwood Green Metallic, Slate Blue Metallic, Deep Night Blue, Sebring Red, and Chestnut Brown Metallic. New graphics were included in the Renegade package. Calendar year CJ sales were 36,308.

For the 1984 model year both the CJ-5 and the Limited Package were dropped. Still available were the Renegade and Laredo trim packages. Rather than admitting that there were no styling changes for 1984, AMC preferred to note that "the Jeep CJ-7's legendary styling ... continues for 1984."

AMC's newly designed 2.5 liter, 150 cubic inch, 4-cylinder engine – which had been under development for over three years – was the standard CJ-7 engine. The 4.2 liter, 258 cubic inch, 6-cylinder was optional. Use of the 2.5 liter engine – the first 4-cylinder engine produced by AMC – increased unit profitability of the CJ-7 by over $300.

This view of the CJ-7 Jamboree instrument panel shows the location of the Commemorative Edition plaque. (Author's collection)

NO. 2000

The Commemorative dash plaque installed on the 2000th Jamboree Edition CJ-7 produced. (Author's collection)

All Jamborees were equipped with a Black padded roll bar and saddle bags. (Author's collection)

"From the standpoint of all-round technology, we feel this is as advanced as any in its class," asserted Roy C Lunn, AMC Vice President of Product Engineering. "We're confident it will be competitive not only today, but for many years to come."

This engine, specifically designed for use in four-wheel drive utility vehicles, combined strong performance with excellent fuel economy. With its standard 4-speed manual transmission, the 2.5 liter CJ-7 had EPA fuel economy ratings of 24mpg estimated and 33mpg highway. "Unlike most engines available today," Lunn explained, "ours was not designed originally for passenger cars and then adapted for trucks. We specifically developed it with our Jeep vehicles and Eagles in mind. That's the reason that performance and durability were of such prime consideration from the very beginning."

AMC asserted that extensive dynamometer testing of the 2.5 liter indicated it had a durability factor substantially better than engines of a similar size and configuration. Lunn summarized the 2.5 liter's performance this way: "This is a high torque engine. It will deliver 132 pound feet of torque at 2800rpm and that certainly translates into a strong acceleration capability for an engine of this size."

In developing the 2.5 liter engine AMC engineers made extensive use of both computer-aided design and the lightweight casting techniques earlier utilized for the CJ's 4.2 liter engine. "However," said Lunn, "this is not just a cut down version of our six-cylinder engine. There is some common componentry, but the four-cylinder includes many unique items such as its own electronic systems. It also has a shorter stroke and larger bore. The valves are larger and the pistons are new."

Specifically, compared to the six-cylinder, the new engine's stroke was shortened to 3.188in from 3.9in, and bore was enlarged to 3.875in from 3.75in. "We wanted as much displacement – for power and torque – as possible within the confinement of bore centers of the tooling," noted Lunn. "The only parameter we could influence substantially was stroke. So we picked the largest bore and stroke in order to get 2.5 liters."

Major features of the new engine consisted of a relatively high, 9.2:1, compression ratio, a double-quench combustion chamber for excellent fuel/air mixing and thermal efficiency, and full electronic controls, including a fuel feedback carburetor for optimum air/fuel ratio control. It also had a breakerless ignition through a conventional distributor. While the spark advance

A close-up of the Jamboree's hood lettering. (Author's collection)

The 1983 CJ-7 was equipped with this standard rear swing-away spare tire carrier. (Author's collection)

Features of the Jamboree's spare tire cover. Mark Smith, leader of the 1979/80 Expedicion De Las Americas and trail master of Jeepers Jamboree Inc, noted that "the Commemorative Edition Jeep CJ is a fine tribute to our Jeepers Jamboree. This is the 30th year for the Jamboree and Jeep Corporation has provided tremendous support all the way." (Author's collection)

These Denim vinyl high-back bucket seats were optional for the standard 1983 CJ interior. They were available in Black, Nutmeg and, as shown here, Blue. (Author's collection)

was achieved by using the customary vacuum system and mechanical centrifugal weight, the ignition system included a unique knock sensor control process which individually sequenced the retard so that each cylinder's retard function was independent of the other three.

"Instead of measuring knock once on average for all four cylinders as is the case with other engines, our system," explained Lunn, "measures the knock each time a cylinder fires. The system then instantaneously determines which cylinder it is, and retards the spark for each one separately." Thus each cylinder operated at its precise knock-free ignition level of optimum power and fuel economy, avoiding pre-ignition damage. This

Displacement:	2.465 liters (150.4cu in)
Bore x stroke:	3.875 x 3.188in
Number of main bearings:	5
Compression ratio:	9.2:1
Valve train:	Hydraulic, overhead
Block material:	Cast iron
Head material:	Cast iron
Piston material:	Autothermic aluminum with steel strut
Rocker arms:	Ball pivot type
Crankshaft:	Nodular
Weight	
With base accessory drive:	315lb
With maximum accessory drive:	341lb
Induction system:	Single barrel carburetor
Fuel:	Regular unleaded
Oil capacity:	4qts
Torque:	132lb/ft@3200rpm

sequence feature was developed by AMC engineers and was not offered on any other vehicles sold in the US.

The 2.5 liter engine was built at AMC's Kenosha, Wisconsin plant where the six-cylinder and V-8 engines were produced. Its specification is shown in the accompanying table.

As an alternative to the standard 4-speed manual transmission, a 5-speed manual was optional. The 3-speed automatic option was only available for the

The 1983 CJ-5 and CJ-7 models in profile. The CJ-5 has a Sebring Red finish; the CJ-7-Laredo's color is Deep Night Blue. (Author's collection)

Transmission	3-speed automatic (Chrysler model 99)	4-speed manual	5-speed manual
Gear ratios			
1st:	2.74:1	4.03:1	4.03:1
2nd:	1.55:1	2.37:1	2.37:1
3rd:	1.00:1	1.50:1	1.50:1
4th:	–	1.00:1	1.00:1
5th:	–	–	0.86:1

6-cylinder engine. A new upshift indicator light – advising the driver when to change gears for optimum fuel efficiency – was standard with the 4-cylinder engine/4-speed manual transmission combination.

The transmissions available for the CJ-7 had the ratios shown in the accompanying table.

The CJ's 1984 calendar year sales totaled 39,547 units.

Standard for the 1985 Renegade and Laredo, and optional for the base CJ-7, were fold and tumble rear seats, which replaced the fixed type seat used in 1984. Up front were new standard high-back bucket seats.

Available exterior colors for the 1985 CJ consisted of four standard choices: Olympic White, Classic Black, Almond Beige and Sebring Red. The extra cost metallic colors were Sterling, Ice Blue, Charcoal, Dark Honey, Dark Brown and Garnet. All extra cost colors had a clear coat finish. One new interior color, Honey, replaced Nutmeg. The two other interior colors were Black and Garnet.

AMC portrayed the absence of any significant change in the 1986 CJ-7 as a virtue. "Celebrating 40 years of Jeep heritage," it noted, "the Jeep CJ-7 for 1986 retains the overall design continuity and its longstanding reputation for ruggedness and durability among small four-wheel drive vehicles." Introducing its full range of 1986 models, AMC reported on the results of an independent survey of owners of 1985 Renault and Jeeps concerning their satisfaction with their vehicles. Maritz Market Research, Inc – a research company with extensive experience in automotive research – undertook the survey. Maritz sent questionnaires to all retail purchasers of 1985 Renault, Jeep and AMC vehicles delivered through April 1985,

This lockable storage compartment was a handy option for the 1983 CJ Jeeps. (Author's collection)

This portrayal of the 1983 CJ-7 Renegade was used by AMC on the cover of one of its 1983 media information packets. Author's collection)

Above: A 1983 CJ-7 Limited in Copper Brown Metallic. The Limited package was not offered the following year. (Author's collection)

This 1984 CJ-7 was equipped with the top-of-the-line Laredo trim package. (Author's collection)

In company with other 1984 Jeep models, a well-optioned CJ-7 shows off its light bar, driving light, Jeep license plate frame, padded roll bars with saddle bags, anodized aluminum running boards, and Warn electric winch. (Author's collection)

The CJ-5 Renegade had new graphics for 1983. Depending on the main body color, they could be Yellow, Blue or Red. The body color of this example is Olympic White. (Author's collection)

This top boot, seen on a 1984 CJ-7, was a popular CJ option for many years. It accommodated both top and vinyl windows. (Author's collection)

A base model 1985 CJ-7 in Classic Black. Its white steel styled wheels were optional. (Author's collection)

A 1985 CJ-7 Renegade in extra cost Dark Honey Metallic clearcoat. New for 1985 was the honey color of its soft top. This example has the standard Renegade P235/7515 black Wrangler tires and 15 x 7in white painted styled steel wheels with chrome hub covers. (Author's collection)

amounting to a total of 153,639. 55,474, or 37 per cent, were completed and returned.

According to Joseph E Cappy, AMC's Executive Vice President of Operations, the overall satisfaction level for Jeep owners was 95.3 per cent. This was, said Cappy, "an extremely high level which demonstrates very forcefully that our products are attuned to the needs of the buyer in

This 1985 CJ-7 Laredo has the optional Black hardtop with 'Gray-Tone' deep-tinted glass for rear quarter and tailgate windows. If the top was ordered in Honey, the windows had a 'Bronze-Tone' tint.

The new fold and tumble rear seat for 1985 made it easy to switch from having room for cargo and gear to accommodating two rear passengers in the CJ-7. This seat was included in the Renegade and Laredo packages and optional for the base CJ-7. (Author's collection)

the areas they consider to be most important."

Whilst ninety per cent of buyers who returned questionnaires considered the condition of their vehicles satisfactory when delivered, only 73 per cent were satisfied with their dealer's ability to fix problems. "While this figure looks respectable," said Cappy, "it should be higher, and we will do everything possible to move the satisfaction level up."

The price of the 1986 CJ-7 and selected popular options (all effective July 1, 1985) were as per the table.

Most Jeep enthusiasts knew that some day the sun would set on the career of the CJ. Others thought that it could, would, and should soldier on indefinitely. The

Model	Manufacturer's suggested retail price
CJ-7	$7500.00
Option	Price
Metallic clear coat paint:	$161.00
Vinyl denim bucket seats:	$123.00
Tires	
P215/75R15 BSW:	$108.00
P235/75R15 RBL:	$346.00
P235/75R15 OWL:	$389.00
4.2 liter engine:	$361.00
5-speed manual transmission:	$250.00
Automatic transmission:	$585.00
Trac-Lok rear differential:	$255.00
California Emission System:	$116.00
Renegade Package:	$1253.00

Option	Price
Laredo Package (soft top):	$2787.00
Laredo Package (hardtop):	$3304.00
Air conditioning:	$804.00
Heavy-duty alternator:	$68.00
Heavy-duty battery:	$55.00
Bumper Accessory Package:	$130.00
Rear bumperettes:	$35.00
Floor carpeting (front and rear):	$125.00
Center console:	$74.00
Cold Climate Group:	$132.00
Convenience Group:	$96.00
Heavy-duty engine cooling:	$57.00
Cruise control:	$204.00
Decor Group:	$99.00
Deep tinted glass:	$138.00
Draw bar:	$50.00
Extra capacity fuel tank:	$57.00
Extra-Quiet Insulation Package:	$199.00
Halogen fog lamps:	$103.00
Halogen headlamps:	$26.00
Metal doors:	$263.00
Outside passenger side mirror:	$18.00
Power disc brakes:	$125.00
Power steering:	$274.00

The 1985 CJ-7 Renegade's standard high-back Denim vinyl front bucket seats in Honey. They were also offered in Black and Garnet. (Author's collection)

Assigned this difficult task was Joseph Cappy, AMC's Executive Vice President of Operations. "The quarter-ton Jeep earned a worldwide reputation for ruggedness and versatility in wartime." he said. "That tradition has continued for the more than four decades that the CJ ... has been sold to the public. Completion of CJ production will signal an end of a very important era in Jeep history".

announcement on November 27, 1985 that CJ Jeep production would cease with the 1986 models marked the end of one of the most remarkable eras in automotive history.

The 1986 CJ-7 Renegade had these standard denim-look vinyl high-back bucket seats. In addition to the Honey color seen here, they were also offered in Black and Garnet. (Author's collection)

Option	Price
Radios	
AM radio:	$123.00
AM/FM stereo radio:	$204.00
AM/FM/cassette:	$348.00
Rear seat:	$275.00
Roll Bar Accessory Package:	$130.00
Heavy-duty shock absorbers:	$40.00
Spare tire lock:	$14.00
Soft Feel steering wheel:	$59.00
Body side steps:	$30.00
Heavy-duty Suspension Package:	$118.00
Soft Ride Suspension:	$56.00
Tachometer and rally clock:	$109.00
Tilt steering wheel:	$118.00
Tops	
Vinyl soft top:	$378.00
Denim soft top:	$402.00
Hardtop with doors:	$889.00
White styled wheels:	$161.00
Chrome styled wheels:	$321.00

This 1986 CJ-7 Renegade has a Dark Honey Metallic finish. Its white styled steel wheels were standard. The color of its optional soft top is Honey. Black, White and Garnet soft tops were also offered. The off-road light bar was a Jeep accessory. (Author's collection)

A 1986 base CJ-7 in Sebring Red, equipped with optional 15 x 7in chrome steel wheels and P235/75R15 white letter Goodyear Wrangler steel radial tires. (Author's collection)

Below: A 1986 CJ-7 Laredo in Garnet Metallic. Many of the Laredo's standard exterior features can be seen, including the chrome front grille and bumper, and 15 x 7in chrome styled steel wheels. (Author's collection)

For more great titles visit ...